New Perspectives in German Political Studies

Series Editors
William E. Paterson
Aston University
Birmingham, UK

Thomas Saalfeld
Universität Bamberg
Bamberg, Germany

Far reaching changes are now taking place in Germany. Stability lay at the core of the German model and much of the writing from Peter Katzenstein and Manfred Schmidt onwards sought to explain this enviable stability. Changes in the external environment have created a number of fundamental challenges which pose a threat to that stability. Germany is now Europe's central power but this has generated controversy about how it is to exercise this new power. Although attention is often centred on German power the migration crisis demonstrates its limits. New Perspectives in German Political Studies aims to engage with these new challenges and to cater for the heightened interest in Germany. The Editors would welcome proposals for single-authored monographs, edited collections and Pivots, from junior as well as well-established scholars working on contemporary German Politics.

More information about this series at
http://www.palgrave.com/gp/series/14735

Hans Vorländer • Maik Herold
Steven Schäller

PEGIDA and New Right-Wing Populism in Germany

palgrave
macmillan

Hans Vorländer
TU Dresden
Dresden, Germany

Maik Herold
TU Dresden
Dresden, Germany

Steven Schäller
TU Dresden
Dresden, Germany

New Perspectives in German Political Studies
ISBN 978-3-319-67494-0   ISBN 978-3-319-67495-7   (eBook)
https://doi.org/10.1007/978-3-319-67495-7

Library of Congress Control Number: 2017958038

Cover illustration: dpa picture alliance / Alamy Stock Photo

Printed on acid-free paper

This Palgrave Macmillan imprint is published by Springer Nature
The registered company is Springer International Publishing AG
The registered company address is: Gewerbestrasse 11, 6330 Cham, Switzerland

PREFACE

This book was written in the context of a research project financed by the Fritz Thyssen Foundation. We would like to thank the director, Dr. Frank Suder, and the responsible coordinator, Dr. Thomas Suermann for the generous support.

There were also others involved in bringing about this book. Dennis Norton translated the German manuscript into English with care and diligence, Ambra Finotello and Imogen Gordon Clark of Palgrave Macmillan patiently supported us throughout and, finally, Marissa Weigle also made a valuable contribution in the form of literary research in Dresden. Our sincere gratitude to them all.

Dresden, Germany

Hans Vorländer
Maik Herold
Steven Schäller

CONTENTS

LIST OF FIGURES

Introduction

A development that had already taken place in Europe since the 1980s also began to emerge in Germany in autumn 2014. Even before the refugee and migration crisis in summer 2015 a protest movement entitled Patriotic Europeans against the Islamisation of the Occident (PEGIDA) had formed on streets and squares. Despite having started as a small group of friends it immediately developed a remarkable dynamic, mobilising thousands of participants. The PEGIDA protests rapidly received media attention, well beyond Dresden, Germany and even Europe. The rallies of protesting citizens chanting shrill slogans were met by strong reactions from those in politics, the media and counter-demonstrators. The pictures of a flag-waving crowd, demonstrating in the darkness and chanting offensive slogans were seen around the world and gave rise to fears that, in a kind of catch-up alignment with other western democracies, right-wing populism was now also able to develop political momentum in Germany.

Although PEGIDA originated in Dresden, and it was also there that it drew the most participants at its weekly demonstrations, the protest movement nevertheless regarded itself as the nucleus of a larger German and European trend. PEGIDA offshoots arose in many German cities, in other European countries and even in Australia. However, in the end they remained insignificant and did not have a lasting impact. And yet, the movement was paradigmatic for a process of political outrage, polarisation and disinhibition. PEGIDA showed how the dynamics of the mobilisation of anger and outrage could unfold, be used for political purposes, and how harsh criticism from politicians and the media can contribute to creating a spiral of mutual escalation. This escalation promoted a division of civil society, furthered the creation of counter-publics on social networks and acted as an accelerant for the protest movement itself. At PEGIDA's rallies communicative power was gained by the purposeful occupation of public spaces. Performative techniques of symbolic staging established rituals that created loyalty and the feeling of belonging to a large community of like-minded people. Here, in a locally concentrated form, PEGIDA made visible the ferment in society, from which a clearly defined potential of support for right-wing populist politics arose throughout Germany—a potential that was later absorbed and converted into electoral successes by the party Alternative for Germany (AfD).

This was in spite of the fact that PEGIDA and the AfD initially had little in common. It was not until the events of 2015 that there were recognisable similar intentions, which were primarily defined by the resistance to "mass migration". In the informal alliance of PEGIDA and AfD, of street and parliament, movement and party, a right-wing populist force took shape which found common ground with the rejection of immigration, mistrust of the religion of Islam, fundamental criticism of the political and media elite, the dissatisfaction with liberal and representative democracy and the fear of heteronomy. As in in other western democracies, new right-wing populism in Germany also came onto the scene, seeking to radically change society through the reactivation and redefinition of central linguistic themes, the assertion of cultural and national identity, the reclamation of a patriotic and ethnic nationalism, the restitution of sovereign statehood and the implementation of plebiscitary democracy.

PEGIDA marked the public appearance of a new type of right-wing populist movement of indignation, which did not articulate a specific protest, but instead staged a diffuse outcry against everything that could be linked with "official" politics and media. The movement's Islamophobic and xenophobic thrust as well as its mobilisation of ethnocentric and national-conservative sentiments made PEGIDA a gathering point for the situationally outraged, the politically alienated and activists from the extreme and the New Right. In the end, PEGIDA achieved little, but it changed a lot: resentment became socially acceptable. The political discourse in Germany became coarser, the protest eventually lost its inhibitions, the lines between rhetorical and physical violence became brittle.

From a contemporary historical perspective this book brings together diverse observations of PEGIDA, of the civic actions to counter it and of the mediating dialogue events, and furthermore the findings and insights gained through the reading of hundreds of letters and e-mails as well as through countless conversations. For a more comprehensive systematic analysis we also come back to our own survey of the Dresden PEGIDA demonstrators, which was the very first empirical study of the movement, and compare its findings with those of numerous other studies. In addition, incorporated into this book are our own observations of the demonstrations, an evaluation of the coverage about PEGIDA in the national and international media, the communication observed on social networks as well as the results of the participatory observation of dialogue rounds between politicians and PEGIDA supporters. Additionally, background talks were conducted with former members of the organisational team involved with the protest events and with actors associated with these events.

In this book the development, structure and effect of PEGIDA are described and the existing empirical findings are brought together with established explanations from research into right-wing extremism and populism as well as more extensive interpretive approaches. First, in Chap. 1 there is a description of the emergence and development of PEGIDA, the contents of its demands and positions, as well as the forms its protest took on the streets and on social media. Subsequently, Chap. 2 addresses the public reactions to the demonstrations, which were characterised above all by strong condemnation. PEGIDA used these reactions in order to present itself as the victim of political and media elites and attempted to provoke them with increasingly radical slogans. The dynamic of alternating escalation that resulted gave the demonstrations media attention and high participation numbers. The relationship between PEGIDA and the existing parties on the right-wing fringe as well as New Right actors in Germany is looked at in Chap. 3, which also describes PEGIDA's contacts with other right-wing populist forces in Europe. Then, in Chap. 4, existing findings on the socio-demographic characteristics, the motivations and the political preferences of the PEGIDA demonstrators are presented and compared with insights into support for the political parties in Germany. Chapter 5 follows on from this with further findings about the political views of PEGIDA supporters and puts them in an interpretative context with research on Islamophobia, right-wing extremism, xenophobia, ethnocentrism, criticism of democracy and populism in Germany. Chapter 6 then brings together the insights gained using the most important explanatory approaches, which trace the new right-wing populism back to recent developments in Germany, to transformations of representative democracy, but also to global economic and social developments. Finally, Chap. 7 summarises the PEGIDA phenomenon: it remains to be seen whether PEGIDA has marked the beginning of the long-term establishment of right-wing populist positions and parties in the democratic system of the Federal Republic of Germany.

CHAPTER 1

The Development of PEGIDA:
From a Movement of the Outraged
to a Protest Ritual

The Patriotic Europeans against the Islamisation of the Occident (PEGIDA) represented something unprecedented in the Federal Republic of Germany. Never before had there been a right-wing protest movement that could mobilise on a massive scale and bring thousands or even tens of thousands of supporters onto the street. Hence, PEGIDA's demonstrations and rallies quickly attracted attention well beyond Germany and Europe. The origin and main location of the protest movement was Dresden, the state capital of the *Bundesland* Saxony. It was from here, starting in October 2014, that every week the same pictures went around the world, of a flag-waving and banner-holding crowd, which cleverly presented itself against a baroque backdrop.

Every Monday evening the same ritual could be observed. In a relaxed, even festival-like, yet partly tense atmosphere, thousands of people streamed into the historic centre of town. These were mainly groups of men, many middle-aged, but also married couples, young people, pensioners, as well as numerous people who appeared to belong to the hooligan or neo-Nazi scene. Influenced by the speakers the atmosphere quickly heated up. Slogans like "We are the people" (*Wir sind das Volk*), "Lying press" (*Lügenpresse*) or "Merkel must go" (*Merkel muss weg*) rang out through the night. Remarks which were xenophobic, nationalist and critical of the elites could be heard, and journalists on the sidelines were

© The Author(s) 2018
H. Vorländer et al., *PEGIDA and New Right-Wing Populism in Germany*, New Perspectives in German Political Studies,
https://doi.org/10.1007/978-3-319-67495-7_1

insulted, which made their coverage even more critical. This image presented to the outside world led to the conclusion that PEGIDA was a narrow-minded, blatantly Islamophobic and xenophobic mob, publicly displaying its diffuse fears. And yet its initiators and supporters always denied that they hated foreigners and Islam. In fact, they thought of themselves as the avant-garde among the citizens, who had the courage to take justified criticisms generally shared by the population to the streets as a public protest. With this in mind, the slogan of the freedom movement from 1989, "We are the people" (*Wir sind das Volk*) was also adopted. PEGIDA believed itself to be the core of a collective German and European movement of the outraged, the new "enraged citizens" (*Wutbürger*).

The development of the protests was marked by highs and lows. Their rapid rise in winter 2014/2015 was followed by a progressive erosion of support, so that in July 2015 it seemed that PEGIDA had already come to an end. Then, the refugee crisis[1] of late summer 2015 provided the impetus for a veritable resurrection of the demonstrations, alongside which a noticeable radicalisation began. One could subsequently observe a brutalisation of the political discourse on the streets and on social media, in which the lines between rhetorical and physical violence threatened to become blurred. Since 2016 the new right-wing populist party Alternative for Germany (AfD) has achieved, at times, spectacular electoral success in elections in a number of German states, whereas the number of participants at PEGIDA events soon declined. The right-wing populist protest, it seemed, had now found its way into parliament via the AfD, whereas on the streets it had stagnated and become an increasingly weary protest ritual. Accompanied by further public quarrels among the organisers, PEGIDA's slow decline into insignificance began.

1.1   EMERGENCE AND FIRST SUCCESSES

What presented itself in autumn 2015 as an anti-immigration movement with international ambitions had started a year earlier as a small, like-minded group of friends and acquaintances. In a Facebook group not visible to the public, established on 11.10.2014, views were exchanged

---

[1] The term "refugee crisis" refers to the events of late summer 2015 when—particularly through Greece and the Balkan states—an ever-increasing stream of refugees reached Central Europe. Angela Merkel eventually decided to let them pass the German borders enabling some 1.2 million asylum seekers to enter the country by summer 2017.

about one's dissatisfaction with the political course of the country. The group's initiator, the trained chef and self-employed advertising entrepreneur Lutz Bachmann,[2] later justified the establishment of this group as a result of a demonstration by supporters of the Kurdistan Workers' Party (PKK), which had recently taken place in Dresden, along with the latest reports of ethnically and religiously motivated conflicts between foreigners in German cities.[3] As a matter of fact, the incidents mentioned were in the context of developments which had led to a broad political debate, not only in the traditional media, but also on social media.

Simultaneously, there was extensive reporting about the successes of the so-called Islamic State (IS) in Syria and Iraq, as well as about the targeted killings shown by the group in videos, which led to a debate about possible German support for Kurdish Peshmerga militias (Leithäuser and Bickel 01.09.2014). Subsequently, on 10.10.2014, also in Dresden, a demonstration did in fact occur in which the participants advocated arms shipments to the PKK, which is banned in Germany.[4] At the same time, already in autumn 2014, the housing of refugees was being discussed at a local level. The authorities had revealed plans to establish new accommodation for asylum seekers. According to those plans, in the Dresden area, for instance, around 2000 places were to be provided. In many affected communities resistance quickly emerged, which was voiced in local discussion rounds, local media and social networks and was frequently consolidated in protest initiatives. The target of the criticism was, above all, a seemingly authoritarian style of administration, the lack of involvement of the local population and the lack of a strategy for the housing and

---

[2]After research by journalists more details about the past of the PEGIDA founder soon came to light. Bachmann was sentenced to prison in 1998 for a number of offences, including burglaries and assault. He initially attempted to avoid imprisonment by fleeing to South Africa. After facing deportation from there, he served his sentence in Germany from 2001. After that he worked, among other things, as a bratwurst vendor and in two advertising companies (Machowecz 2015, p. 21f.).

[3]This was stated in an interview for the internet portal of the weekly newspaper *Junge Freiheit* (12.12.2014).—In Celle on 06.10.2014 a "mass brawl" between Kurdish Yazidis and Chechen Muslims had occurred. In the Hamburg district of St. Georg on 08.10.2014 a similar clash took place between Kurds and Salafists (Knoche 08.10.2014; Knaack 08.10.2014; Dostal 2015, p. 24ff.).

[4]Lutz Bachmann had spread footage of this demonstration on social media (Cf. https://www.youtube.com/watch?v=d6aFr9GVE2c).

integration of asylum seekers (Baumann-Hartwig et al. 26.11.2014; Wolf and Llanque 08.08.2014).[5]

Against the backdrop of this mix of developments in global politics, national debates and local conflict situations in the population, a decision was made in Lutz Bachmann's Facebook group to take their outrage to the streets in a protest event. By choosing the label "Patriotic Europeans" the aim was to create the image of a middle-class initiative.[6] Even the first public call for a demonstration in Dresden's city centre, which the PEGIDA organisers distributed among their friends and acquaintances on Facebook, was heeded by around 300 to 350 people on 20.10.2014. In the following weeks the number of participants then rose exponentially. As it turned out, the threat scenarios that were then under discussion and captured in the name "Patriotic Europeans against the Islamisation of the Occident" acted as an emotional catalyst for a fast and successful mobilisation of thousands of supporters (Fig. 1.1).[7]

In the wake of these successes, offshoots of the Dresden PEGIDA initiative were soon also established in other large German cities. As

[5] The problematic nature of these conflicts can be illustrated with the example of the small municipality of Perba. Only around 180 inhabitants lived in the community, without any kind of public infrastructure, such as doctors or shopping facilities, to fall back on. When the housing of 50 predominantly male asylum seekers from North Africa was ordered, protest erupted among local residents. From then on, Perba featured in headlines such as "The anger is growing" or "A village is being overwhelmed" (Scharf 20.11.2014, 17.12.2014a, 17.12.2014b).

[6] The original name of the Facebook group was "Peaceful Europeans against the Islamisation of the Occident" (Friedliche Europäer gegen die Islamisierung des Abendlandes) (Popp and Wassermann 10.01.2015).

[7] The numbers in Fig. 1.1 were calculated by the police (from October 2014 until July 2015) as well as a group of researchers from TU Dresden. Cf. the media information from the Dresden police, accessible at: https://www.polizei.sachsen.de/de/medieninformationen_pdd.htm as well as the blog of the TU-research group, accessible at: https://durchgezaehlt.org. The counting method used by the police was not without controversy and the results were the focus of criticism in the media (Springer 24.12.2014; Keilholz 13.01.2015). The PEGIDA organisers themselves stated figures that were considerably higher in some cases. Also included in Fig. 1.1, for the purposes of comparison, are the numbers of counter-demonstrators who were mobilised in Dresden parallel to the PEGIDA events. Apart from that, there were further large-scale events in the city, where there were protests against PEGIDA. For instance, on 10.01.2015, at an event entitled "For Dresden, for Saxony—for openness to the world, humanity and dialogue in cooperation", there were approximately 35,000 people in attendance according to the event organiser, the Saxon State Chancellery. On 26.01.2015 the association "Dresden—place to be" organised the rally "Open-minded and diverse—Dresden for all" with approximately 22,000 participants. Cf. Sect. 2.2 in Chap. 2.

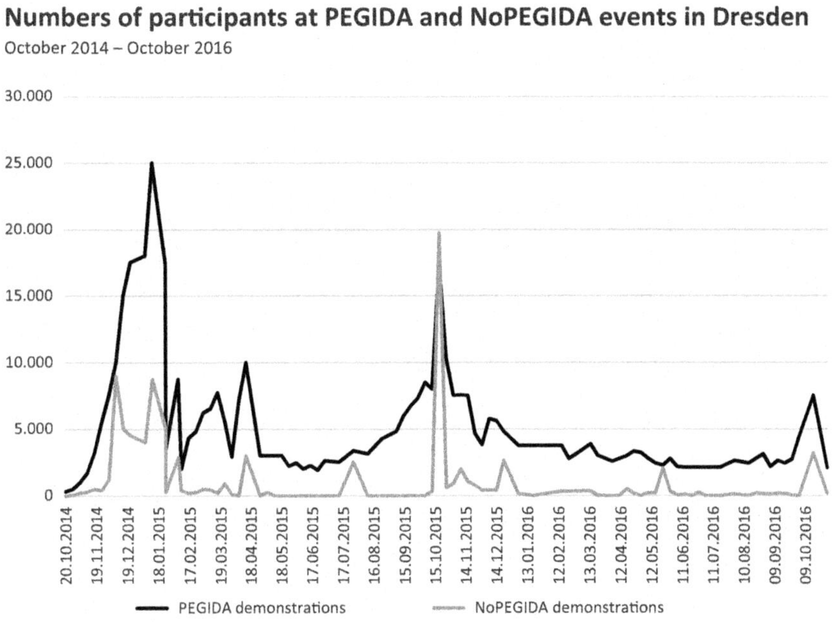

Numbers of participants at PEGIDA and NoPEGIDA events in Dresden
October 2014 – October 2016

Fig. 1.1 Numbers of participants at PEGIDA and NoPEGIDA events in Dresden (October 2014–October 2016)

early as mid-November 2014 a group in Würzburg took to the streets. In December Kassel, Bonn, Munich and Düsseldorf followed, and in early 2015 Hanover, Leipzig, Kiel, Saarbrücken, Braunschweig and further cities joined. In addition to the offshoots throughout Germany, eventually even international groups emerged, which adopted the same general thrust as the Dresden movement, some even taking the name PEGIDA, for example in Great Britain, Spain, Austria, Poland, the Netherlands and even Australia (see Fig. 1.2).[8] However, it was mainly in Dresden that PEGIDA was successful. There the Patriotic Europeans achieved rapid growth until mid-January and on 12.01.2015 ultimately reached the peak of their mobilisation with approximately 25,000 demonstrators.

[8] In Great Britain and Australia existing Islamophobic and xenophobic groups demonstrated under the label of PEGIDA. For example, on 04.04.2015 in Sydney, demonstrators from "Reclaim Australia" carried a PEGIDA banner during protests. A comparison of PEGIDA-offshoots beyond Germany can be found in Berntzen and Weisskircher (2017).

Fig. 1.2 One of the many offshoots, PEGIDA UK, with its spokesperson Tommy Robinson giving a speech at a rally in Birmingham on 6.2.2016. Image credit: Guy Corbishley/Alamy Stock Photo

One week later all PEGIDA-related events in Dresden were cancelled at short notice, because the security authorities had detected a "concrete threat", a planned attack against a member of PEGIDA's organisational team.[9] Sunday, 25.01.2015, was the last time the high level of the previous weeks was close to being achieved with approximately 17,500 participants. After internal conflicts and a first split in PEGIDA's organisational team, considerably fewer people joined the Monday demonstrations from February 2015. With the exception of 13.04.2015, when the Dutch right-wing populist Geert Wilders spoke at a PEGIDA rally in Dresden, by the end of June 2015 the weekly participant numbers had stabilised at approximately 2000 to 3000.

The number of participants at the numerous PEGIDA offshoots in other German cities remained far below the numbers in Dresden. Often

---

[9]This was probably Lutz Bachmann, even though it was neither officially confirmed nor denied by the security authorities.

they were gatherings of only a few hundred people. The demonstrations were often abandoned entirely after disappointing initial events or because of disputes among the local organisers (Kollenberg 06.05.2015; Crolly 16.03.2015). Among the most successful PEGIDA offshoots were two other organisations in Saxony—LEGIDA in Leipzig and PEGIDA-Chemnitz/Erzgebirge. But even this apparent success was marginal in comparison to Dresden: Leipzig only managed to get around 500 to 1000 demonstrators to regularly take to the streets in spring 2015, Chemnitz-Erzgebirge between 300 and 500, and from summer 2015 both experienced a steady downward trend (Freie Presse 19.05.2015; Döring 05.05.2015). After the number of participants dropped further, the organisers of LEGIDA finally announced the official end of the street protests on 09.01.2017, the second anniversary of the Leipzig offshoot.

In Dresden, too, the protests seemed to have passed their peak in spring 2015. After the rapid growth phase, internal disputes about the future course of the movement at the end of January 2015 led to a public row within the organisational team. In this group, up until that point, all decisions had been made based on a simple majority—from questions about the thematic orientation of speeches, or the procedure for Monday demonstrations, right through to dealing with the public and politicians. Only a fragmentary socio-demographic profile of the 12 founding members of PEGIDA can be obtained.[10] At the time of the first demonstrations in autumn 2014 they were all—with the exception of the slightly younger wife of Lutz Bachmann, Vicky Bachmann—between 37 and 55 years old. At least nine of them were self-employed entrepreneurs in small businesses, mainly in the service industry. Some of them had repeatedly suffered existential setbacks in these occupations. There were only two women among the founding members. Three people had already been active in political parties before PEGIDA.[11] Some had professional links to the Dresden party scene, some were active among the supporters of locally

---

[10]The available information is based in part on the research of journalists (in particular Wolf et al. 02.12.2014, 22.12.2014; Wolf and Schawe 10.01.2015; Dresdner Neueste Nachrichten 15.12.2014; Machowecz 2015), but also the information and activities shared in social networks by key figures, as well as behind-the-scenes talks with individuals from the organisational team of PEGIDA or sources close to them.

[11]One for the conservative Christian Democratic Union of Germany (CDU), one for the Social Democratic Party of Germany (SPD) and one for the liberal Free Democratic Party (FDP).

well-known football (SG Dynamo Dresden) and ice hockey clubs (Dresdner Eislöwen). Through these and other connections[12] most of the members of the organisational team are likely to have been acquainted long before PEGIDA. The commitment and collaboration of this group of people was institutionalised with the founding of the PEGIDA association (PEGIDA e.V.) on 19.12.2014; additionally, on 05.03.2015, a "PEGIDA-Förderverein" (a PEGIDA support association) was founded, in which supporters and sympathisers were also meant to become involved through membership in order to support the work of the protest movement through membership fees and donations (Cf. Vorländer et al. 2016, p. 10ff.).

On 28.01.2015 an internal dispute culminated in a split of the Dresden organisational team. The powers more strongly aiming for a moderate, middle-class, conservative image turned their backs on the movement. Among them were René Jahn and Kathrin Oertel, two of the board members of PEGIDA e.V. The cause of the split visible to the public was the publication of text and photographic material associating Lutz Bachmann with xenophobic comments and an imitation of Adolf Hitler.[13] Bachmann initially stepped down, but wanted to continue pulling the group's strings in the background. However, retrospective statements made by the actors involved indicated that it was mainly underlying conflicts about the future course of the movement that had provoked the public dispute.[14] The

---

[12] During the Elbe flood in early summer 2013, Lutz Bachmann was one of the organisers of the flood relief centres set up in the stadium of the football club SG Dynamo Dresden. Contacts were also made there which later gained in importance in the context of PEGIDA. For the dedication he showed during the flood relief Bachmann was awarded the non-monetary "Sächsischer Fluthelferorden" (an award—of a medal and a certificate—for flood relief helpers in Saxony) on 17.01.2014. At an official ceremony the Mayor of Dresden presented this award to deserving flood relief helpers on behalf of Saxony's Minister President Stanislaw Tillich. Bachmann was among them (Fischer 09.12.2014).

[13] An older chat history, which was made public, contained entries in which Bachmann allegedly called asylum seekers "cattle" (*Viehzeug*), "trash" (*Gelumpe*) and "filthy rabble" (*Dreckspack*). Furthermore, a photo surfaced in which Bachmann was posing with a "Hitler hairstyle". According to research by the *Sächsische Zeitung* the moustache was only added to the photo later (Wolf 16.02.2015). On 30.11.2016 Bachmann was convicted in court (Landgericht Dresden) of inciting racial hatred because of the aforementioned statements about asylum seekers (Sächsische Zeitung 30.11.2016b).

[14] The open outbreak of these conflicts took place at a time when individual members of the PEGIDA organisational team had begun to seek contact with political representatives and had started opening themselves up to the media. On 07.01.2015 some of the PEGIDA organisers met with the Saxon AfD parliamentary group (Saft 08.01.2015) and on

consequences of these events were grave for PEGIDA in terms of personnel. Six of the total 12 members left the Dresden organisational team. A
few days later, five of the members who had left founded their own movement, entitled Direct Democracy for Europe (DDfE), which, however,
remained insignificant.

Just two weeks after these events, on 09.02.2015, PEGIDA returned
to the streets. However, the number of participants had nosedived, and
only about 2000 demonstrators gathered. The organisers consequently
employed various measures in an attempt to regain political momentum
and to draw back the media's attention. One such measure was the appearance of the Dutch right-wing populist Geert Wilders on 13.04.2015,
which mobilised around 10,000 PEGIDA supporters. Another measure
was the decision to contest the Dresden mayoral election on 07.06.2015
with the group's own candidate. The candidate chosen was Tatjana
Festerling, who after the organisational team's split first appeared as a
speaker in March 2015, and shortly thereafter became part of the leadership in Dresden.[15] For the subsequent election campaign around €30,000
was provided from the income from donations received by PEGIDA e.V.
(Schenk 03.06.2015). In the first round of voting on 07.06.2015,
Festerling received 9.6 per cent of the valid votes (in absolute numbers:
21,311 votes). She did not contest the second round of voting on
05.07.2015, but did endorse the later victorious liberal candidate Dirk
Hilbert (FDP). Even during the election campaign in April and May 2015
the number of participants still continued to decrease. In June 2015 there
were only between 2000 and 2500 participants. Neither the final phase of
the mayoral electoral campaign nor the announcement of further political
initiatives could alter the fact that interest was dwindling. The PEGIDA
organisers announced plans on 15.06.2015 to enter local and state parliaments via direct mandates and, over the medium term, to found their own

---

27.01.2015 they met the Saxon Minister of the Interior, Markus Ulbig (Spiegel Online
31.01.2015). On 18.01.2015 Kathrin Oertel was the first representative of PEGIDA to have
a guest appearance on a major German television show (*Günther Jauch*). On 19.01.2015, in
a high-profile press conference, Lutz Bachmann and Kathrin Oertel answered questions
asked by representatives of the media.

[15]Tatjana Festerling, a well-educated entrepreneur with a professional career as consultant
and marketing expert, had already appeared as a founding member of the Hamburg branch
of the AfD party. However, a short time later she resigned from the party to avoid impending
expulsion proceedings.

party. PEGIDA had, however, clearly lost its initial momentum and observers expected the protest movement to soon come to an end (Alexe 16.06.2015; Schenk 21.05.2015).

This picture did not change until August 2015 when an ever-increasing stream of refugees reached Germany and Angela Merkel eventually enabled the entry of hundreds of thousands of asylum seekers. In many parts of Germany this sparked a new wave of protest against the refugee policy, which was also accompanied by a significant increase in violent attacks on refugees and their accommodation.[16] Against this background, PEGIDA was able to profit from the heated political situation and create new interest in the demonstrations. The movement's initiators, Lutz Bachmann and Tatjana Festerling, now attempted to position it as the leading platform for protest against the refugee policy of the Federal Republic. Thus, speeches and comments on social media now focused almost exclusively on the issue of refugees, fuelling the fear of rising crime, social disadvantage and of being culturally overwhelmed by foreigners. In this context, reference was frequently made to alleged incidents which then quickly spread on social media, but the truthfulness of these claims was difficult to determine. The protest movement addressed existing feelings of resentment towards refugees and attempted to make targeted use of them. At the same time, on 10.08.2015, PEGIDA released a new list of demands concerned exclusively with asylum policy.[17] Thus, by the end of September 2015, PEGIDA had turned into a clear anti-immigration movement and, against the backdrop of the refugee crisis, was in fact again able to achieve the high number of participants that it had in winter 2014/2015. On 19.10.2015, the first anniversary of the protests, between 17,000 and 20,000 participants watched a comparatively professional stage production with elaborate video output, a specially composed hymn, as well as numerous speeches by international guests.

---

[16] In Saxony such attacks seemed to occur with particular frequency. Media attention focused in particular on incidents in Freital, where a citizens' initiative protested vehemently against the local initial reception camp for refugees; in Heidenau, where, on 22.08.2015, a right-wing extremist mob was involved in a street fight with the police; in Clausnitz, where, on 18.02.2016, a protesting crowd of people blocked the access to accommodation for a bus carrying refugees; as well as in Bautzen, where on 14.09.2016 there were violent clashes between local youths and north African asylum seekers (Cf. Lindner 28.06.2015; Locke 25.08.2015, 21.02.2016, 16.09.2016).

[17] The paper entitled "Ten demands for German asylum policy" is available at http://www. tatjanafesterling.de/download/PEGIDA_10_Forderungen_DE.pdf (Accessed 01.06.2017).

The organisers subsequently attempted to sustain this success by connecting the orientation of PEGIDA as an anti-immigration movement with increasingly radical statements about Islam and Muslims and to tie PEGIDA in content-wise with the established right-wing populist movements in Europe (cf. Sect. 3.4 in Chap. 3). Even in terms of organisation PEGIDA attempted to consolidate. A mobile stage with high-performance sound technology and a wireless mobile communications system were purchased. This technology was paid for with the help of donations, money which came partly from the donation boxes regularly set up at each rally. Since spring 2017 PEGIDA has generated revenue from its own online shop, which commercially exploits the brand "PEGIDA" in the form of printed t-shirts, sweaters and lanyards for keys. Additionally, PEGIDA has built up its presence on social media. Alongside its already exisiting Facebook page, a YouTube channel, a Twitter account and a website were added, on which every rally could now be followed via livestream on the internet. The hymn composed especially for the first anniversary was made available from an online music provider as an MP3 file.[18]

Efforts to appear more professional were, however, often counteracted by contradictory statements and amateurish practices. The founding of a political party was announced a number of times, without being carried out; a planned collection of signatures against the fee collection service of Germany's public broadcasting institutions (GEZ) failed; defamation charges against political opponents which were announced in front of supporters failed to materialise; and, contrary to announcements, the PEGIDA Förderverein e.V. (PEGIDA support association) was never opened for supporters. Emerging tensions between Lutz Bachmann and Tatjana Festerling eventually led to Festerling's departure from PEGIDA's organisational team at the beginning of May 2016. Bachmann accused Festerling of having put off the demonstrators with her aggressive rhetoric thereby squandering the recent mobilisation successes. Reciprocal hostilities, disputes and numerous speculations about the reasons for the rift were spread publicly on social media over a period of several months.

In autumn 2016 the official Day of German Unity celebrations took place in Dresden, providing PEGIDA with the opportunity to once again

---

[18]The internet presence can be found at: http://www.pegida.de, the YouTube channel at: https://youtube.com/channel/UC65Iv3g2t8a8oQqWkSh5aYg and the Twitter account at: https://mobile.twitter.com/official_pegida.

attract media attention and to stage an effective public protest in front of the prominent German politicians and many foreign guests who were gathered in Dresden. Accordingly, on 03.10.2016, attendees of the ceremony for the Day of German Unity were offensively abused, mobbed, and harassed with whistles by an enraged, yet purposeful and controlled crowd (Locke 03.10.2016). In light of this, the President of the Bundestag Norbert Lammert mentioned the protests in his ceremonial address in the Semperoper in Dresden and pointed out that a defence of the west is still bound by minimum standards, which were obviously not being observed by the protestors.[19]

Effective public actions of this kind were, however, unable to hide that PEGIDA had become disorientated both organisationally and in terms of its programme. Whilst the, by now, small number of participants went through the same ritual of speeches, slogans and a protest march week after week, the right wing populist party AfD entered the parliaments of Hamburg and Bremen as well as Baden-Württemberg, Rhineland-Palatinate, Saxony-Anhalt, Mecklenburg-Vorpommern and Berlin in the state elections in 2015 and 2016.[20] Thus, in politics, the media and the public, the AfD had finally become representatives of the diffuse motivations for protest and indignation which had originally given rise to PEGIDA's foundation.

1.2   POSITIONS

Between December 2014 and January 2016 the Patriotic Europeans conveyed their thematic orientation through position papers, lists of demands and statements. Individual demands, which were initially only presented in speeches, were followed on 10.12.2014 by a first position paper, consisting of 19 points and published via Facebook.[21] Due to the fact the paper did not have the desired impact in the media, on 12.01.2015 it was

---

[19]The speech by the President of the Bundestag Norbert Lammert is available at: http://www.bundestag.de/parlament/praesidium/reden/2016/004/462296 (Accessed 01.06.2017).

[20]The AfD's share of votes was as follows: Hamburg (15.02.2015): 6.1 per cent, Bremen (10.05.2015): 5.5 per cent, Baden-Württemberg (13.03.2016): 15.1 per cent, Rhineland-Palatinate (13.03.2016): 12.6 per cent, Saxony-Anhalt (13.03.2016): 24.3 per cent, Mecklenburg-Vorpommern (04.09.2016): 20.8 per cent and Berlin (18.09.2016): 14.2 per cent.

[21]The *19 points* paper can be accessed at: http://www.i-finger.de/pegida-positionspapier.pdf (Accessed 01.06.2017).

followed by an abbreviated version entitled "Six demands to policy-makers", which was also shared on Facebook. After the split in the Dresden organisational team, there was a meeting of PEGIDA offshoots from throughout Germany in mid-February 2015, which took place in Moritzburg near Dresden. As a result of this meeting, on 15.02.2015 a new position paper entitled "Dresden theses" was presented, which had been devised as a thematic platform for all PEGIDA offshoots. There were no new topics in the paper. Instead the demands, which were already known from the *19 points*, had been presented in a systematic form.[22] Then in summer 2015, the transition from a diffuse protest movement to an anti-immigration movement manifested itself in the so-called "10 demands for German asylum policy". These ten demands were first presented on 10.08.2015 in a speech by Tatjana Festerling and subsequently released by PEGIDA as a further position paper.[23]

In total, the demands made by PEGIDA in their position papers covered six thematic areas: refugees and immigration, Islam and Islamisation, internal security, direct democracy, foreign policy as well as so-called political correctness. The topic "Refugees and immigration" was addressed in most detail in all papers.[24] Here, it was stated first of all that PEGIDA supported the right to asylum for "war refugees" and those suffering political or religious persecution, as well as expedited asylum proceedings, but also accelerated deportation proceedings for asylum seekers who have been turned down. There were demands for adequate, decentralised housing and a better care ratio for asylum seekers, a pan-European allocation of refugees, but also "a zero tolerance policy towards asylum seekers and immigrants who have committed a crime". Furthermore they called for an "obligation to integrate" to be incorporated into the Basic Law. Then, in the *Dresden theses*, came the demand for an immigration law "based on the Swiss or Canadian model" according to demographic, economic and cultural factors, which would allegedly enable a "qualitative control" of immigration. Also to be found here was the theory that a change in family policy could be the key to reversing demographic change and preventing

---

[22] The *Dresden theses* can be accessed at: http://www.pegida.de/ (Accessed 01.06.2017).

[23] http://www.tatjanafesterling.de/download/PEGIDA_10_Forderungen_DE.pdf (Accessed 01.06.2017).

[24] In the *19 points* there were nine associated demands, in the *Dresden theses* there were three. In the *10 demands for German asylum policy* the topic of refugees was the only one addressed and the stance also became tougher.

a feared minoritisation of "indigenous Germans". In contrast, the *10 demands for German asylum policy* resorted to uncompromising language, making the previous papers seem comparatively moderate. Against the backdrop of the refugee crisis in autumn 2015, in this paper the apparently uncontrolled migration, described as illegitimate immigration to a welfare state, as well as a perceived threat of foreign criminals and Islamist terrorists, had been condensed into a manifesto of a right-wing populist and Islamophobic anti-immigration movement. Stemming from this were demands for an asylum emergency law, suspension of the Schengen Agreement, deportation of all rejected asylum seekers as well as a withdrawal from the European Union (EU), "the useless outfit that oppresses"[25] all member states.

The "Islamisation" which gave the protest movement its name was also addressed in several respects: the demands were said to be directed at Islam as a "misogynist, violent political ideology but not against Muslims living here who are integrating", against "parallel societies/parallel courts in our midst, like Sharia courts, Sharia police" or Muslim "justices of the peace" as well as against "those who preach hate, regardless of what religion they belong to".[26] In the *Dresden theses* from February 2015, the topic of "Islam and Islamisation" had received much less attention and was to be found in just a single demand, which was of a general nature.

Demands for a police budget increase and an end to reductions in staff, for referendums according to the Swiss model and for a suspension of weapon shipments to war zones the topics "Internal Security", "Direct Democracy" and "Foreign Policy" were represented in PEGIDA's position papers. In addition, there were commitments "to sexual self-determination" and against the "obsessive, politically correct gender-neutralisation of our language". In particular, the topic of "Foreign policy" was greatly expanded in the *Dresden theses* from February 2015. Firstly, there was a demand for a normalisation of the relationship with Russia. Secondly, there was a statement against supranationalisation, demanding the replacement of the EU with a bond between "strong sovereign national states in free political and economic self-determination". Here Eurosceptic positions merged with the call for more democratic participation. Thirdly, PEGIDA also included

---

[25] This is the actual wording in the tenth demand. Cf. http://www.tatjanafesterling.de/download/PEGIDA_10_Forderungen_DE.pdf (Accessed 01.06.2017).

[26] Cf. in the *19 points* 10, 16, 18 and 19.

reservations about the Transatlantic Trade and Investment Partnership (TTIP), which were widespread and intensely discussed at the time, because an agreement of this kind would be harmful to "European self-determination and the European economy".

In politics and the media the position papers were met with fierce criticism, mainly tied to their inconsistency and vagueness. The general consensus was that with the *19 points* PEGIDA was trying to disguise its radical demeanour. The much too general demands were said to invite "free riders from splinter parties on the right-wing fringe" to use the PEGIDA movement for their own dubious goals. Finally, it was said that the organisers were using this paper and their apparently middle-class slogans in an attempt to conceal their own right-wing extremist intentions (Sächsische Zeitung 11.12.2014; Anderson 16.01.2015; Frigelj 13.12.2014).[27] In addition, the media and the general public hardly took any notice of the content of the position papers, even though the demonstrators from Dresden referred to the papers again and again as the basis for their participation. In particular, the first two position papers, the *19 points* and the *Dresden theses*, constituted a regular point of reference, whereas the *10 demands* were soon forgotten.

With their position papers the PEGIDA organisers wanted, above all, to demonstrate the sincerity of their concerns as well as to clearly distance themselves from extremist activities through relatively moderate demands. The papers were thus somewhat in contrast to the speeches held at PEGIDA events, in which blanket criticism of Islam and populist attacks on politicians were used to stoke the mood of the crowd. The speeches held on stage by PEGIDA only rarely had a direct function in the programme. Instead, through the exaggerated expression of indignation, they served to drive the mood among the demonstrators. At the same time, they were part of a recurring sequence of events, which constituted an important element in the enactment of the protest with the weekly repetition of familiar positions by known speakers. Ultimately, while PEGIDA used the speeches to present itself as a victim of a political and media elite, its positions were also expressed. The first speeches at the Dresden PEGIDA demonstrations were usually given by the initiators of the protests themselves. It was not until later that they were joined by non-local

---

[27]For the conceptual fuzziness of the contemporary European radical right, cf. Önnerfors (2017).

guests. The early versions of these speeches in October and November 2014 took up, with slight thematic variations, those points that were written in the first position papers. The departure of the moderate organisers at the end of January 2015, however, finally influenced the choice of external speakers to the extent that now even speakers who previously would not have gained majority support in the organisational team due to their proven radicalism were invited.

Some of these speakers were frequently invited by PEGIDA from then on and they started to shape the movement's image with their different respective areas of focus. Among these speakers was, for instance, Edwin Wagensveld, born in the Netherlands but based in Germany, proprietor of an internet-based retailer for pneumatic weapons, "self-defence articles" and outdoor products. He mainly made the topic of "Islamisation" the focal point and claimed that the spread of Muslim customs and conventions was displacing German culture and that this was willingly tolerated by politicians. A remarkable naivety in dealing with Islam on the part of the media-political establishment was also claimed by Udo Ulfkotte. The former *Frankfurter Allgemeine Zeitung* journalist and author of a critical, conspiracy theory-laden bestseller about the German media landscape spoke on 05.01.2015 on the stage in Dresden. René Stadtkewitz, a former Berlin CDU member and founder of the former party Die Freiheit, intensified the thrust of PEGIDA's criticism of Islam on 23.02.2015 by characterising Islam as a politically totalitarian ideology. On 13.04.2015 the Dutch right-wing populist Geert Wilders endorsed these theories and also warned about the consequences of an aggressive Islam, which, if necessary, would need to be combatted by also restricting the right to asylum.[28] Another exponent of a blanket criticism of Islam at PEGIDA was Michael Stürzenberger, the author of the Islamophobic news portal "Politically Incorrect". His speeches reflect a defamation of the religion and all its followers, which can hardly be seen as compatible with the Basic Law. With the use of speakers like Stürzenberger, a more radical Islamophobic and xenophobic position within PEGIDA became apparent, with which it opposed any and all forms of Muslim immigration as an alleged threat to one's own western culture. Other speakers focused their criticism above all

[28] See the transcripts of the speeches by Edwin Wagensveld (called "Ed uit Utrecht") on 22.12.2014, Udo Ulfkotte on 05.01.2015, René Stadtkewitz on 23.02.2015 and Geert Wilders on 13.04.2015.

on the political and media elites in Germany. Götz Kubitschek, proprietor of a national-conservative publisher and protagonist of the so-called New Right in Germany, for example,[29] linked his scolding of the media-political class in several appearances in Dresden with a semantically barely disguised ethno-nationalistic position.

As of spring 2015, however, Tatjana Festerling became the most important speaker at PEGIDA. Her condemnation of the political-cultural establishment was particularly shrill and defamatory. She, for instance, referred to the political personnel of the Federal Republic as a "swearing plague of apparatchiks in our parliaments" and lashed out at the conventions of so-called political correctness calling it "minority terror" and "an attitude dictatorship".[30] In view of the immigration and integration policy, she spoke of "fantasies of self-destruction" in "left-wing green strongholds". In this context she dismissed Chancellor Angela Merkel and Vice Chancellor Sigmar Gabriel as being "destroyers of Germany".[31] She said that "gender mainstreaming", "early sexual education" and similar were the work of "screwed up gender ladies", a radical "socialist queer-sexual minority lobby", which had set itself the goal of "already traumatising our children with their excessive sexual crap in primary school".[32] All this, according to Festerling, would justify a new wall between the East and the West, which would protect the "patriotic East" from the "green empire" in the West.[33] As a candidate in the Dresden mayoral electoral campaign at the beginning of May 2015, Festerling initially adopted a more moderate tone, only later again attract attention through her disparaging rhetoric.[34] As a reaction to the refugee crisis Festerling distinguished herself with her speeches as a tough critic of German refugee policy. Central to this were the rising numbers of refugees, whose misconduct and dubious reasons for fleeing were almost exclusively interpreted as a desire to migrate to a welfare state, and the Federal Government, which was accused of poli-

---

[29] See the information about Götz Kubitschek in Chap. 3.
[30] See the transcripts of her speeches at PEGIDA on 09.03.2015 and 30.03.2015.
[31] See the transcripts of her speeches at PEGIDA on 09.03.2015 and 06.04.2015.
[32] See the transcripts of her speeches at PEGIDA on 30.03.2015 and 06.04.2015.
[33] See the transcript of her speech at PEGIDA on 09.03.2015.
[34] Festerling, on 01.06.2015, labelled "our opponents", the politicians in Brussels and Berlin as "alcoholics". Their parties were said to be riddled with "communists" and "kid fuckers". (See the transcript of her speech on 01.06.2015).

cies to harm the German people. In particular Chancellor Angela Merkel became the target of biting, at times even insulting, criticism.[35]

After Festerling left PEGIDA's organisational team in June 2016 the content profile of the speeches once again began to shift. PEGIDA now increasingly prioritised the topic of "Criticism of journalism". Beyond that, however, the protest movement no longer attracted attention with its own topics. Instead, it mainly concentrated on commenting on current, day-to-day, political headlines and events. An attempt was thereby made to divert a noticeable protest potential towards PEGIDA, namely in the context of the so-called Bilderberg conference in June 2016 in Dresden, during the festivities of the Day of German Unity in Dresden on 03.10.2016 and, for instance, on the occasion of several controversial art installations in the historic centre of Dresden.[36]

1.3   THE STAGING OF THE PEGIDA PROTEST

The, in many areas, seemingly moderate demands of PEGIDA's position papers were not only in contrast to the speeches, but also to the appearance of the rallies on the streets. Here, the protest movement became visible above all through the public display of anger and indignation. Crowds marching in the darkness, flags waving, aggressively recited chants with unsettling contents, a defiant, in part even violent, rejection of journalists: this side of PEGIDA dominated the media coverage, even though an impartial, on the spot observer could clearly perceive a more differentiated picture.

The Dresden demonstration events were characterised by a calm and orderly, almost strictly organised, procedure. The event concept usually consisted of three parts: a stationary starting rally, followed by a protest

---

[35] In this time, for the first time in one of her speeches, Festerling also took up the concept of "Umvolkung" (the replacement of an ethnicity), which stems from a strategy of the New Right to recode political language. This term suggests a deliberate conspiratorial strategy of the political elites against one's "own people", who are to be replaced by a new majority-securing constituency. In general terms, the speeches at PEGIDA rallies reflected to a large extent topics of the New Right. Speakers, for instance, emphasised the values of German and Saxon culture and traditions, their endangerment by foreign influences, especially by a massive refugee influx (Del Giudice et al. 2018). Cf. to the corresponding analysis on ethnocentrism in Sect. 5.4 in Chap. 5.

[36] For example, the art installation "Monument" by the artist Manaf Halbouni, which generated national and international attention, and which stood in front of the Frauenkirche in Dresden between February and April 2017. The installation consisted of three vertically placed buses, which were supposed to be a reminder of how the civilian population in the Syrian city of Aleppo sought shelter from snipers (Kirschbaum 11.02.2017).

march described as an "evening stroll", which in turn was concluded with a closing rally. At the initial events, main speakers were used before the organisers eventually asked participants to walk peacefully and silently through Dresden, along an announced route. At the closing rally there were greetings and further short speeches were delivered. The final act of a PEGIDA event often consisted of participants holding their mobile phones or lighters into the dark evening sky, so that a "light would dawn on" the opponents of PEGIDA, in other words they would become enlightened.[37] This "sea of light" in the evening darkness as a conclusion to proceedings had a strong symbolic and inclusive effect for participants. It was not until spring 2015 when the lighting conditions in the early evening no longer allowed this illumination effect that the organisers attempted to find a replacement by singing the national hymn as a conclusion.

This recurring sequence led to a uniform and ritualised protest, which had the effect for the demonstrators of building a community. The regular demonstrations developed into a kind of "regulars' street table", which afforded an opportunity to exchange political views with friends and like-minded people. One found confirmation for one's own position in the positions of others. The generation of communicative power by the high-profile occupation of prominent streets and squares, the repetition of certain processes along with the weekly combination of rallies and an evening stroll created a feeling of belonging to a group, a community that was able to generate national and international attention and thereby gain political relevance.

The PEGIDA offshoots in other cities attempted to copy this three-part event concept. However, there the counter-protest was often so fierce that PEGIDA remained limited to holding only a stationary rally.[38] In Dresden, on the other hand, the organisation and implementation of the individual events was based on a meticulously planned security concept, which was intended to ensure the event would run smoothly without disruption. In this way, PEGIDA attempted both to avoid external interference, but also to have a disciplinary influence on its demonstrators, in order to emphasise

---

[37] This was the request that Lutz Bachmann first made to the demonstration participants on 24.11.2014 and which later was varied in several ways. See the transcript of the speech by Bachmann on 24.11.2014.

[38] Even in Dresden it was not always possible to stick to this concept because counter-demonstrations and sit-ins occasionally forced a change of the demonstration route or a relocation of the closing gathering.

the impression of a peaceful, middle-class, evening stroll. Tasked with the development and implementation of this security concept were those organisers who had professional experience in holding major events and who had the relevant contacts to recruit the necessary security personnel. Thus, the stewards employed at PEGIDA probably came mainly from the extended group of friends and acquaintances of the organisers who were well-connected in Dresden and the surrounding area—for instance, from those associated with a Radebeul American Football club, a motorcycle club or from the supporter scene of the football club SG Dynamo Dresden. The plan was for there to be one steward to 50 demonstrators, which at the large demonstrations in December 2014 and January 2015 meant that on some Mondays as many as 300 PEGIDA wardens were on duty.[39] These people wore a white armband and their primary task was to see to it that the legal regulations and the requirements laid down by the authorities were adhered to. They enforced a ban on alcohol and glass bottles, for example, and formed a frame around the march in order to quickly defuse critical situations—such as contact with counter-demonstrators. This is the reason why hardly any violent incidents occurred at the demonstrations.

Although the protest could thus be described as predominantly peaceful and non-violent, one could nevertheless regularly observe an angry if not aggressive mood at the events. This impression was created above all by the combative, partly aggressive slogans, which were chanted by the demonstrators and often recited as part of the interaction between a speaker and the audience. Approval of the speeches was expressed through calls like "We are the people!" (*Wir sind das Volk!*), "Yes!" (*Jawohl!*), "Shame!" (*Pfui!*) and "Traitors of the people!" (*Volksverräter!*),[40] and the closing rally was usually closed with the slogan "We will be back". With its regular repetition, the joint chanting of these and other slogans soon took on the form of a weekly ritual. With the exclamation "Lying press" (*Lügenpresse*) contempt for journalists was expressed, which also often erupted into insults and aggressive harassment of representatives of the media who were on the spot (cf. only Thurau 12.01.2015). When

---

[39]When PEGIDA was at its peak some individuals were also recruited as wardens from the midst of the demonstrators with a loudspeaker announcement made at the site of the rally calling for assistance before the beginning of the opening event.

[40]In particular the use of the slogan "We are the people!" earned the demonstrators criticism and the accusation of presumptuousness from former GDR civil rights campaigners. Cf. for instance Baumann-Hartwig (26.11.2014), Zweigler (27.01.2015).

PEGIDA again gained numbers in the course of the refugee crisis, the protest movement also became radicalised in terms of its slogans. Thus, from summer 2015 its disdain for the German Federal Chancellor and her asylum policy were expressed with cries in unison of "Merkel must go!" (*Merkel muss weg!*) and "Resistance!" (*Widerstand!*).

Alongside the slogans, the image of PEGIDA on the streets was also shaped by banners and signs. As a conglomeration of demands, mottos and invectives they were directed against an impending "Islamisation" of Germany,[41] against the immigration and asylum policy at the time and came out in favour of the preservation of traditions, one's homeland and own identity.[42] On other placards there was criticism of the political system, the parties and politicians, and in particular the German Chancellor Angela Merkel and the German President at the time, Joachim Gauck. More opportunities for democratic co-determination were demanded,[43] the media coverage[44] as well as the supposed dictates of political correctness[45] were denounced and the foreign policy course of the Federal Government was criticised.[46] Quotations from well-known personalities were intended

[41]Cf. mottos like "Against religious fanaticism and every kind of radicalism! Together without violence" (22.12.2014); "Peace treaty & constitution instead of Sharia & Jihad", "Better upright to PEGIDA, than tomorrow on your knees towards Mecca", "Islam = carcinoma" (12.01.2015).

[42]"Preserve homeland and identity, stop asylum fraud" (08.12.2014); "For the future of our children", "No room for economic refugees and foreign criminals", "More money for our children, instead of for foreigners" (15.12.2014); "Stop war-mongering and refugee flows" (05.01.2015); "Multiculture kills", "Stop excessive immigration! We want a secure, social, German homeland", "1989: We are the people! 2014: We are still the people. 2039: We were the people" (12.01.2015).

[43]Cf. slogans like "Courage to be democratic now" (01.12.2014); "Parties good night, citizens to power", "Plebiscites into the Basic Law" (15.12.2014); "End EU diktat—introduce direct democracy", "All politicians are elected SERVANTS of the people! And not the other way around" (12.01.2015).

[44]"An end to lies and deception. The courage to be truthful" (22.12.2014).

[45]"For free expression of opinion—PEGIDA" (12.01.2015); "Genderism is western decadence" (09.03.2015).

[46]"Peace with Russia! Never again war in Europe!" (08.12.2014); "Democrats respect freedom; do not commit genocide; respect the freedom of the press; do not instigate wars, like: Libya, Syria, Iraq; respect the law; do not murder political opponents; do not lie to the people" (05.01.2015); "USA, NATO, EU, Germany—If you want peace, you have to make peace" (12.01.2015); "For world peace: no export of weapons of war; no un-Christian CDU" (09.03.2015); "Gospodin Putin! Help us, save us, from the corrupt anti-popular regime of the Federal Republic of Germany, and also from America and Israel" (13.04.2015).

to lend authority to the demonstrators' own opinions.[47] Lastly, many placards and numerous flags were intended to show the origin of the demonstrators carrying them. Alongside the colours of various German
Bundesländer, the flags of other countries were regularly displayed, including French, Ukrainian, Israeli and (most frequently) Russian flags. Some
flags were deliberately chosen with the intent of making political statements. These included, against the backdrop of the attacks in Paris on
07.01.2015, the French flag or, in the context of the war in Ukraine, the
Russian flag, but also countless German flags. They were meant to be interpreted as a commitment to one's own country, as an expression of national
sentiment or—as in the case of a regularly carried, black-red-gold cross—as
a symbolic display of one's own "Christian-occidental (guiding) culture".

Furthermore, the flag of the Identitarian Movement developed symbolic political power—a group with a New Right ethno-nationalistic
background—as well as the frequently seen so-called Wirmer flag. The
flag of the Identitarian Movement is a black lambda in a circle, depicted
on a yellow background (or the same symbol with the colours reversed).
This flag is used as a symbol of the resistance against a perceived invasion
of the western world by "conquerors from a foreign culture from the
Orient", especially from Muslim-Arab regions. With the Greek letter
lambda the flag creates a mythologically transfigured reference to the
ancient Lacedaemonians or Spartans, whose elite military troops, the
Spartiates, according to Herodotus, prevented the Persian conquest and
oppression of civilised Greece at the Battle of Thermopylae in 480 BC. The
Wirmer flag, on the other hand, shows—similar to the flag of Norway—a
black, gold-framed cross on a red background. Originally used as a symbol of the resistance of those German army officers who attempted to
assassinate Hitler on 20.07.1944, this flag has undergone a series of rein-
terpretations and attempts to appropriate it as a symbol over the past years
in Germany, for instance in the context of the so-called New Right. Also,
in the case of PEGIDA, the carriers of this flag have evidently attempted
to tap into the symbolic reservoir of the resistance, whereby the Federal
Republic was thus equated with a totalitarian system (Kellerhoff
20.01.2015; see Fig. 1.3).

---

[47] "PEGIDA. First they ignore you, then they laugh at you, then they fight you, then you
win. (Mahatma Gandhi)" (05.01.2015); "He who does not learn to adapt himself to the
laws, must leave the region where they prevail. (Johann Wolfgang von Goethe 1749–1823)"
(06.04.2015).

Fig. 1.3 Wirmer flags that have become iconic for the PEGIDA protests, seen at a rally on 31.10.2016 in Dresden. Cover credit: PACIFIC PRESS/Alamy Stock Photo

1.4   PEGIDA on Social Media

The public perception of PEGIDA was also based to a significant extent on the image that the protest movement and its supporters presented on social media. In particular the PEGIDA "fan page" found on Facebook was relevant for evaluating the protest movement. Unlike the demonstrations on the streets, here the culture of discussion that could be observed was, to a substantial degree, uninhibited and coarsened, and also crossed the line of what would be a punishable offence. This was amplified by the communication effects particular to social media. The page acted as a filter bubble, thus hardly any information contrary to the viewpoints of PEGIDA supporters could enter. At the same time, a space with the opinions of like-minded people was formed, a so-called echo chamber, in which the already polarised supporters mutually reinforced each other's views and became radicalised. While PEGIDA sometimes conveyed the image of a completely deteriorated culture of discussion on its website, this platform was, however, connected with the opportunity to create a counter-public independent of the traditional media, and to engage in direct interaction with supporters. The Facebook page served as a platform for communication among like-minded people as well as for the integration and involvement of supporters. Lastly, the social networks also provided an "alternative opportunity structure", with which the PEGIDA organisers could disseminate content economically and with a wide coverage (Kneuer and Demmelhuber 2012, p. 33).

The huge response to PEGIDA's Facebook fan page also influenced the perception of the protests outside of social media. Initially, there was interest in the immense growth in supporter numbers, which in the first months through to February 2015 grew to as many as 160,000. In summer 2015 the 200,000 supporter mark was reached. At the beginning of 2016 the PEGIDA account had considerably more "likes" than the parties represented in the Bundestag, even more than the internet-savvy Pirate Party and more than the AfD, which is also very active on Facebook.[48] Within the space of a few months the PEGIDA page on Facebook had become the most far-reaching platform from the right of the political spectrum in the Federal Republic.[49] Thus, PEGIDA supporters on Facebook were more active than the supporters of AfD and of the extremist right-wing National Democratic Party of Germany (NPD).[50] Moreover, overlaps in the interactions between PEGIDA supporters and the Facebook pages of political parties showed that supporters of PEGIDA much more frequently "liked" something on the pages of AfD and the Christian Social Union in Bavaria (CSU), than, for instance, on the pages of other German parties. And vice versa, the entries on the "fan page" of PEGIDA registered most "likes" from supporters of AfD and CSU (Stier et al. 2017, p. 1372f.). The supporters of the PEGIDA movement on Facebook differed, however, from those who protested on the streets. The former were considerably younger

[48] On 01.01.2016 the CDU had 98,989 "likes", the SPD 92,371, the Greens 77,912, The Left (Die Linke) 125,749, the Pirate Party 83.128 and the AfD had 180,786 "likes".

[49] The reach of such a page is expressed in the interactions carried out by the users of the page, for instance when a post is commented on, shared and "liked". In this respect the PEGIDA "fan page" achieved record high numbers between December 2014 and February 2016. However, only around 50 per cent of the digital followers of PEGIDA engaged in at least one interaction. Only every tenth user interacted ten times or more on the PEGIDA "fan page" (Pleul and Scharf 2016, p. 344).

[50] On the "fan page" of the AfD it was 9.3 per cent of all supporters who interacted ten times or more, on the "fan page" of the NPD, 7.6 per cent of the users. In comparison to these figures the interaction rates for both the big parties, CDU and SPD, with 2.1 per cent and 1.2 per cent respectively proved to be absolutely marginal (Institut für Demokratieforschung 2016, p. 50).

than the demonstrators, which is not atypical for internet users in comparison with the population as a whole. Their places of residence were spread throughout the entire Federal Republic (Pleul and Scharf 2016, pp. 333–338).

On 23.07.2016 the PEGIDA page was removed from the internet because posts had contravened the Facebook Community Standards. In this way the protest movement lost the digital following of approximately 200,000 supporters and sympathisers in one fell swoop (Sächsische Zeitung 23.07.2016). This was a bitter blow for the movement's reach on social media and the connected possibilities to set agendas. By May 2017 there were only around 45,000 supporters following the new PEGIDA fan page which was subsequently created.

The original, first PEGIDA page had also been able to develop into a counter-public in no small part because the organisers were able to pass on their messages directly to their supporters without the filter of journalistic editing and classification. On the one hand, the administrators regularly published invitations to upcoming demonstration there, including announcements of particularly prominent speakers or other special items in the programme. On the other hand, the PEGIDA organisers used their page to share appeals with their supporters—such as the appeal to activate a still "silent majority" of like-minded people, which needed to be exploited for PEGIDA to achieve its goals or to disseminate certain pertinent news items. In these reports the alleged consequences of immigration were denounced (mostly with an undercurrent of scandal), the criminality of immigrants was emphasised, proponents of immigration were made to look like naive "do-gooders" and morally self-centred "people who clap at railway stations",[51] and politicians were accused of condescension, contempt and conspiratorial intentions towards their "own people".

The PEGIDA Facebook posts shared by the administrators of the PEGIDA page could also be quantitatively evaluated and sorted according to certain main topics. What came up the most was criminality, own

---

[51] This referred to the events of the refugee crisis in summer 2015 in Germany when pictures went around the globe showing people applauding trains at Munich's central station arriving with Syrian refugees. Later, critics of the generous German immigration and refugee policy sarcastically referred to these events calling supporters of the policy naïve "railway station clappers".

demonstration activities and Islam as well as the distorted coverage by the media. In contrast, welfare state policies, gender equality and the EU (Stier et al. 2017, p. 1375) were much more rarely addressed. These main topics were, however, not all deemed to be equally relevant by the users of the page. In 2015 posts about the topics "PEGIDA and its opponents", the "policies of the established parties" and also "refugees and immigrants" received the most comments with shares between 21 and 24 per cent. Other topics, such as "Islam", the "media" or pessimistic "expectations for the future" remained stuck at a lower level, between 4 and 6 per cent. The proportion of commentators who made inflammatory and dehumanising statements, was, however, comparatively low here (Stefanowitsch and Flach 2016, p. 2).[52]

With the online presence on Facebook the protest organisers succeeded in effectively using social networks for the coordination, mobilisation and integration of their support. At the same time, PEGIDA made itself independent of the conventional media by using such a "counter-public". Bypassing intermediary media institutions when addressing one's supporters can be seen as an important feature of populist movements in general (Urbinati 2015; Müller 2016). It should, however, be noted that, in terms of supporters, PEGIDA on social media was only identical in part with the demonstrators on the streets of Dresden. The PEGIDA protest marches on the streets had to reassemble on a weekly basis, whereas PEGIDA on the internet proved to be an outraged protest community in perpetuity. Here a homogenous and closed world view was maintained, one which can be described in just a few sentences. The starting point for holders of this view was an Islamisation of Germany, which was classified as a conspiratorial act of unnamed powers. Refugees were seen as a tool of this Islamisation, and the solution to the problem was consequently to be sought above all in the expulsion of the refugees. PEGIDA, as the authentic representation of the will of the people, had the task of leading the resistance to what it perceived as adverse developments (Stefanowitsch and Flach 2016, p. 1).

---

[52] This is in contrast with the public perception of right-wing populist outbursts on social media and the resulting efforts of the Federal Government to regulate so-called hate speech with a controversial social network enforcement law ("Netzwerkdurchsetzungsgesetz").

REFERENCES

Alexe, Thilo. 16.06.2015. Pegida will in die Parlamente. *Sächsische Zeitung*: 13.

Anderson, Peter. 16.01.2015. Verwirrung um angeblichen Meißner Pegida-Sprecher. *Sächsische Zeitung*: 17.

Baumann-Hartwig, Thomas, Hauke Heuer, and Ingolf, Pleil. 26.11.2014. Die Debatte um neue Asylbewerberheime spaltet Dresden und treibt unter dem Schirm von Pegida Tausende auf die Straße. *Dresdner Neueste Nachrichten*: 3.

Berntzen, Lars, and Manès Weisskircher. 2017. Anti-Islamic PEGIDA Beyond Germany: Explaining Differences in Mobilisation. *Journal of Intercultural Studies* 37: 556–573.

Crolly, Hannelore. 16.03.2015. Lutz Bachmann dreht Frankfurter Pegida den Saft ab. *Welt Online*. Accessed 3 July 2017. http://www.welt.de/politik/deutschland/article138465853/Lutz-Bachmann-dreht-Frankfurter-Pegida-den-Saft-ab.html

Del Giudice, Lukas, Nick Ebner, Lea Knopf, and Max Weber. 2018. Was sagt Pegida? Eine Analyse von Reden bei Pegida in Dresden. In *Hochburg des Rechtsextremismus? Sachsen im interregionalen und internationalen Vergleich*, ed. Uwe Backes and Steffen Kailitz (in preparation).

Döring, Frank. 05.05.2015. Islamkritiker wollen bei Bürgermeisterwahl antreten. *Leipziger Volkszeitung*: 13.

Dostal, Jörg Michael. 2015. The Pegida Movement and German Political Culture: Is Right-Wing Populism Here to Stay? *The Political Quarterly* 4: 523–531.

Dresdner Neueste Nachrichten. 15.12.2014. Zur Person: Lutz Bachmann. *Dresdner Neueste Nachrichten*: 3.

Fischer, Christian. 09.12.2014. Hier zeichnet OB Orosz den PEGIDA-Chef aus. *Bild Online*. Accessed 3 July 2017. http://www.bild.de/regional/dresden/helmaorosz/ob-orosz-zeichnete-pegida-chef-aus-38901524.bild.html

Freie Presse. 19.05.2015. Pegida-Kundgebung verläuft friedlich. *Freie Presse*: 10.

Frigelj, Kristian. 13.12.2014. Subtil. Infam. Pegida. *Welt Online*. Accessed 3 July 2017. http://www.welt.de/politik/deutschland/article135316848/Subtil-Infam-Pegida.html

Institut für Demokratieforschung. 2016. Büchse der Pandora? Pegida im Jahr 2016 und die Profanisierung rechtspopulistischer Positionen. *Institut für Demokratieforschung*. Accessed 3 July 2017. http://www.demokratie-goettin-gen.de/content/uploads/2016/10/Pegida2016_Göttinger_Demokratieforschung.pdf

Junge Freiheit. 2014. JF-TV veröffentlicht Film-Dokumentation über Pegida. *Junge Freiheit Online*. Accessed 3 July 2017. https://jungefreiheit.de/sonder-thema/2014/jf-tv-veroeffentlicht-film-dokumentation-ueber-pegida

Keilholz, Christine. 13.01.2015. Sachsens Innenminister Ulbig über Halbwahrheiten Pegidas und die Herausforderungen für die Polizei. *Dresdner Neueste Nachrichten*: 5.

Kellerhoff, Sven F. 20.01.2015. Pegida maßt sich das Erbe des 20. Juli an. *Welt Online*. Accessed 3 July 2017. http://www.welt.de/geschichte/article136523616/Pegida-masst-sich-das-Erbe-des-20-Juli-an.html

Kirschbaum, Erik. 11.02.2017. Art Sparks Dresden's Bitter Divide. A Dramatic Syrian Art Installation Fuels Debate and Protests in the German City. *Los Angeles Times*: 3.

Knaack, Benjamin. 08.10.2014. Kurden gegen Salafisten in Hamburg: Die Chaos-Nacht von St. Georg. *Spiegel Online*. Accessed 3 July 2017. http://www.spiegel.de/politik/deutschland/hamburger-steindamm-randale-zwischen-kurden-und-salafisten-a-996055.html

Kneuer, Marianne, and Thomas Demmelhuber. 2012. Die Bedeutung Neuer Medien für die Demokratieentwicklung. *Informationen zur Politischen Bildung* 35: 30–38.

Knoche, Kai. 08.10.2014. Geste der Versöhnung zwischen Eziden und Muslimen in Celle. *Cellesche Zeitung Online*. Accessed 3 July 2017. http://www.celleschezeitung.de/S3392767/Geste-der-Versoehnung-zwischen-Eziden-und-Muslimen-in-Celle

Kollenberg, Kai. 06.05.2015. Pegida Freiberg sagt geplante Demo ab. *Freie Presse*: 9.

Leithäuser, Johannes, and Markus Bickel. 01.09.2014. Berlin will 4000 Mann bewaffnen. *Frankfurter Allgemeine Zeitung*: 4.

Lindner, Nadine. 28.06.2015. Freitaler Demos gegen Flüchtlinge. Politiker lassen einfach gewähren. *Deutschlandfunk Online*. Accessed 3 July 2017. http://www.deutschlandfunk.de/freitaler-demos-gegen-fluechtlinge-politiker-lassen-einfach.720.de.html?dram:article_id=323812

Locke, Stefan. 25.08.2015. Nach den Krawallen. *Frankfurter Allgemeine Zeitung*: 3.

———. 21.02.2016. Die Flüchtlinge hatten sich Ruhe erhofft. *Frankfurter Allgemeine Sonntagszeitung*: 2.

———. 16.09.2016. Eskalation mit Ansage. *Frankfurter Allgemeine Zeitung*: 3.

———. 04.10.2016c. Den Pöblern zum Trotz. *Frankfurter Allgemeine Zeitung*: 2.

Machowecz, Martin. 2015. Busen, Bier und Islamismus. Zeit Magazin 15: 16–25.

Müller, Jan-Werner. 2016. *Was ist Populismus?* Berlin: Suhrkamp Verlag.

Önnerfors, Andreas. 2017. Between Breivik and PEGIDA: The Absence of Ideologues and Leaders on the Contemporary European Far Right. *Patterns of Prejudice* 51: 159–175.

Pleul, Clemens, and Stefan Scharf. 2016. Pegidas Entwicklung auf der Straße und im Netz. In *PEGIDA: Warnsignale aus Dresden*, ed. Werner J. Patzelt, Joachim Klose, and PEGIDA, 295–368. Dresden: Thelem Verlag.

Popp, Maximilian, and Andreas Wassermann. 2015. Rechte Spaßgesellschaft. *Der Spiegel* 3: 34.

Reinhard, Doreen. 16.01.2015. Uns bleibt keine Wahl als Pegida. *Sächsische Zeitung*: 3.

Sächsische Zeitung. 11.12.2014. Pegida veröffentlicht Positionspapier. *Sächsische Zeitung.* 6.
———. 23.07.2016. Pegida verliert Facebook-Seite. *Sächsische Zeitung Online.* Accessed 3 July 2017. http://www.sz-online.de/sachsen/pegida-verliert-facebook-seite-3450503.html?desktop=true
———. 30.11.2016. Bachmann rechtskräftig wegen Volksverhetzung verurteilt. *Sächsische Zeitung Online.* Accessed 3 July 2017. http://m.sz-online.de/sachsen/bachmann-rechtskraeftig-wegen-volksverhetzung-verurteilt-3552673.html
Saft, Gunnar. 01.08.2015. AfD und Pegida spielen verstecken. *Sächsische Zeitung.* 6.
Scharf, Christoph. 17.12.2014a. Die Wut wächst. *Sächsische Zeitung.* 13.
———. 17.12.2014b. Ein Dorf wird überfordert. *Sächsische Zeitung.* 3.
———. 20.11.2014. Das Asylheim mitten im Dorf. *Sächsische Zeitung.* 13.
Schenk, Winfried. 21.05.2015. Politikwissenschaftler Werner Patzelt: Ende der Pegida-Bewegung absehbar. *Menschen-in-Dresden.de.* Accessed 3 July 2017. https://menschen-in-dresden.de/2015/politikwissenschaftler-werner-patzelt-ende-der-pegida-bewegung-absehbar/
———. 03.06.2015. OB-Kandidatin Tatjana Festerling: Ein gut zweistelliges Ergebnis wäre eine Überraschung. *Menschen-in-Dresden.de.* Accessed 3 July 2017.http://www.menschen-in-dresden.de/2015/ob-kandidatin-tatjana-festerling-ein-gut-zweistelliges-ergebnis-waere-eine-ueberraschung
Spiegel Online. 31.01.2015. Anti-Islam-Bewegung: Sächsisches Ministerium hatte direkten Draht zur Pegida-Spitze. *Spiegel Online.* Accessed 3 July 2017. http://www.spiegel.de/politik/deutschland/pegida-hatte-direkten-draht-in-sachsens-innenministerium-a-1015935.html
Springer, Christoph. 24.12.2014. Beamte räumen einzelne Fehler bei Durchlasskontrollen zu Anti-Pegida-Kundgebung am Montagabend ein. *Dresdner Neueste Nachrichten.* 15.
Stefanowitsch, Anatol, and Susanne Flach. 2016. Auswertung von Userkommentaren auf der offiziellen Facebook-Seite von PEGIDA, Januar bis Dezember 2015. *FU Berlin.* Accessed 3 July 2017. https://drive.google.com/file/d/0B9mLol0BxIQ_Z053SXZ6S2NVR3M/view?pref=2&pli=1
Stier, Sebastian, Lisa Posch, Arnim Bleier, and Markus Strohmaier. 2017. When Populists Become Popular: Comparing Facebook Use by the Right-wing Movement Pegida and German Political Parties. *Information, Communication & Society* 20: 1365–1388.
Thurau, Carsten. 2015. Live-Bericht von der Pegida-Demonstration. *Heute Journal.* Accessed 3 July 2017. https://www.youtube.com/watch?v=3VXH9b64Ca8
Urbinati, Nadia. 2015. A Revolt against Intermediary Bodies. *Constellations* 22: 477–486.
Vorländer, Hans, Maik Herold, and Steven Schäller. 2016. *PEGIDA. Entwicklung, Zusammensetzung und Deutung einer Empörungsbewegung.* Wiesbaden: Springer VS.

Wolf, Ulrich. 16.02.2015. Waschen, Schneiden, Blödeln. *Sächsische Zeitung*: 3.

Wolf, Ulrich, and Morgane Llanque. 08.08.2014. Zimmer frei. *Sächsische Zeitung*: 3.

Wolf, Ulrich, and Andrea Schawe. 10.01.2015. Pegida etabliert sich. *Sächsische Zeitung*: 3.

Wolf, Ulrich, Alexander Schneider, and Tobias Wolf. 22.12.2014. Pegida—wie alles begann. *Sächsische Zeitung*: 3.

Wolf, Ulrich, Alexander Schneider, Tobias Wolf, and Heinrich M. Löbbers. 02.12.2014. Pegida persönlich. *Sächsische Zeitung*: 3.

Zweigler, Reinhard. 27.01.2015. Bürgerrechtlerin Freya Klier hält nicht aufgearbeitete Vorurteile für eine Wurzel der Pegida-Proteste. *Dresdner Neueste Nachrichten*: 4.

CHAPTER 2

Dealing with PEGIDA: Between Demarcation and Dialogue

The rapid spread and immense growth of the Patriotic Europeans against the Islamisation of the Occident (PEGIDA) in Dresden generated feedback in the media, which by November 2014 was no longer restricted to regional coverage. Soon the Dresden demonstrators dominated the comment columns of the newspapers nationwide and the public broadcasted evening talk shows. Even international media paid attention to PEGIDA.[1] At the same time, the weekly protests had long seemed puzzling from the viewpoint of observers, and the dismissive and in some cases aggressive sentiments towards journalists who were present made a disturbing impression. The tone of national reporting was accordingly negative. The crowds "marching" in the evening darkness with their national flags and populist slogans were seen as a danger to democratic order, its moral foundations and Germany's reputation in the world.[2] This image was further strengthened by the explicit rejectionist stance of the PEGIDA organisers towards the mass media and the maxim enforced on their supporters that

---

[1] Cf. the corresponding reports in *Le Monde* (Martel 2015), *El País* (Doncel 05.01.2015), *The Times* (Charter 15.12.2014), the *New York Times* (Smale 07.12.2014), the *Washington Post* (Noack 16.12.2014) and on CNN (Amanpour 05.01.2015).

[2] Given the disconcerting behaviour of the demonstrators, in Dresden in particular, certain parallels with the annually occurring neo-Nazi marches in the city were obvious. Dresden regularly becomes the location for "memorial marches" of German and European right-wing extremists on 13 February, the anniversary of the Allied bombardment of the city.

© The Author(s) 2018
H. Vorländer et al., *PEGIDA and New Right-Wing Populism in Germany*, New Perspectives in German Political Studies,
https://doi.org/10.1007/978-3-319-67495-7_2

Fig. 2.1 Flag waving demonstrators in front of the nightly scenery of baroque Dresden, 22.12.2014. Image Credit: dpa picture alliance/Alamy Stock Photo

they were not to speak to media representatives on the sidelines of the demonstrations.[3] The PEGIDA organisers did, on the other hand, know how to use the mechanisms of media coverage for their own ends. The intention was to further strengthen the negative political and media response through calculated provocation, in order to be able to present as innocent victims of an elite detached from the real life of "ordinary people" (Fig. 2.1).

[3] The explanation for the PEGIDA organisers' refusal to cooperate with the media was that it was a reaction to the critical reporting of the regional press (Wolf et al. 02.12.2014; *Dresdner Neuesten Nachrichten* 15.12.2014). The advice to the demonstrators not to speak with media representatives was mainly based on the assumption that journalists usually intend to distort their statements, exploiting them for their own hidden political agenda. In order to nevertheless obtain meaningful information about the Dresden demonstrators within the scope of an undercover investigation, on 15.12.2014 an employee of the television station RTL mingled with the PEGIDA participants, copied their slogans and in the role of a supposed protestor even gave a detailed interview to a team from a competing station (ARD) (which was unaware of his true identity), in which he, in his role as a PEGIDA demonstrator, also expressed xenophobic feelings of resentment (*Panorama* 18.12.2014). After the identity of the interviewed journalist became known there was corresponding outrage in the media and he was eventually sacked by his employer. The PEGIDA organisational team subsequently took up this incident on several occasions in order to criticise the allegedly scandalous methods of the lying press (Hanfeld 22.12.2014).

The explosive political impact that this dynamic of alternating escalation could develop became clear even at the beginning of the protests due to several surveys. According to a representative study on behalf of *Zeit Online* in mid-December 2014, around half of Germans expressed understanding for demonstrations against an imminent "Islamisation of the Occident". In total, three-quarters of all respondents even acknowledged having a positive or open-minded attitude towards PEGIDA. A representative survey conducted a little later revealed that the levels of sympathy for PEGIDA in the old *Bundesländer* were at a similarly high level to those found in the East. The survey found that around a third of western Germans shared some of PEGIDA's views.[4] Even in 2016, the findings of a further representative study showed that around 40 per cent of the population agreed, at least in part, with the goals of PEGIDA.[5]

Against this backdrop, dealings with PEGIDA proved to be difficult. On the one hand, there was a dominant stance in favour of a clear isolation of the protesters and their slogans. This position mapped out the fundamental disagreements and alleged that the protest movement blatantly disregarded the shared basic political consensus of the Federal Republic. On the other hand, there were proponents of a dialogue with PEGIDA. They interpreted the protests as a symptom of social and political developments which needed to be taken seriously, and felt that some criticisms addressed by the demonstrators were by all means important, and emphasised that a hasty moral condemnation of the protestors would only further intensify existing tendencies towards a division in society. For that reason the supporters of PEGIDA and their concerns, insofar as they were reasonable, could not be ignored, defamed or marginalised.

[4]The surveys were carried out by YouGov. In a survey by TNS Forschung on behalf of *Spiegel Online* a good third of the respondents were of the view that a growing Islamisation was taking place in Germany. A representative survey conducted by the opinion research institute Forsa on behalf of *Stern* and published on 01.01.2015 confirmed these results. It found that almost a third of Germans feel that the influence of Islam in their own country is too great and that protests against it are justified (*Zeit Online* 15.12.2014; *Frankfurter Allgemeine Zeitung* 19.12.2014; *Spiegel Online* 13.12.2014; *Süddeutsche Zeitung* 01.01.2015; Baumgärtner 15.12.2014; Barth and Lemke 04.12.2014).

[5]According to the so-called Leipzig Mitte Studies the figure was 46.2 per cent in eastern Germany, and in western Germany 38.5 per cent (Yendell et al. 2016, p. 139).

2.1   Dynamics of the Outrage

Within the space of a few weeks in autumn 2014, the combination of a rapid growth in demonstrations and their disconcerting appearance put the protest movement on the agenda of politicians, associations, churches and civil society actors. PEGIDA was described as a "disgrace for Germany" (Heiko Maas). Its demonstrators and sympathisers were said to be a "strange clan of lowlifes" (Cem Özdemir), a "crude bunch" (Gerhard Schröder), "rabble" (Sigmar Gabriel) and "anarchists" (Joachim Gauck). The organisers, in turn, were called "rabble-rousers" (Markus Ulbig) and "Nazis in pinstripes" (Ralf Jäger), whose hearts house much "cold, even hate" (Angela Merkel) and who employ a "culture of scaremongering" (Joachim Gauck). Their use of the words "patriot" and "patriotism" was called "impudence" (Thomas de Maizière).[6] Even churches and trade unions took the same tone. While the Federation of German Trade Unions (DGB) called for counter-protests in many places and the dean of the Cologne Cathedral darkened the place of worship in protest against a demonstration by the Cologne PEGIDA offshoot KÖGIDA on 05.01.2015, representatives of the Evangelical Church in Germany described the demonstrations of the "Patriotic Europeans" as "intolerable" and "unchristian": Christians had "no business being at these rallies" (Dörries 05.01.2015; Rheinische Post 05.01.2015).[7] The chairman of the German Bishops' Conference (*Deutsche Bischofskonferenz*), cardinal Reinhard Marx, also criticised PEGIDA, however—unlike his Bamberg colleague Ludwig Schick—he expressed his opposition to a "PEGIDA ban" for Catholics ordered by a spiritual leader (Gierth 28.12.2014; Münchner Kirchennachrichten 21.12.2014). Other comments, on the other hand, used popular clichés in their condemnation of the Dresden demonstrators, namely of "dim", "ungrateful" eastern Germans with extremist tendencies—for instance, when the PEGIDA demonstrators were called the "outraged relatives of

---

[6]Evidence of the quotes: Joachim Gauck (Burger 13.12.2014; Spiegel Online 12.12.2014), Heiko Maas (Rossmann 15.12.2014), Markus Ulbig (Kochinke 26.11.2014) Cem Özdemir (Maybritt Illner 17.12.2014), Ralf Jäger (Süddeutsche Zeitung 13.12.2014), Gerhard Schröder (Waurig 20.12.2014), Sigmar Gabriel (Locke 25.08.2015), Thomas de Maizière (Meier and Niewendick 09.12.2014) and Angela Merkel (Bundesregierung.de 31.12.2014).

[7]The lighting of the Dresden Frauenkirche was also turned off on the occasion of the PEGIDA demonstrations on 09.02.2015 (Lohse 09.02.2015).

the Zone-Gabi",[8] when their statements were quoted in broad Saxon dialect or when their seeming "rage, unfriendliness and coldness" was diagnosed as part of a general, eastern German, mental state (Martin 19.12.2014; Yücel 16.12.2014; Machowecz 04.02.2015).

This was followed in turn by wide-ranging (remote) diagnoses about the background to the remarkable success of PEGIDA. People were quick to talk about Saxony as a region of typical intolerance and about Dresden as a "Valley of the Clueless" (*Tal der Ahnungslosen*) following a historically rooted "special path" (*Sonderweg*) of self-centredness, fear of facts and a mythical transfiguration of its own historical role as a victim.[9] In the heated atmosphere, numerous speculations about the social background of the demonstration participants and their political attitudes soon did the rounds. PEGIDA was presumed to be the articulation of "outsiders' profound distrust of the traditional, middle class public". It was thought to feed off "the fear of social decline" in a world, in which "globalisation and technology mercilessly wipe out low-skilled jobs". The anger of the demonstrators was said to be typical for people who "at all times are at risk of social exclusion and precarity". Furthermore, many of the demonstrators were said to not fully understand the political significance of their actions. Therefore, it was seen as correspondingly important to unmask the organisers of PEGIDA and their real goals, because, according to the assumption of, for instance, the then North-Rhine Westphalian Minister of the Interior, Ralf Jäger, "many demonstrators are simply tagging along out of ignorance" (Altenbockum 20.12.2014; Joffe 23.12.2014; Marschall and Quadbeck 24.12.2014; Schwan 30.12.2014; Frigelj 13.12.2014).

---

[8] "Zonen-Gaby" refers to a fictitious East German woman named Gaby, who was depicted on the cover of a West German satire magazine from 1989 for the purpose of making fun of the supposed simple-mindedness and naïvety of the East Germans. In the picture the young woman is proudly holding a half-peeled cucumber in her hand saying "my first banana". "Zone" is in reference to the Soviet occupation zone and was used as a colloquial term for East Germany.

[9] Aly (15.12.2014), Lühmann (16.12.2014), Petzold (17.12.2014), Birgel (20.12.2014), Müller et al. (20.12.2014) and Carstens (21.12.2014). "Valley of the clueless" refers to the special location of Dresden in the Elbe valley reviving a polemical label which was used in the everyday language of the former German Democratic Republic (GDR). Due to the city's location in the valley, television and radio programmes from western media could not be received before 1989, which is why the inhabitants of Dresden had to rely on the information from the GDR state media. Therefore, they were said to be 'clueless' about what was really going on in the world. Cf. also Sect. 6.1 in Chap. 6.

Diagnoses of this kind, which were mostly made from a distance and did not differentiate between organisers, followers and the various groups of demonstrators, often acted like an accelerant and initiated a real spiral of escalation. The very people who with their protest first and foremost wanted to criticise a perceived notorious ignorance, one-sidedness and moral impertinence of politicians and media representatives, only saw themselves vindicated by such generalisations and were motivated to protest further. The organisers of PEGIDA in turn were able to use the statements by public figures, politicians and journalists, which ranged from distancing to derogatory, specifically for their own purposes. On the one hand, critical statements by politicians were made a topic of discussion at the PEGIDA events on a weekly basis, in order to thereby highlight supporters' role as victims.[10] On the other hand, speeches and placards incorporated the criticism with a view to polemicise and appropriated it as positive and identity-building. For instance, when repeated xenophobic incidents in the region surrounding Dresden occurred in summer 2015, in the media the cause was sought in the specific politico-cultural make-up of Saxony. In this context, one fantasised about the *Bundesland* leaving the Federal Republic. PEGIDA, however, used the idea of a "Säxit" polemically, appropriated the suggestion and justified it, saying that political sanity in terms of refugee policy was obviously now only present in Saxony (Schirmer 21.08.2015; Dresdner Neueste Nachrichten 12.10.2015). Even the derogatory description of the demonstrators as a "brown mob" and as "rabble" (Pack) were confidently appropriated by PEGIDA. Thus, for weeks a brown-dyed mop stood on the stage and the speaker referred to it ironically amid the howling of the demonstrators.[11] Other protesters had the motto "We are the rabble" (*Wir sind das Pack*) printed on t-shirts and placards and expressed in this way ridicule and mockery (Meisner 22.08.2015; Gathmann 24.08.2015).

When, in summer 2015, the severe condemnation from politicians and the media first abated, it became clear that PEGIDA was reliant on constant new provocations in order to permanently remain in the public eye and to guarantee continued mobilisation of its own supporters. For this

[10]This hit rock bottom with a speech by the author Akif Pirinçci on the first anniversary of the protest movement. He claimed that there was a prevailing social climate in the Federal Republic based on which critics of the asylum policy were at risk of becoming interred in concentration camps in the future.

[11]In German "mop" sounds like "mob" when spoken.

reason the organisers now tried to be conspicuous by making increasingly radical statements, some of which in the end could also be interpreted as calls for violence. An example was in autumn 2015 when Tatjana Festerling stated the demand that Germans finally needed to do the mucking out "in the German offices". This demand was made more vivid by a real pitch-fork, which temporarily became a symbolic accessory in her public appearances. On top of that came the call for "resistance", with which all Germans were called upon to resist the refugee policy, in particular the police and soldiers who were supposed to refuse to work and no longer immediately obey the orders of their superiors. This increasingly radical rhetoric by PEGIDA led in turn to even harsher forms of condemnation, which soon even drew parallels with National Socialism. After Lutz Bachmann had compared the incumbent Minister of Justice Heiko Maas with the NS Minister of Propaganda Josef Goebbels, the Secretary-General of the Social Democratic Party of Germany (SPD), Yasmin Fahimi, described the PEGIDA organisers as "crazy fascists" engaging in "disgusting rabble-rousing". Other SPD party functionaries added that PEGIDA was preparing the ground "for the pack of thugs that attacks refugees or sets accommodation on fire" (Gathmann and Trenkamp 03.11.2015).

These sorts of examples show how the supporters and critics of the protest movement repeatedly riled each other with their reactions. With sensationalist media coverage and the need to scandalise on the one hand, and radical provocation on the other, an escalating dynamic of alternating intensification arose, which the protest movement in particular was able to profit from, in the form of demonstrable mobilisation successes.[12]

2.2   Division of Civil Society

These dynamics of escalation did not remain limited to the demonstrations in Dresden. Anger and indignation also manifested themselves in other forms and other contexts. For example, the offices of elected officials and other holders of political office, but also the editorial teams of the mass media, vilified as the "Lying press", found themselves confronted with numerous aggressively insulting and defamatory readers' letters, e-mails and phone calls, in which their critical stance towards PEGIDA was denounced. In the city of Dresden's population and civil society, on the

[12]This link was also able to be empirically proven by systematically interviewing PEGIDA demonstrators (Vorländer et al. 2015, p. 67ff.).

other hand, the public disputes about PEGIDA led to a real formation of opposing camps, with an irreconcilable division between the backers of PEGIDA on the one hand and those who opposed PEGIDA on the other. In the population there was soon a veritable obligation to declare one's allegiance. Everyone seemed to have to position themselves with regard to PEGIDA in some way. Whoever was on the "wrong" side was, from the perspective of the other camp, considered to be either a "naive do-gooder" or "a latent Nazi". Circles of friends were divided, friendships were ended.[13]

The enormous polarisation of the political discourse in Germany was also evident on the internet. Below almost every article about the topic on the websites of news portals and daily newspapers the comments sections and reader forums were overflowing—mostly with indignant reactions to (in the eyes of the commentators) incorrect and uncritical handling of topics like "asylum", "refugees" or "Islam" as well as "disparaging" media coverage about PEGIDA. On the social networks PEGIDA sympathisers and PEGIDA opponents gathered on the relevant sites and gave free rein to their resentment of the other side. On the one hand, there were rants about the "system", the "politicians", the "filthily red-green media" made in an indignant, inflammatory manner, sometimes also employing concrete conspiracy theories, while the PEGIDA critics ranted about the "antisocial elements", "traitors of the people", "anarchists" or ideologically blinded "do-gooders". On the other hand, PEGIDA and the demonstrators who joined the marches were confronted with the accusation that the positions represented there and the slogans used were incompatible with the rules of humanity, tolerance and liberal democracy, and that they revealed all PEGIDA sympathisers' right-wing extremist, racist and neo-Nazi body of thought. Any kind of sympathy with the PEGIDA movement was therefore unacceptable and could only be met with resolute condemnation. This went so far that in national daily newspapers there were soon calls to cleanse one's "list of friends" on applicable social media by removing PEGIDA sympathisers

---

[13] The charged political atmosphere in the city was evident when an Eritrean asylum seeker was murdered on 13.01.2015. Shortly after this incident came to light, speculation was rife in national and international media about a racist motive for the crime and subsequent suspected cover-up by the police as well as a possible connection to PEGIDA. Vigils, memorial events and solidarity rallies were organised by political activists prior to the outcome of the police investigations. As it eventually turned out, however, the victim was stabbed to death in self-defence by his Eritrean flatmate after an argument about the running of the household. (Springer 15.01.2015).

and to delete those who "like" PEGIDA (Stern Online 17.12.2014; Tanriverdi 17.12.2014).[14]

The polarisation initiated by PEGIDA also made itself felt in the public debates. Not only was there debate about the topics which the protest movement had put on the agenda, but the debate culture itself also had a noticeably coarser character. An increase in vulgar remarks and the general deterioration of etiquette could be observed, especially on social media. That was accompanied by a very real "normalisation" of comments which were critical of immigration, xenophobic and sometimes even glorified violence. Here the formation of a digital "defamation community" became apparent, one which was simply a communicative merger of those harbouring feelings of resentment.[15] The discursive loss of inhibition also led to a softening of the boundaries with regard to the use of physical violence. As the rapid increase in acts of violence motivated by xenophobia showed, PEGIDA seemed to have created a climate in which right-wing extremist offenders felt emboldened. Between 2014 and 2015 the number of acts of violence in Germany with a right-wing motivation rose by 42 per cent. As a matter of fact, in Saxony this increase was 142 per cent, the *Bundesland* was thereby (behind North Rhine-Westphalia) the region, in which the most incidents were recorded (Federal Ministry of the Interior 2016, p. 27ff.).[16]

---

[14]Cf. additionally the posts, comments and chat histories on the Facebook pages of PEGIDA (https://www.facebook.com/pegidaevdresden), NOPEGIDA (https://www.facebook.com/nopegida) or PEGIDA#watch (https://www.facebook.com/pegidawatch) among others.

[15]This public display of hatred and the normalisation of defamatory statements even resulted in a legislative initiative to reduce hate speech in social media. In autumn 2016, Federal Minister of Justice, Heiko Maas (SPD), provided a draft bill to make it mandatory for Facebook (and other social media platforms) to delete so-called hate speech. The bill passed through the Bundestag on 01.07.2017 (Wieduwilt 06.04.2017, 01.07.2017).

[16]For the development of politically-motivated violence in Germany cf. Sect. 5.3 in Chap. 5, for the political conditions in Saxony cf. Sect. 6.1 in Chap. 6. In the Saxon town of Freital, for instance, a so-called "Bürgerwehr Freital/360" ("Home Guard Freital/360") had formed in early summer 2015. It carried out numerous attacks on political opponents and refugee accommodation with illegal firecrackers, small explosive devices and butyric acid and was also involved in riots in Heidenau. On 05.11.2015 a special unit of the Federal Police, arrested members of the militia which had been classified as a right-wing terrorist organisation by the Federal Prosecutor General. Since 07.03.2017 they have had to stand trial, among other things, for the formation of a terrorist group (Locke 24.08.2015, 13.04.2016, 07.03.2017).

While the willingness to participate in demonstrations continually grew in the camp of the PEGIDA sympathisers in the winter months of 2014/2015, the resistance to PEGIDA also grew from numerous initiatives.[17] With the goal of confronting the right-wing populists on the street, between the beginning of November 2014 and May 2015 weekly counter-demonstrations took place in Dresden. The organisers were, however, unable to outnumber PEGIDA at any point, nor were they able to get high numbers of participants onto the streets as consistently (cf. Fig. 1.1). It was only on the first anniversary of PEGIDA, in October 2015, that the counter-protest was able to mobilise its own supporters on a similar scale. In other German cities the demonstrations directed against PEGIDA were in fact on a similar scale to those in Dresden, but here they were always clearly in the majority.[18]

The forms of protests against PEGIDA were diverse. They ranged from loud confrontations with its supporters within view and earshot, to the occupation of squares where rallies were scheduled to be held, right through to sit-ins with the goal of stopping the PEGIDA marches. Others chose more symbolic forms of expression for their counter-protests. For example, from December 2014, the Semperoper in Dresden, which served as a backdrop for PEGIDA, began campaigning for "cosmopolitan attitudes and tolerance" during the demonstrations using flags and light installations with messages. Even the Saxon state chancellery, as well as the political leadership of the city of Dresden, attempted to confront PEGIDA with its own format, in order to counteract the negative public image of Dresden. The event organisers opted for a mix of concerts by well-known performers and short political statements, and were able to attract up to 35,000 participants.[19] The aim was to show the world that the majority of the population of Dresden did not agree with PEGIDA's goals and positions. Among the manifold forms of protest against the

---

[17] Among them were, for example, "Bündnis Dresden für Alle" (Alliance Dresden for all), whose central actors came from the context of the local university, "Dresden nazifrei" (Dresden Nazi-free), a group which has existed for years in opposition to the symbolic misuse of the city of Dresden on 13 February, the day of Dresden's destruction in the Second World War, as well as the "Initiative Weltoffenes Dresden" (Liberal-minded Dresden Initiative), an association of the Dresden cultural institutions.

[18] Various groups and individuals appeared as registrants and organisers of counter-demonstrations, such as students, political activists and left-wing extremists, but also members of parliament, representatives of cultural and art institutions and the Rector of the Technische Universität Dresden.

[19] The association "Dresden—place to be" employed a similar concept and was able to mobilise around 22,000 participants with an event on 26.01.2015.

"Patriotic Europeans" there were also activities with satirical connotations. In 2015 a "New Year's Cleaning Campaign", an initiative of artists from Dresden, regularly made an appeal to the citizens, as part of a "symbolic expulsion", to "clean" the inner city with a broom after every PEGIDA event. In addition, reporters from satirical shows repeatedly mingled with the participants of the PEGIDA demonstration marches and attempted to ridicule the protests using humorous banners (Leubecher 02.12.2014).

However, the unbroken continuity of the weekly PEGIDA demonstrations gradually caused a certain feeling of helplessness to grow in the counter-protest camp. The focus of the engagement in counter-protest was consequently shifted from the streets to the support of welcome initiatives, which had as their goal supporting arriving refugees and asylum seekers and facilitating their integration into German society with appropriate offers. Specifically, work in voluntary associations of this kind was also seen as an indirect form of addressing the PEGIDA issue.[20]

2.3   Attempts at Dialogue

Alongside the already mentioned tactics of isolation, polarisation and counter-protest, the question of how best to handle the PEGIDA demonstrations was also answered in other ways. A plea made by numerous prominent figures from politics and society was to not play down the fears of PEGIDA supporters, but to instead confront them with a certain openness.[21] The Minister President of Saxony, Stanislaw Tillich, repeatedly made the case for having "understanding for citizens who are worried" about how the integration of refugees could be successful. Tillich, however, did not take the organisational team up on its offer, made on 05.01.2015, for him to attend a PEGIDA event: he stated that "to speak on a stage from which the Federal Chancellor and other politicians have repeatedly been personally insulted and from which hatred of foreigners was incited" was out of the question (Hebel 06.01.2015).[22] The Dresden

---

[20]Cf. Fuchs and Klein (2016).

[21]They included, for example, the Federal Ministers Thomas de Maizière (CDU) and Gerd Müller (CSU), or FDP vice chairman Wolfgang Kubicki, (Exner 05.01.2015; Sigmund 01.01.2015; Tagesthemen 11.12.2014).

[22]In this context, however, Tillich also attracted attention with his remark that "Islam is not a part of Saxony". In saying this, he explicitly distanced himself from a statement made by Angela Merkel, who on 12.01.2015 after the terrorist attack on the satirical magazine *Charlie Hebdo* had declared that Islam is a part of Germany (Detjen 21.12.2014; Kammholz 25.01.2015; Wiegel and Ross 13.01.2015).

mayor at the time, Helma Orosz, also initially expressed a certain under-standing for the protests. On 11.12.2014 she stressed, in the Dresden city council, that the freedoms of expression and assembly enshrined in the German constitution also enabled PEGIDA supporters to express their protest on the street. Whoever makes use of this right is not automatically right-wing radical, Orosz claimed. On the other hand, she said that the boundaries of legitimate protests were clear: inhuman forms of expression cannot be tolerated, human dignity and the right to asylum was not up for discussion (Orosz 2014).

In addition, there were warning voices which feared the negative con-sequences of reactions which sought to isolate and polarise. The former leader of the parliamentary group for the Green Party (Bündnis90/Die Grünen) in the Saxon state parliament, Antje Hermenau, urged people not to hastily discredit the PEGIDA demonstrators. "Those are my peo-ple in Saxony, who, in a knee-jerk response, are to be clubbed to death with ideology. The questions pertaining to real life, that they ask, cannot be slain by moralising. To claim that one is on the right side and 'the oth-ers' on the wrong one, is historicising and unworldly" (Hermenau 24.01.2015). Similarly, the publisher of Germany's leading feminist mag-azine *Emma*, Alice Schwarzer, also publicly made a case for sincerely dis-cussing the matters concerning the Dresden demonstrators. Politicians, said Schwarzer, in view of surveys which indicated great sympathy for PEGIDA in the population, should not "continue to ignore" the uneasi-ness of this overwhelming majority, punish or even demonise—even though it is currently "good form" to be outraged about PEGIDA (Schwarzer 06.01.2015). Many of those who publicly called for under-standing for PEGIDA supporters were heavily criticised for doing so, hav-ing to endure outright barrages of condemnation—which themselves became the subject matter of media coverage (Altenbockum 07.01.2015; Sturm 24.01.2015; Tageszeitung 25.01.2015; Jacobsen 29.01.2015).

Others tried to establish a direct dialogue with PEGIDA. Already at the turn of 2014/2015 various political actors were working in the back-ground, trying to establish contact with the leaders of the movement. Among them was the parliamentary group of the Alternative for Germany (AfD) in the Saxon state parliament under the leadership of Frauke Petry and also the Minister of the Interior for Saxony, Markus Ulbig (Saft 08.01.2015; Spiegel Online 26.01.2015). In addition, Saxon state politi-cians from all parties attended podium discussions with PEGIDA sym-pathisers and PEGIDA opponents. Political foundations, educational institutions and the TU Dresden organised a series of information events to bring experts and members of the public together to talk about the topics which PEGIDA had put on the agenda.[23]

It was above all the Saxon Agency for Civic Education, led by then director Frank Richter, that emerged as an intermediary between supporters and opponents of PEGIDA by organising several dialogue events. Its objective was to give members of the public who sympathised with PEGIDA the opportunity to present their points of view as objectively as possible in the presence of professional observers, journalists and academics, but also local, state and even federal politicians.[24] Similar events, which were run by the Saxon state government in various cities from January 2015, conversely had the goal of bringing members of the public in direct contact with political, administrative, judicial and cultural functionaries.[25] In the course of a series of Dresden city dialogue events starting at the end of 2015, the aim was to initiate direct discussion between supporters and opponents of PEGIDA, in order to enable a change in the situation of polarisation in the city through mutual understanding of the positions of the respective opposing side.[26]

The dialogue events all took place in a difficult environment and became topics of further discussion themselves. Observers seemed unsure as to what goals discussions of this kind should be pursuing. It was asked whether it was appropriate to sit down at a table with people who were

[23] Meetings, panels and conferences about PEGIDA were held with topics like "The phenomenon of Pegida: Sociological interpretations", "What truth is there to the accusation of the 'lying press'?" and "What do the people want?" Cf. in detail Vorländer et al. 2016, p. 27).

[24] The foundation of these events, which had between 150 and 200 participants, was a so-called "aquarium" or "fishbowl": A table with four chairs was placed in the middle of the room, around which further chairs were placed, on which the participants were seated. The people who sat at the table in the middle were recruited from the audience, and they then spoke publicly about their motivation for supporting or rejecting PEGIDA.

[25] The participants, who numbered as many as 300, were allocated to the individual tables, which each had seven chairs, by drawing lots. Seated at each table were six members of the general public with various attitudes towards PEGIDA, as well as one "expert". The planned course of events was to start with two consecutive rounds of discussion, termed "table dialogues", a subsequent round of interviews of chosen tables and a fishbowl-podium discussion as a conclusion.

[26] In this discussion format the contributions were organised based on the model of a town hall meeting. The moderators let as many as possible of the up to 750 members of the public in the audience have their say on a given topic within the scope of severe time constraints. Politicians, journalists and experts who were present could react to the contributions.

obviously inciting antipathy towards asylum seekers, immigrants and Muslims in the first place (Amman et al. 24.01.2015). Furthermore, the quality of the discussions did not live up to expectations. At the events only a fraction of the participants got a chance to speak, it was only seldom that reference was made to the previous speaker and, what is more, frequently an opportunity to talk about the topic at hand was wasted. There was scant evidence of a mutual desire to understand one's dialogue partner. The fundamentally confrontational atmosphere between supporters and opponents of PEGIDA remained, just as it did between citizens who felt misunderstood and "aloof" political representatives. Furthermore, the dialogue formats ran the risk of being abused as a platform for agitation by groups acting in co-ordination. It could be observed several times how representatives of the so-called New Right with training in rhetoric used the event to set their agenda and to influence the public discourse as they wished with inflammatory comments.

Despite these obvious deficits the dialogue events had a calming effect which dampened the protest mood in the heated and polarised atmosphere in spring 2015. Their existence had created an outlet through which pent-up frustration and anger could be released. The rounds of dialogue succeeded in bringing members of the public and political elites to the table and contributed to the—sometimes also emotionally charged—debate of opposing positions. Due to the events being very structured and moderated it was possible to keep the debates largely on point. The dialogues were, however, unable to overcome the extremely polarised political climate.

REFERENCES

Altenbockum, Jasper v. 20.12.2014. Die Verdummung des Abendlands. *Frankfurter Allgemeine Zeitung*: 8.

Altenbockum, Jasper. v. 07.01.2015. Shitstorm gegen Alice Schwarzer. *Frankfurter Allgemeine Zeitung Online*. Accessed 3 July 2017. http://www.faz.net/aktuell/pegida-shitstorm-gegen-alice-schwarzer-13357475.html

Aly, Götz. 15.12.2014. Pegida, eine alte Dresdner Eigenheit. *Berliner Zeitung Online*. Accessed 3 July 2017. http://www.berliner-zeitung.de/kolumne-zur-fremdenangst-in-dresden-pegida--eine-alte-dresdner-eigenheit-482290

Amanpour, Christiane. 2015. German Minister: Don't Overestimate 'PEGIDA' Movement. *CNN*, January 5. Accessed 3 July 2017. http://edition.cnn.com/videos/tv/2015/01/05/intv-amanpor-thomas-de-maiziere-germany-pegida-anti-islam-protests.cnn

Amman, Melanie, Markus Deggerich, Sven Röbel, and Steffen Winter. 01.01.2015. Therapie an Tisch 26. *Der Spiegel*: 30.

Barth, Rafael, and Johanna Lemke. 04.12.2014. Pegida-Märsche gefährden Dresdens Ansehen. *Sächsische Zeitung*: 1.

Baumgärtner, Maik, Jörg Diehl, Frank Honig, Maximilian Popp, Sven Röbel, Jörg Schindler, Wolf Wiedmann-Schmidt, and Steffen Winter. 15.12.2014. Neue deutsche Welle. *Der Spiegel*: 23–26.

Birgel, Dirk. 20.12.2014. Dresden—wo sonst. *Dresdner Neueste Nachrichten*: 18.

Bundesregierung.de. 2014. Neujahrsansprache der Bundeskanzlerin: Stärker zusammenhalten. *Bundesregierung*, December 31. Accessed 3 July 2017. http://www.bundesregierung.de

Burger, Reiner. 13.12.2014. Scharfe Kritik an Anti-Islam-Bündnis Pegida. *Frankfurter Allgemeine Zeitung*: 1.

Carstens, Peter. 21.12.2014. Das Abendland ist eine Scheibe. *Frankfurter Allgemeine Sonntagszeitung*: 7.

Charter, David. 15.12.2014. Germans March on Mondays to Oppose Rising 'Islamisation'. *The Times Online*. Accessed 3 July 2017. http://www.thetimes.co.uk/tto/news/world/europe/article4297087.ece

Detjen, Stephan. 21.12.2014. Tillich: "Organisatoren sind nicht zum Dialog bereit". *Deutschlandfunk Online*. Accessed 3 July 2017. http://www.deutschlandfunk.de/pegida-proteste-tillich-organisatoren-sind-nicht-zum-dialog.868.de.html?dram:article_id=306804

Doncel, Luis. 05.01.2015. La marea islamófoba polariza Alemania. *El País*. Accessed 3 July 2017. http://internacional.elpais.com/internacional/2015/01/05/actualidad/1420489196_231287.html

Dörries, Bernd. 05.01.2015. Kölner Dompropst stellt das Licht ab. *Süddeutsche Zeitung Online*. Accessed 3 July 2017. http://www.sueddeutsche.de/politik/protest-gegen-pegida-koelner-domprobst-stellt-das-lichtab-1.2290719

Dresdner Neueste Nachrichten. 15.12.2014. Zur Person: Lutz Bachmann. *Dresdner Neueste Nachrichten*: 3.

———. 12.10.2015. Festerling fordert "Säxit"—Morddrohungen gegen Politiker. *Dresdner Neueste Nachrichten Online*. Accessed 3 July 2017. http://www.dnn.de/Dresden/Lokales/Pegida-Festerling-fordert-Saexit-Morddrohung-gegen-Politiker

Exner, Ulrich. 05.01.2015. Pegida-Anhänger haben ernst zu nehmende Sorgen. Interview mit Wolfgang Kubicki. *Die Welt*: 5.

Federal Ministry of the Interior. 2016. Verfassungsschutzbericht 2015. *Bundesministerium des Inneren*. Accessed 3 July 2017. https://www.verfassungsschutz.de/embed/vsbericht-2015.pdf

Frankfurter Allgemeine Zeitung. 19.12.2014. Ein Drittel der Westdeutschen teilt Pegida-Positionen. *Frankfurter Allgemeine Zeitung Online*. Accessed 3 July 2017. http://www.faz.net/aktuell/politik/inland/pegida-findet-auch-in-westdeutschland-zustimmung-laut-umfrage-13331060.html

Frigelj, Kristian. 13.12.2014. Subtil. Infam. Pegida. *Welt Online*. Accessed 3 July 2017. http://www.welt.de/politik/deutschland/article135316848/Subtil-Infam-Pegida.html

Fuchs, Petra, and Ansgar Klein. 2016. Ohne Engagement keine Integration—Bedarfe der Engagementförderung in der Flüchtlingshilfe. *NDV—Nachrichtendienst* 96 (4): 175–178.

Gathmann, Florian. 24.08.2015. Gabriel über Rassisten in Heidenau: "Das ist Pack". *Spiegel Online*. Accessed 3 July 2017. http://www.spiegel.de/politik/deutschland/heidenau-sigmar-gabriel-besucht-fluechtlingsunterkunft-a-1049582.html

Gathmann, Florian, and Oliver Trenkamp. 03.11.2015. Goebbels-Vergleich bei Pegida-Demo: SPD-Generalsekretärin nennt Bachmann "wahnsinnigen Faschisten". *Spiegel Online*. Accessed 3 July 2017. http://www.spiegel.de/politik/deutschland/pegida-yasmin-fahimi-nennt-lutz-bachmann-wahnsinnigen-faschisten-a-1060780.html

Gierth, Matthias. 28.12.2014. EKD-Chef: Pegida ist "unerträglich". *Deutschlandfunk Online*. Accessed 3 July 2017. http://www.deutschlandfunk.de/bischof-bedford-strohm-ekd-chef-pegida-ist-unertraeglich.868.de.html?dram:article_id=307267

Hanfeld, Michael. 22.12.2014. Ich bin Pegida. RTL-Reporter fällt aus der Rolle und verliert den Job. *Frankfurter Allgemeine Zeitung*: 9.

Hebel, Christina. 06.01.2015. Proteste in Dresden: Ministerpräsident Tillich will nicht auf die Pegida-Bühne. *Spiegel Online*. Accessed 3 July 2017. http://www.spiegel.de/politik/deutschland/pegida-in-dresden-stanislaw-tillich-lehnt-einladung-ab-a-1011504.html

Hermenau, Antje. 24.01.2015. "Das sind meine Leute". *Die Tageszeitung*: 20.

Jacobsen, Lenz. 29.01.2015. Wo es brodelt und stinkt. *Zeit Online*. Accessed 3 July 2017. http://www.zeit.de/politik/deutschland/2015-01/pegida-dialog-gefuehlspolitik-essay

Joffe, Josef. 23.12.2014. Rechte raus! *Die Zeit*: 10.

Kammholz, Karsten. 25.01.2015. Der Islam gehört nicht zu Sachsen. *Welt Online*. Accessed 3 July 2017. http://www.welt.de/politik/deutschland/article136740584/Der-Islam-gehoert-nicht-zu-Sachsen.html

Kochinke, Jürgen. 26.11.2014. CDU und SPD in Sachsen richten Lenkungsausschuss ein. Schwarz-Rot will Asyldebatte entschärfen. *Sächsische Zeitung*: 3.

Leubecher, Marcel. 02.12.2014. "Die Partei" kapert Pegida-Marsch mit Homo-Plakat. *Welt Online*. Accessed 3 July 2017. http://www.welt.de/politik/deutschland/article134940066/Die-Partei-kapert-Pegida-Marsch-mit-Homo-Plakat.html

Locke, Stefan. 24.08.2015a. Hier regiert der nationale Widerstand. *Frankfurter Allgemeine Sonntagszeitung*: 2.

———. 25.08.2015b. Nach den Krawallen. *Frankfurter Allgemeine Zeitung*: 3.

———. 13.04.2016. Unter Terrorverdacht. *Frankfurter Allgemeine Zeitung*: 4.

———. 07.03.2017. Waren doch nur ein paar Böller. *Frankfurter Allgemeine Zeitung*: 3.

Lohse, Stephan. 09.02.2015. Protest gegen Pegida: Frauenkirche wird ab 18.30 verdunkelt. *Dresdner Neueste Nachrichten Online*. Accessed 3 July 2017. http://www.dnn-online.de/dresden/web/dresden-nachrichten/detail/-/specific/Protest-gegen-Pegida-Frauenkirche-wird-ab-18-30-verdunkelt-377517058

Lühmann, Michael. 16.12.2014. Pegida passt nach Sachsen. *Zeit Online*. Accessed 3 July 2017. http://www.zeit.de/politik/deutschland/2014-12/pegida-dresden-politische-tradition

Machowecz, Martin. 04.02.2015. Pegida und ich. *Zeit Online*. Accessed 3 July 2017. http://www.zeit.de/2015/06/pegida-dresden-ostdeutschland

Marschall, Birgit, and Eva Quadbeck. 24.12.2014. Wolfgang Schäuble im Interview: "Nur Russland kann die Krise beenden". *Rheinische Post Online*. Accessed 3 July 2017. http://www.rp-online.de/politik/deutschland/nur-russland-kann-die-krise-beenden-aid-1.4760264

Martel, Clément. 2015. A Dresde sur les pas de PEGIDA. *Le Monde*. Accessed 3 July 2017. http://www.lemonde.fr/europe/visuel/2015/01/21/a-dresde-sur-les-pas-de-pegida_4559085_3214.html

Martin, Marko. 19.12.2014. Sachsen und Araber. *Die Welt*: 2.

Maybritt Illner. 11.12.2014. Aufstand für das Abendland—Wut auf die Politik oder Fremdenhass? *ZDF*.

Meier, Albrecht, and Martin Niewendick. 09.12.2014. Kundgebung der Islam-Hasser in Dresden. Innenminister de Maizière: "Pegida ist eine Unverschämtheit". *Tagesspiegel Online*. Accessed 3 July 2017. http://www.tagesspiegel.de/politik/kundgebung-der-islam-hasser-in-dresden-innenminister-de-maiziere-pegida-ist-eine-unverschaemtheit/11091188.html

Meisner, Matthias. 22.08.2015. Der braune Mob von Heidenau. *Zeit Online*. Accessed 3 July 2017. http://www.zeit.de/gesellschaft/zeitgeschehen/2015-08/heidenau-fluechtlinge-ausschreitungen-polizei

Müller, Ann-Katrin, Maximilian Popp, and Andreas Wassermann. 20.12.2014. Im Zentrum. *Der Spiegel*: 30–32.

Münchner Kirchennachrichten. 21.12.2014. Kardinal Marx: Pegida-Phänomen ist diffus. *Münchner Kirchennachrichten*. Accessed 3 July 2017. http://www.muenchner-kirchennachrichten.de/meldung/article/kardinal-marx-pegida-phaenomen-ist-diffus.html

Noack, Rick. 16.12.2014. What's Behind the Astonishing Rise of an Anti-Islam Movement in Germany? *Washington Post Online*. Accessed 3 July 2017. https://www.washingtonpost.com/news/worldviews/wp/2014/12/16/

whats-behind-the-astonishing-rise-of-an-anti-islam-movement-in-germany/?utm_term=.5ee19cab8fef

Orosz, Helma. 2014. Rede der Oberbürgermeisterin vor dem Stadtrat am 11. Dezember 2014 zum Thema Asyl. *Landeshauptstadt Dresden.* Accessed 3 July2017.http://www.dresden.de/media/pdf/presseamt/OB-Rede-Stadtrat-11122014.pdf

Panorama. 2014. Kontaktversuch: 'Lügenpresse' trifft Pegida. *ARD*, December 18. Accessed 3 July 2017. http://daserste.ndr.de/panorama/archiv/2014/Kontaktversuch-Luegenpresse-trifft-Pegida-,pegida136.html

Petzold, Andreas. 17.12.2014. Immer noch im Tal der Ahnungslosen. *Stern Online.* Accessed 3 July 2017. http://www.stern.de/politik/deutschland/pegida-demonstrationen-in-dresden-immer-noch-im-tal-der-ahnung-slosen-2160827.html

Popp, Yvonne. 11.11.2016. Harte Strafen für Heidenau-Randalierer. *Sächsische Zeitung:* 13.

Rheinische Post. 05.01.2015. Schneider: "Christen haben bei diesen Demos nichts zu suchen". *Rheinische Post Online.* Accessed 3 July 2017. http://www.rp-online.de/panorama/deutschland/nikolaus-schneider-christen-haben-bei-den-demos-nichts-zu-suchen-aid-1.4775318

Rossmann, Robert. 15.12.2014. Interview mit Heiko Maas: "Die Argumente von Pegida sind doch wirklich hanebüchen". *Süddeutsche Zeitung:* 5.

Saft, Gunnar. 08.01.2015. AfD und Pegida spielen verstecken. *Sächsische Zeitung:* 6.

Schirmer, Stefan. 21.08.2015. Dann geht doch! Hass, Extremismus und Abschottung in Sachsen: Ist es Zeit für einen "Säxit"? *Zeit Online.* Accessed 3 July 2017. http://www.zeit.de/2015/34/sachsen-austritt-bundesrepublik-rechtsextremismus-pegida

Schwan, Gesine. 30.12.2014. Pegida ist überall. *Die Zeit:* 44.

Schwarzer, Alice. 2015. Sie fliehen vor den Islamisten! *Alice Schwarzer*, January 6. Accessed 3 July 2017. http://www.aliceschwarzer.de/artikel/sie-alle-fliehen-vor-den-islamisten-318215

Sigmund, Jörg. 01.01.2015. Minister Müller: Es gibt keinen Grund für Fremdenhass. *Augsburger Allgemeine Online.* Accessed 3 July 2017. http://www.augsburger-allgemeine.de/politik/Minister-Mueller-Es-gibt-keinen-Grund-fuer-Fremdenhass-id32489802.html

Smale, Alison. 07.12.2014. In German City Rich with History and Tragedy, Tide Rises Against Immigration. *The New York Times Online.* Accessed 3 July 2017. http://www.nytimes.com/2014/12/08/world/in-german-city-rich-with-history-and-tragedy-tide-rises-against-immigration.html

Spiegel Online. 12.12.2014. Bundespräsident zu Flüchtlingen: Gauck wünscht sich weniger Beachtung für Pegida. *Spiegel Online.* Accessed 3 July 2017.

http://www.spiegel.de/politik/deutschland/pegida-bundespraesident-gauck-fordert-weniger-beachtung-a-1008161.html
———. 13.12.2014. SPIEGEL-Umfrage zur Flüchtlingspolitik: Deutsche fühlen sich von Regierung übergangen. *Spiegel Online.* Accessed 3 July 2017. http://www.spiegel.de/politik/deutschland/deutsche-kritisieren-fluechtlingspolitik-ein-drittel-stimmt-pegida-zu-a-1008274.html
———. 26.01.2015. Sächsischer Minister trifft Pegida-Team: Auch Kathrin Oertel gehört zu Sachsen. *Spiegel Online.* Accessed 3 July 2017. http://www.spiegel.de/politik/deutschland/sachsens-innenminister-ulbig-trifft-pegida-sprecherin-kathrin-oertel-a-1015127.html
Springer, Christoph. 15.01.2015. 20-Jähriger aus Eritrea starb nach mehreren Messerstichen in den Hals und die Brust. *Dresdner Neueste Nachrichten*: 11.
Stern Online. 17.12.2014. Hier können Sie sehen, ob Ihren Freunden Pegida gefällt. *Stern Online.* Accessed 3 July 2017. http://www.stern.de/politik/deutschland/pegida-auf-facebook-hier-koennen-sie-sehen-ob-ihren-freunden-pegida-gefaellt-2160772.html
Sturm, Daniel F. 24.01.2015. Genossen rüffeln Gabriel für seinen Pegida-Dialog. *Welt Online.* Accessed 3 July 2017. http://www.welt.de/politik/deutschland/article136734129/Genossen-rueffeln-Gabriel-fuer-seinen-Pegida-Dialog.html
Süddeutsche Zeitung. 13.12.2014. Gemeinsame Gegenwehr. Bundespräsident und Politiker sehen Pegida-Proteste mit Sorge. *Süddeutsche Zeitung*: 7.
———. 01.01.2015. Fast jeder Dritte hat Verständnis für Pegida. *Süddeutsche Zeitung Online.* Accessed 3 July 2017. http://www.sueddeutsche.de/politik/umfrage-zu-anti-islam-bewegung-fast-jeder-dritte-hat-verstaendnis-fuer-pegida-1.2287619
Tagesthemen. 2014. De Maizière im tagesthemen-Interview: "Sorgen von 'PEGIDA' ernst nehmen". *ARD*, December 11. Accessed 3 July 2017. https://www.tagesschau.de/inland/de-maiziere-interview-101.html
Tageszeitung. 25.01.2015. Hanebüchen, verharmlosend, naiv. *taz Online.* Accessed 3 July 2017. http://www.taz.de/Gruenen-Frau-kommentiert-Pegida-/!5022617
Tanriverdi, Hakan. 17.12.2014. Löscht Facebook-Freunde, die Pegida liken. *Süddeutsche Zeitung Online.* Accessed 3 July 2017. http://www.sueddeutsche.de/digital/like-button-loescht-facebook-freunde-die-pegida-liken-1.2271851
Vorländer, Hans, Maik Herold, and Steven Schäller. 2015. *Wer geht zu PEGIDA und warum?* Dresden: Zentrum für Verfassungs- und Demokratieforschung.
———. 2016. *PEGIDA. Entwicklung, Zusammensetzung und Deutung einer Empörungsbewegung.* Wiesbaden: Springer VS.
Waurig, Tom. 2014. Altkanzler fordert "Aufstand der Anständigen". *couragiert. Magazin für demokratisches Handeln und Zivilcourage*, December 20. Accessed

3 July 2017. http://www.couragiert-magazin.de/me/schroeder-interview.html

Wieduwilt, Hendrik. 06.04.2017. Kabinett beschließt Regeln für ein sauberes Facebook. *Frankfurter Allgemeine Zeitung*: 18.

———. 01.07.2017. Bundestag entschärft Hassrede-Gesetz. *Frankfurter Allgemeine Zeitung*: 20.

Wiegel, Michaela, and Andreas Ross. 13.01.2015. Paris verschärft nach Terroranschlägen Sicherheitsvorkehrungen. *Frankfurter Allgemeine Zeitung*: 1.

Wolf, Ulrich, Alexander Schneider, Tobias Wolf, and Heinrich M. Löbbers. 02.12.2014. Pegida persönlich. *Sächsische Zeitung*: 3.

Yendell, Alexander, Oliver Decker, and Elmar Brähler. 2016. Wer unterstützt Pegida und was erklärt die Zustimmung zu den Zielen der Bewegung? In *Die enthemmte Mitte. Autoritäre und rechtsextreme Einstellungen in Deutschland*, ed. Oliver Decker, Johannes Kiess, and Elmar Brähler, 137–152. Gießen: Psychosozial-Verlag.

Yücel, Deniz. 16.12.2014. Ich geh ooch ma zum Döner. *taz Online*. Accessed 3 July 2017. http://www.taz.de/Pegida-Demonstration-in-Dresden/!5026039

Zeit Online. 15.12.2014. Jeder Zweite sympathisiert mit Pegida. *Zeit Online*. Accessed 3 July 2017. http://www.zeit.de/politik/deutschland/2014-12/islam-pegida-fluechtlinge-deutschland-umfrage

CHAPTER 3

PEGIDA in the Context of German Right-wing Populism

Right-wing populist movements and extreme right-wing parties have thus far failed to permanently establish themselves in Germany. The reasons for this can be found mainly in the specific political culture of the Federal Republic. After the experiences of National Socialism, an anti-totalitarian and anti-extremist fundamental consensus was established in the 1950s, which has functioned as a bulwark against radical parties on the right (as well as the left) side of the political spectrum until the present. An example of this is the *Socialist Reich Party* (SRP), the extreme right-wing successor of the National Socialist German Workers' Party (NSDAP), which was banned by the Federal Constitutional Court (FCC) in 1952. At the end of the 1960s an extreme right-wing party, in the form of the National Democratic Party of Germany (NPD), did in fact enter the state parliaments of Bavaria, Hesse, Bremen, Lower Saxony, Rhineland-Palatinate, Schleswig-Holstein and Baden-Württemberg, but was unable to establish itself long-term.[1] The NPD was isolated by the parties from the democratic spectrum in the state parliaments. Furthermore, the voters from the right-wing fringe were integrated with some success by the big conservative parties, the Christian Democratic Union (CDU) and the Christian Social Union in Bavaria (CSU) in the 1970s and 1980s. For instance, the CSU had early on issued the message that there should be no other party

---

[1] The NPD only just failed to enter the Bundestag in 1969 with 4.3 per cent in the Bundestag elections.

© The Author(s) 2018

H. Vorländer et al., *PEGIDA and New Right-Wing Populism in Germany*, New Perspectives in German Political Studies, https://doi.org/10.1007/978-3-319-67495-7_3

further to the political right. However, a volatile right-wing fringe, which could be mobilised, always remained. This was evident at the beginning of the 1990s through the temporary electoral successes of the parties Die Republikaner and German People's Union (DVU). One reason was the uncertainty which had arisen in parts of the German population because of the high number of immigrants and refugees from areas of the former Soviet Union and the Balkan region. Xenophobic arson attacks and acts of violence in German cities like Mölln (Schleswig-Holstein), Solingen (North Rhine-Westphalia) and Hoyerswerda (Saxony) further added to a heated social climate, whereby there were certain similarities to the sensitivities that resulted from the refugee crisis of 2015. After the Peaceful Revolution of 1989/1990 it also became evident that the eastern German party system exhibited less party attachment and higher voter volatility. In some instances, right-wing radical and right-wing populist parties achieved significant success. In Saxony-Anhalt in 1998 the DVU achieved a sensational election result with 12.9 per cent. In Saxony, the NPD entered the state parliament in both 2004 (with 9.2 per cent) and 2009 (with 5.6 per cent), before it fell just short of the threshold at the 2014 elections.

3.1   The AfD as a New Right-wing Populist Party in Germany

With the emergence of the Alternative for Germany (AfD) it seems that for the first time there is now a party which, through its numerous electoral successes, has the prospect of becoming established long-term. The reasons for this are complex.[2] The AfD started as an opponent of the federal government's Euro rescue policy and was able to mobilise a general suspicion towards the European Union (EU) (Arzheimer 2015; Franzmann 2016). Drawing its vitality mainly from disgruntled members and supporters of the CDU, the party succeeded in swiftly building up a party organisation throughout Germany. In 2013 the AfD had only just failed to enter the Bundestag because of the threshold clause, but already in 2014 the European election saw it enter the European Parliament with 7.1 per cent of votes. Thereafter the party was able to secure entry into the

---

[2] The success of the AfD is mainly associated with its clear stance in certain policy fields, for instance its forthright Euroscepticism (Arzheimer 2015) and its ability to draw on groups of voters that were neglected by the other parties in Germany (Schmitt-Beck 2017). The German developments can be put into a European perspective, cf. Decker and Lewandowsky (2017).

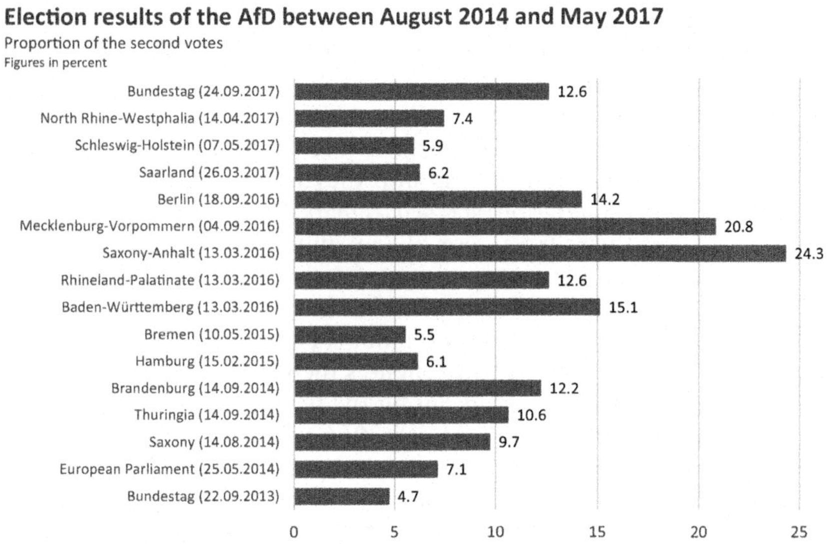

Election results of the AfD between August 2014 and May 2017
Proportion of the second votes
Figures in percent

Fig. 3.1 Overview of the electoral successes of the AfD between August 2014 and September 2017

parliaments of the Länder in every election it contested between 2014 and 2017. During this time it had, however, changed significantly in terms of its personnel and its programme. While the AfD still presented itself as a Eurosceptical party during the regional and European elections in 2014, it then made clear changes to its profile in the course of the protests of the Patriotic Europeans against the Islamisation of the Occident (PEGIDA) (cf. Sect. 3.2 in Chap. 3). During the refugee crisis in late summer 2015 the AfD was then able to create a distinctive image as an alternative to the refugee-friendly policy of the Federal Chancellor Angela Merkel. With its political agenda having undergone a shift to right-wing populism the AfD contested elections in Baden-Württemberg, Rhineland-Palatinate and Saxony-Anhalt on 13.03.2016. With voter shares of 15.1, 12.6 and 24.3 per cent respectively these results represent the party's greatest successes till then (see Fig. 3.1).[3] In summer 2017 the AfD was represented in 13 state parliaments and on 24.09.2017 it finally entered the Bundestag with remarkable 12.6 per cent of the votes. With this development even in the

[3] Cf. data from the statistical offices of the Länder and the Federal Returning Officer.

national parliament an entrenched political cleftavage became visible, in which differing concepts of cultural identity and social cohesion were negotiated as issues of refugee and immigration policy.[4]

The electoral successes of the AfD could be traced back to two effects in particular. Firstly, with its new right-wing populist profile, the party was, to a large extent, able to tap into the group of non-voters. Here analyses of voter migration showed remarkable differences between before and after the refugee crisis of September 2015. Before the refugee crisis in the five state elections in the Saxony, Brandenburg, Thuringia, Hamburg and Bremen Länder the AfD gained between 0.63 and 1.26 per cent of the absolute numbers of second votes from the camp of former non-voters. These figures then rose considerably in the state elections which were held during the height of the refugee crisis. In five state elections between March 2016 and September 2016, held in Baden-Württemberg, Rhineland-Palatinate, Saxony-Anhalt, Berlin and Mecklenburg-Vorpommern the party was able to mobilise as many as 8.8 per cent of votes from the camp of the former non-voters. This effect then subsequently weakened again when the borders were closed in the Balkans and the issue of refugees retreated into the background in the public debate.[5] In the elections in Saarland, in Schleswig-Holstein and in North Rhine-Westphalia between March and May 2017 only around 1.5 per cent of the votes for the AfD came from the camp of former non-voters.[6] On the other hand, the AfD was also able to draw away voters belonging to a range of segments from the other parties: in particular from both of the large parties (CDU and SPD), but also from the left-wing Die Linke, and, to a much lesser extent, from the Greens

---

[4]For the debate about the classification of the AfD cf. Lewandowsky (2015). For the attitudes of AfD supporters and AfD candidates cf. Berbuir et al. (2015); Schmitt-Beck (2014, 2017). For similarities and differences between the right-wing populist parties in Europe cf. Mudde (2007, 2017) and Ennser (2012).

[5]While at the height of the refugee crisis in autumn 2015 more than half of the population (53 per cent) were very worried about the refugee situation; this figure had sunk to only 31 per cent by autumn 2016 (Köcher 20.10.2016).

[6]The basis for the calculation are the second votes cast as well as the voter migration flows ascertained on election day by Infratest dimap through post-election surveys. Cf. the data from the returning officers in the state statistical offices and also the overview of the data from Infratest dimap on the election pages of the ARD, which can be accessed at: https://wahl.tagesschau.de/landtag.shtml

and the FDP.[7] In the first state elections directly after the refugee crisis on 13 March 2016 the flow of voters from the conservative CDU to the AfD was particularly dramatic. In Baden-Württemberg, for example, almost 200,000 former CDU voters switched their allegiance to the AfD.[8]

The AfD managed to channel the political protest that PEGIDA had taken to the streets and to convert it into parliamentary mandates. This meant not only that the party could establish itself in the *Bundesländer* with considerably greater resources for political work, but further to that, with its election successes, in some instances, the AfD even gained the status of leader of the opposition, as was the case in Baden-Württemberg, Mecklenburg-Vorpommern, Saxony-Anhalt and Rhineland-Palatinate. However, a dispute soon started within the AfD with regard to the manner in which it should perform its role as a political opposition party. A radical, ethno-nationalistic wing in the regional associations of both Thuringia and Saxony-Anhalt declared in favour of a fundamental opposition which could not be given up until the party had achieved "51 per cent" in elections.[9] A more pragmatically orientated wing led by then

---

[7] It was particularly remarkable that former left-wing voters also defected to the AfD in large numbers. In Saxony-Anhalt the Die Linke party recorded the second highest losses after the CDU with 28,000 voters who changed their allegiance and in Rhineland-Palatinate the third highest losses after the SPD with 12,000 voters going to the AfD. The party chairwoman Sarah Wagenknecht had already attempted to confront these losses in the run-up to the elections by saying that refugees seeking protection who committed crimes in Germany would no longer have the right to hospitality (Küppers and Leithäuser 13.01.2016).

[8] This was followed, some distance behind, by the losses of the SPD to the AfD (around 90,000 in Baden-Württemberg). Cf. the data of the returning officers in the state statistical offices and also the overview of the data from Infratest dimap on the election pages of the ARD, accessible at: https://wahl.tagesschau.de/landtag.shtml. As a reaction to their losses there were conflicts between CDU and CSU about the refugee policy, which was determined to be the cause of the election losses. Cf. the discussion paper of the Berliner Kreis in der Union (an association of members of the Bundestag from the CDU/CSU) at: http://dynamic.faz.net/download/2016/erklaerungberlinerkreis.pdf (Accessed 01.06.2017). The CSU, in turn, demanded a tougher asylum policy from Angela Merkel and the CDU, namely by the setting of an upper limit for the reception of refugees (Bannas 16.12.2016). These disputes also refer to deeper conflicts within the German Christian Democrats since 1990, cf. Green (2013).

[9] This was advocated by the Thuringian state chairman Björn Höcke in a speech on 17.01.2017.

party chairwoman Frauke Petry, on the other hand, sought to take on the responsibilities of government within the framework of coalitions (Hensel et al. 2017, p. 17f.). However, in the state parliaments many AfD representatives did not play their part adequately. Parliamentary work was used to stage protests and to provoke political opponents. The local party organisations in the *Bundesländer* only slowly became more professional as parliamentary advisers, experts and lawyers could not be recruited to the required extent. The work of the AfD parliamentary groups was predominantly focused on "minor interpellations", more time-consuming and more complex "major interpellations" were started by the members of parliament of the AfD to a lesser extent than their colleagues from the other parties (Schroeder et al. 2017, p. 30ff.). Nevertheless, the AfD satisfies all the prerequisites to secure itself a place in the German party landscape for the time being. And PEGIDA must be viewed as having paved the way for this development.

3.2   PEGIDA AND THE RIGHT-WING PARTIES IN GERMANY

The relationship between PEGIDA and the two right-wing parties relevant in Germany in 2014 was unsettled and full of tension. The AfD and NPD initially stated that they supported the protest movement and praised its achievements. Advances and attempts to instrumentalise PEGIDA, however, soon led to a competitive relationship.

Within the AfD the question of how to deal with the PEGIDA demonstrators was contentious at first. The suggestions ranged between clear differentiation, benevolent approval, informal support and official co-operation. The parliamentary group of the AfD in the Dresden city council had already stressed in a press release at the end of October 2014, that the PEGIDA protest—unlike that of the counter-demonstrators—was "carried out non-violently, peacefully and objectively", and explicitly welcomed the fact "that citizens make use of their right to demonstrate as guaranteed in the Basic Law and that they use it to articulate issues as well as their concerns" (Lommel 2014). In addition, close ties between the PEGIDA organisers and local party groupings of the AfD had existed very early on. There were several members of the party who were actively associated with PEGIDA from the beginning of the Monday demonstrations and who supported the work of the organisational team on site—for instance by providing a mobile shop which had been converted into a stage and equipped with a sound system (Vorländer et al. 2016, p. 42). At the level of the Saxon regional party association, however, collaboration was prevented by personal animosity between the AfD chairwoman Frauke Petry and the founder of PEGIDA Lutz Bachmann. A meeting between members of the AfD parliamentary group and PEGIDA organisers, which took place on 07.01.2015, did not deliver any concrete results—aside from the conclusion that there were "intersections as regards content" (Lachmann 08.01.2015). Instead, Bachmann publicly adopted the position that the AfD was a failed protest party, which had been elected into the different parliaments on the basis of the citizens' trust, only to subsequently be occupied with "internal fights about posts, with debates about the direction the party is taking and with taking care of itself". This meant that the AfD was no longer any different from the other established parties, which was why co-operation was not possible for a citizens' movement like PEGIDA.[10]

For a long time the party leadership did not present a co-ordinated position on the matter. Instead, its speakers engaged in debate, partly conducted in public, about the right way to deal with the protests, thereby fuelling party in-fighting. On the one hand, a position formed which warned about PEGIDA's xenophobic and racist motives. This more liberal economic wing of the party expressly advised against AfD members joining the protest marches (Meier and Niewendick 09.12.2014). Other representatives of the AfD came to the defence of PEGIDA in the face of public criticism. The then party chairman, Bernd Lucke, for instance, declared that the knee-jerk reaction of the "old parties and many media sources" which was a rejection of the protests, "without seriously taking a closer look at the demands of the demonstrators", was "proof of their shortcomings" (Neuerer 11.12.2014). The deputy AfD spokesperson and Brandenburg state chairman Alexander Gauland even went one step further by describing his own party as the "natural allies of this movement" (Lachmann 11.12.2014). After he had observed a Dresden PEGIDA demonstration in person on 15.12.2014, he stated for the record that he had discerned more of a "grass-roots movement", not right-wing extremists—nor had he heard slogans along those lines. The *19 points* of PEGIDA, were, according to Gauland, "in part very reasonable" (Weiland 19.12.2014).

---

[10]Cf. transcript of the speech by Lutz Bachmann on 11.05.2015.

The question of how to evaluate PEGIDA uncovered a divide within the party and this rift continued to deepen in the first half of 2015. While the representatives of the AfD's national-conservative oriented, eastern German state associations, which were strengthened after successful results in the state elections, clearly sympathised with the concerns of the PEGIDA participants, the federal party leaders increasingly distanced themselves from the demonstrations and soon made harsh judgements about parts of their own party's supporter base.[11] This dispute about principles between the camps finally became personalised through the open competition between the two party chairpersons, Bernd Lucke and Frauke Petry. It was resolved in a public power struggle both for the leadership and the future orientation of the party. At a party conference in July 2015, Frauke Petry was finally able to emerge victorious from the confrontation, whereupon Markus Pretzell, the state chairman of the AfD in North Rhine-Westphalia and Member of the European Parliament, declared that the AfD was also the "PEGIDA party" (Bender and Lohse 06.07.2015). Numerous AfD members and functionaries from the outnumbered moderate wing then left the party, among them Bernd Lucke who had been voted out of his position as chairman. Regarding his reasons, Lucke stated that he did not wish to be misused as a "bourgeois advertisement" for political ideas which he strongly repudiated. He had recognised too late the "extent members who want to reshape the AfD into a protest party for angry citizens had pushed their way into the party".[12]

This reorientation opened up the possibility for the AfD to raise its profile with right-wing populist slogans; however it did not lead to a rapprochement with PEGIDA. Instead the federal executive of the AfD adopted an extensive ban on co-operation in May 2016.[13] When Bachmann

---

[11]With regard to the PEGIDA supporters who were still demonstrating at the rallies which had shrunk considerably by spring 2015 the party executive member Hans-Olaf Henkel stressed on 17.04.2015, that by now "even the most obstinate extreme right-winger in the AfD [must] recognise what kind of people they are". The AfD should "look very closely at who is walking around there and keep at a distance from all these diffuse movements". PEGIDA had now crossed a line and become openly xenophobic (Weiland 17.04.2015).

[12]Cf. Bernd Lucke's written statement regarding his resignation from AfD at http://berndlucke.de/austrittserklaerung-aus-der-alternative-fuer-deutschland-afd (Accessed 10.07.2015).

[13]Cf. the summary of the various decisions made by the federal executive of the AfD on the relationship of the party with PEGIDA and the Identitarian Movement at: https://cdn.afd.tools/sites/75/2017/05/15144844/2017-05-15_afd-bundesverband_zusammenfassung-beschlusslage_gida-ib.pdf

then announced that he intended to found his own PEGIDA party,[14] the latent conflict between the AfD and PEGIDA turned into a definite relationship of open competition (Locke 19.07.2016; AfD Sachsen aktuell 2016, p. 6). Subsequently, PEGIDA became actively involved in new power struggles within the AfD and supported an even more radical ethno-nationalistic wing. In May 2016 representatives of this group spoke at PEGIDA events and a representative from PEGIDA spoke at a rally of the Thuringian AfD. One year later the first joint rally of PEGIDA and the AfD took place in Dresden. These evident breaches of the co-operation ban could not be prevented by the—now severely weakened—party leadership headed by Frauke Petry (Wolf and Alexe 08.05.2017).

Shortly after PEGIDA had emerged, the NPD as well as individuals from extreme right-wing comradeships (*Kameradschaften*) also sought a special, close relationship with the protest movement and attempted to take advantage of the demonstrations. Press reports covering the first Dresden demonstrations had already reported the participation of people known in the city to be neo-Nazis and former members of parliament from the NPD, without there being any outcry from the demonstrators (Pleil et al. 25.11.2014; Baumann-Hartwig et al. 26.11.2014). Furthermore, neither in any of the speeches at the demonstrations nor in other public contexts was there a clear distancing from the National Democrats. The Saxon regional association of the NPD, in turn, affirmed the PEGIDA demonstrations very early and characterised them as a sign of dissatisfaction with the "German policy on foreigners and asylum", which had always been denounced by the party (Schimmer 26.11.2014). Functionaries of the NPD expressed the view that "a lasting political climate change" could be read from the protests (Wonka and Riecker 17.12.2014). PEGIDA was said to be driven by "patriotic and courageous citizens", it had supposedly "plunged the immigration lobbyists and their media propaganda apparatus into real uncertainty" and was thereby pursuing similar goals to the party. Like the NPD the Dresden demonstrators were said to show "a firm, clear stance against asylum fraud and being overrun by foreigners" (Regional branch of the NPD in Saxony 05.01.2015).

However, the NPD's closeness to PEGIDA met with little approval from the protest movement. After the split of the organisational team in January 2015 there were increasing signs that the relationship was moving

---

[14]The name of this new party was to be Freiheitlich Direktdemokratische Volkspartei (Liberal Direct Democratic People's Party). The plans, however, came to nothing.

in the direction of competition instead of co-operation (Saft 30.01.2015). This was evident, for instance, in the Dresden mayoral election campaign 2015, when the unilateral call from the NPD to support the PEGIDA candidate (Weller 21.04.2015)[15] was dismissed as an attempt to discredit. Tatjana Festerling described the recommendation by the NPD as a predictable attempt "to make [her] unelectable", by trying to give her "a bit of an NPD flavour". For her part, she made conspiratorial allegations and accused the NPD of working against PEGIDA on behalf of government authorities. Festerling described the party as untrustworthy due to it being secretly controlled by the German domestic security agency (Verfassungsschutz).[16]

Subsequently the competition between the NPD and PEGIDA culminated in an open conflict over the sovereignty of interpretation in the right-wing nationalist camp. Two meaningful opponents had arisen against the NPD in the form of PEGIDA and the AfD, whose successes had proved to be an existential threat for the party. Since losing its presence in the Saxon state parliament in 2014, the NPD had already been battling for its political survival and had now been superseded on the political stage by the AfD. Against this background PEGIDA turned into another competitor, one which exhibited large overlaps on the issues of asylum, integration and immigration policy, and in part served a similar political clientele. PEGIDA, on the other hand, was determined to consistently differentiate and isolate itself from the NPD because its own middle-class image would be jeopardised by a relationship that was too close.

3.3   PEGIDA AND NEW RIGHT CURRENTS IN GERMANY

The protest movement of the Patriotic Europeans against the Islamisation of the Occident ventured, with its contents, into a realm of social expression in Germany which over the previous years had already been marked

[15] Cf. also the press release by the district executive of NPD Dresden made on 19.04.2015: https://npd-sachsen.de/dem-patriotischen-protest-in-dresden-eine-stimme-geben/

[16] By this Festerling alluded to the fact that a recent effort to ban the NPD was unsuccessful because during the case at the German Federal Constitutional Court (FCC) it had turned out that the German domestic security agency (Verfassungsschutz) had been closely linked with the party through having recruited many party officials as secret informants. Hence, the FCC refused to consider a ban in 2003. Another attempt to ban the NPD failed in 2017. Cf. the relevant Facebook post made by Tatjana Festerling on 20.04.2015: https://www.facebook.com/tatjana.festerling/posts/882926931773664 (Accessed 08.06.2015).

out by other actors and which the new protest movement was able to build on. Particularly influential in that respect was a book full of argument based on biologism and criticism of immigration entitled *Deutschland schafft sich ab* ("Germany is Doing Away With Itself"), with which the former member of the Executive Board of the Deutsche Bundesbank and member of the German Social Democratic Party (SPD), Thilo Sarrazin, was able to achieve bestseller status in 2010. In addition, right-wing orientated protest movements with Islamophobic and xenophobic themes had already attempted to mobilise on Germany's streets even before the emergence of PEGIDA, but without finding much support in the population.[17] Yet, in magazines and online blogs an alternative public had begun to form, catering to positions which were critical of the media and aggressive towards other cultures (Weiß 2011; Hunger 2016; Pfeiffer 2016).

The political and cultural environment, which enabled the rapid mobilisation successes of the PEGIDA protests in autumn 2014 had also been shaped by various intellectuals. They are mostly termed the so-called New Right. As a political current the New Right in Germany refers back to the German Conservative Revolutionary movement of the 1920s as well as to the French school of Nouvelle Droite which was founded mainly by the philosopher Alain de Benoist in 1968 (Cf. Mohler 1972; Benoist 1985). The exponents of the New Right see themselves as spearheading the fight against the so-called '68 generation and their left-wing, alternative, sociopolitical programme, which emphasised principles like individualisation, emancipation and equality (including same-sex partnerships), pursuing the expansion of democratic participation rights as well as a post-national integration of Germany into Europe. In its criticism the New Right accuses these developments of promoting the disintegration of cultural and national identities, while shifting between libertarian, conservative, *völkisch* or rather ethno-nationalistic, and ethnopluralist positions—with the aim of establishing a counter-culture (Kellershohn 2015a, p. 439). In terms of organisation a firmly established structure is not as apparent. The New Right can rather be described as a kind of network with many decentralised hubs, which attempt to create links to many further milieus. In

---

[17]These included, for example, the so-called "PRO" movement, which had been active since 1996 in Cologne and from 2005 further afield, mainly in North Rhine-Westphalia, and demonstrated against a supposed Islamisation (Sager and Peters 2008) or the so-called Hooligans against Salafists (HoGeSa), which agitated against Salafism predominantly on the internet, starting in spring 2014, and began to call for street protests at approximately the same time as PEGIDA (Gensing 2015).

Germany, there are publications available which serve this purpose, such as the magazines *Sezession* (Secession), *eigentümlich frei*[18] as well as *Tumult. Vierteljahresschrift für Konsensstörung* (*Tumult. Quarterly magazine for the disruption of consensus*), which are also available on the internet with up-to-date entries discussing the topics of the day.[19] In these forums spokespeople of the New Right publish both theoretical texts on the organisation of a political-cultural counter-revolution as well as current commentaries of political, social and cultural events.

One of the main spokespeople of the New Right in Germany is the publisher and political activist Götz Kubitschek.[20] With the advent of the PEGIDA protests he saw the chance to convey New Right ideas to a wider public: "They had the dynamism and masses and we knew the path to take, we knew the adversary—we could give it shape" (Somaskanda 22.06.2017). Starting in March 2015 Kubitschek repeatedly made appearances as a speaker at PEGIDA events in Dresden. Beyond that he was active as a networker with his publishing house Antaios, as well as the magazine *Sezession* and in many places he was the organiser of civil society initiatives against the immigration policy of the federal government. Among these was the initiative *Ein Prozent* (One percent), with which, in the style of a grassroots movement, 1 per cent of the population of Germany was to be successfully encouraged to form a "patriotic network of citizens".[21] Furthermore, Kubitschek founded the so-called Institut für Staatspolitik (Institute for State policy), which carries out training sessions in his place of residence, the small village of Schnellroda in Saxony-Anhalt, not least also for newly elected parliamentary representatives of the AfD (Kellershohn 2016; Speit 2016, p. 199ff.).

Alongside Götz Kubitschek the Identitarian Movement in Germany is a second important actor from the New Right with which PEGIDA co-operated. The movement is set in the context of a recent pan-European spread of ideas pursuing the protection of homeland, culture and identity. These terms are to be understood as ciphers, with which older nationalistic concepts and right-wing ideological backgrounds are semantically

---

[18] The title involves an apparent play on words based on the German word *eigentum* meaning property.

[19] Cf. the online blog "Sezession im Netz" (Secession on the Internet) at https://sezession.de as well as the online edition of "eigentümlich frei" at https://www.ef-magazin.de

[20] For information about Götz Kubitschek cf. Kellershohn (2016).

[21] *Ein Prozent* appears mainly on a professionally made website: https://einprozent.de

recoded.[22] The Identitarian Movement originally started in France in 2002 as the youth organisation of the conservative Bloc Identitaire which in turn was derived from the Nouvelle Droite school of thought. Its positions include, for example, the desire for a small-scale regional economy, the demand for an end to the so-called *Großer Austausch* ("big exchange" of population of all ethnic groups and cultures around the world)—a transformation of the French term of *Grand Replacement*[23]—as well as the idea of a world order which is based on the principles of so-called ethnopluralism.[24] The Identitarian Movement in Germany is under observation by the German domestic security agency (Verfassungsschutz), which sees "indications of right-wing extremist aspirations" (Federal Ministry of the Interior 2017, p. 64). The first evident co-operation between the Identitarian Movement and PEGIDA was the appearance of Martin Sellner in Dresden on 06.02.2016. Sellner is one of two speakers from the Identitarian Movement in Austria and is closely linked with ethno-nationalistic and right-wing populist intellectual circles. He has since made repeated appearances in Dresden. Sellner's political repertoire includes making use of popular culture on the street, publishing activities in association with Götz Kubitschek's publishing house Antaios, as well as subversive political performance art following the example of left-wing protest forms, attempting to achieve the largest possible effect in the media with little effort. The ideological purpose of these forms of political action is defined by the struggle of the New Right for so-called cultural hegemony.[25]

Since 2016 the so-called Reichsbürgerbewegung (Reich Citizens' Movement) has also attracted attention in Germany. Supporters (known as Reichsbürger) deny the existence of the Federal Republic of Germany, reject its police, courts and legislation, and see themselves as belonging

[22]For the Identitarian Movement's Greek lambda symbol and its origin cf. Sect. 1.3 in Chap. 1.

[23]Cf. the work of Renaud Camus, who is renowned for his warnings of a forthcoming replacement of the French people by Muslim immigrants (Camus 2011). The presence of the concept of a replacement of a people by another can be observed in French politics and literature: party officials of the Front National refer to it (Farand 07.12.2015) as does Michel Houellebecq's controversial novel *Soumission* (*Submission*).

[24]According to ethnopluralism every single culture is worthy of preservation in its own right, and in order to protect itself from external, allegedly corrupting influences a culture is allowed to separate itself on its own home territory and should strive to maintain its own cultural purity (Strobl and Bruns 2016, p. 106).

[25]Cf. Minkenberg 2011, p. 115f.

to a still existent German Reich. For a long time, Reichsbürger were only perceived to be troublemakers, who occupied the country's courts, authorities and offices with unnecessary queries and constant refractoriness. After two gunfights occurred between the police and avowed Reichsbürger in summer 2016, which resulted in a police officer being fatally wounded, the assessment of the danger changed however (Lohse 21.10.2016; Schaaf 11.09.2016; Lohse and Schäffer 03.11.2016). Since November 2016 Germany's domestic security agency has been monitoring the Reichsbürger scene, parts of which represent a potential danger with anti-constitutional dimensions due to some being armed.[26] The ideology-based strict rejectionist stance towards representatives and institutions of the Federal Republic of Germany could also be found in a more moderate form among PEGIDA demonstrators. In addition there were also occasional indications of an ideological closeness between Reichsbürger and PEGIDA demonstrators—for example placards, on which Germany was referred to as "BRD GmbH" (BRD Ltd).[27]

On this spectrum of New Right trends in Germany PEGIDA functioned as a catalyst. The protest movement made it clear that mobilisation successes which traditionally would have been expected more in association with the political left-wing, were also possible with right-wing positions. As a consequence, the movement became somewhat of a role model. Numerous protest initiatives started and attempted to imitate the concept of PEGIDA, in the hope that they would be able to attract similarly high numbers of participants.[28] First and foremost these protest initiatives included so-called GIDA offshoots, which were also formed in other German cities just a few weeks after the first successes of the Dresden protests. Initially they included some "official" offshoots

---

[26] The Verfassungsschutz estimates the Reichsbürger scene at around 10,000 people in the whole of the Federal Republic (Federal Ministry of the Interior 2017, p. 97).

[27] "BRD GmbH" (Federal Republic of Germany Ltd) is meant to indicate that the Federal Republic is not a sovereign State, instead it is a company with limited liability which is active in the economy. According to this the citizens of the Federal Republic are only employees of this 'GmbH', the shareholders of which are said to be the Allied Forces or global elites pursuing sinister interests.

[28] The initiative We are Germany—it is only together that we are strong (*Wir sind Deutschland—nur gemeinsam sind wir stark*), for example, organised demonstration events in the Saxon towns of Plauen and Bautzen in 2015 and 2016, with up to 5000 participants in Plauen.

recognised by PEGIDA in Dresden, such as LEGIDA in Leipzig or KAGIDA in Kassel. Other GIDA initiatives, on the other hand, were founded by people from the right-wing radical milieu and openly or covertly controlled by them, which, for the organisers in Dresden, meant significant damage to the carefully cultivated middle-class image of the PEGIDA "brand". This became clear in the case of the BOGIDA protests in Bonn, which were initiated by a right-wing radical activist who was well known in the region, or MVGIDA in Schwerin,[29] where not only registrants and speakers came from the extreme right NPD, but also parts of the NPD parliamentary group from the state parliament in Schwerin openly took part in the demonstrations (Kiesel 21.01.2015). It was also scarcely concealed that SÜGIDA in Thuringian Suhl was controlled by the local neo-Nazi scene (Haak 15.01.2015); in this case it remained unclear as to whether there was any contact with the organisers in Dresden. In other cases it is known that PEGIDA Dresden maintained existing contacts, although it had to be assumed that there had been an infiltration by right-wing radical forces—for example in BAGIDA (Munich) and LEGIDA (Leipzig) (Götte 07./08.03.2015; Klaubert 22.01.2015).

Other actors also profited from the attention that PEGIDA had attracted. Representatives of the New Right established contact with the PEGIDA organisers and made appearances at the protest demonstrations (cf. Sect. 1.2 in Chap. 1). Numerous previously fringe publications, both in print and online, were consumed by PEGIDA supporters as alternative media, and articles were shared on social media. For their part, the organisers of PEGIDA raised the profile of these publications. The Islamophobic online blog *Politically Incorrect* was regularly advertised on the PEGIDA stage. Jürgen Elsässer, editor of the monthly magazine *Compact*, which combines positions which are nationalistic and critical of capitalism, organised discussions with Götz Kubitschek, Lutz Bachmann and Tatjana Festerling in Dresden. PEGIDA, in turn, gave away monthly magazine subscriptions to its supporters.[30]

---

[29]The "MV" in the name stands here for the federal state Mecklenburg-Vorpommern.
[30]For information about Jürgen Elsässer cf. Lang (2016).

3.4   PEGIDA's Contacts with European Right-wing Populists

The PEGIDA organisers also attempted to establish contact with well-known actors in other European countries early on. The goal of these efforts to make connections was to establish the protest movement as the German counterpart of these parties and movements. The numerous activities, which were intended to lead to a political and institutional network, did not achieve any lasting success however. European right-wing populist parties and movements kept their distance, even though they did partially maintain contacts for a short time. Apparently they did not view PEGIDA as a serious partner, with which it could have been worthwhile entering into longer-term co-operation.[31] Faced with this reluctance PEGIDA was forced to turn to smaller movements and parties in Europe, which in part exhibited unmistakable extreme right-wing tendencies. Furthermore, PEGIDA's networking attempts were in competition with those of the AfD party. Due to its representation in the European Parliament and its membership in the political group Europe of Nations and Freedom the AfD already had an institutionalised forum for co-operation, for instance, with the French Front National (FN), the Dutch Partij voor de Vrijheid (PVV), the Italian Lega Nord and the Freiheitliche Partei Österreichs (FPÖ) of Austria. The co-operation of these parties was also evident outside of the European Parliament, for example at a high-profile gathering in January 2017 in Koblenz (Bender 23.01.2017).

Because PEGIDA did not have these forms of co-operation at its disposal, attempts were made to carry over the street protest into lasting structures in other ways. For that purpose there were appearances from speakers belonging to the Italian Lega Nord, the Belgian Vlaams Belang, the Irish Identity Ireland and the Czech Blok Proti Islámu. Additionally, there were numerous speakers from right-wing populist alliances such as

---

[31] For example, Lutz Bachmann and Siegfried Däbritz took part in the New Year's meeting of the Austrian FPÖ in Wels on 16.01.2016 and motivated their participation with the goal of international networking. At the same time, however, the FPÖ denied that Bachmann and Däbritz were official guests of the party (Die Presse 16.01.2016; Meisner 20.01.2016).

the Identitarian Movement in Austria and PEGIDA offshoots from Denmark and Great Britain.[32] However these appearances by international speakers did not in any way result in fixed institutional structures. The hope that the visit by Geert Wilders in April 2015 would change this was soon disappointed. In addition, Bachmann's attempts to recruit further prominent representatives of European right-wing populism as speakers—such as Nigel Farage from the British UK Independence Party (UKIP) or Marine Le Pen from the French Front National—failed.

Instead, PEGIDA took an even stronger line and became more radical. Above all Tatjana Festerling played a decisive role here. She, for instance, appeared on the Bulgarian-Turkish border where she showed herself in military camouflage clothing together with the paramilitary group Bulgarian Military Veterans Union, Vasil Levski and presented herself as a capable fighter ready to "track down illegal intruders and hand them over to the border police", hardly leaving any doubt as to her intention to make PEGIDA the spearhead of a militant movement to save the Occident.[33]

In this context, PEGIDA made a great effort to establish its own pan-European platform called Fortress Europe. With this alliance the movement attempted to integrate offshoots from Austria, the Netherlands and Bulgaria as well as the right-wing conservative Estonian Eesti Konservatiivne Rahvaerakond and the Italian Lega Nord. Also included were parties and movements with even more clear-cut, extreme, right-wing tendencies: the Czech party Úsvit—Národní Koalice, the Czech movement Blok Proti Islámu and the Polish movement Ruch Narodowy (Spanka and Kahrs 2014). In the founding document of Fortress Europe, the so-called

---

[32] Vincenzo Sofo spoke for the Lega Nord, Marek Černoch for the Blok Proti Islámu, Filip Dewinter and Anke van Dermeersch for Vlaams Belang. Peter O'Loughlin represented Identity Ireland, Tommy Robinson, Paul Weston and Ann Marie Waters spoke for PEGIDA UK. PEGIDA Denmark was represented by Tania Groth. Gavin Boby, lawyer and representative of the Islamophobic Law and Freedom Foundation, also spoke at PEGIDA in Dresden. The Law and Freedom Foundation supports those who oppose the construction of new mosques in Great Britain. For further international PEGIDA offshoots cf. Sect. 1.1 in Chap. 1.

[33] Festerling's presentation of herself as such a "freedom fighter" is documented on her Facebook page with a report about her "deployment". Cf. https://www.facebook.com/tatjana.festerling/media_set?set=a.1112401432159545&type=1&l=277a381b58 (Accessed 01.06.2017).

Prague Declaration, the usual themes of European right-wing populism were to be found. Refugees were described as a "migration weapon", which was being pointed at the peoples of Europe. Islam was labelled a "conqueror from an alien culture" that needed to be repelled in order to safeguard the preservation of the peoples of Europe (Strobl and Bruns 2016; Bouron 2016; Kellershohn 2015b). Fortress Europe however did not turn out to be a platform for the desired internationalisation of PEGIDA. Instead, after Festerling's departure it also split away from the protest movement.[34] Thus, for PEGIDA the short episode of connection with parts of European right-wing populism (and right-wing extremism) was over. Since the European expansion of PEGIDA offshoots was not making headway either, the efforts towards an international network had finally failed.

References

AfD Sachsen Aktuell. 2016. Ja zum Parteitag, Nein zu Pegida. *AfD Sachsen aktuell* 25: 6.

Arzheimer, Kai. 2015. The AfD: Finally a Successful Right-Wing Populist Eurosceptic Party for Germany? *West European Politics* 38: 535–556.

Baumann-Hartwig, Thomas, Hauke Heuer, and Ingolf Pleil. 26.11.2014. Die Debatte um neue Asylbewerberheime spaltet Dresden und treibt unter dem Schirm von Pegida Tausende auf die Straße. *Dresdner Neueste Nachrichten*: 3.

Bender, Justus, and Eckart Lohse. 06.07.2015. Flugversuche mit einem Flügel. *Frankfurter Allgemeine Zeitung*: 2.

Berbuir, Nicole, Marcel Lewandowsky, and Jasmin Siri. 2015. The AfD and Its Sympathisers: Finally a Right-Wing Populist Movement in Germany? *German Politics* 24: 154–178.

de Benoist, Alain. 1985. *Kulturrevolution von rechts. Gramsci und die Nouvelle Droite*. Krefeld: Sinus.

Bouron, Samuel. 2016. The Strategy of the French Identitaires. In *Trouble on the Far Right*, ed. Maik Fielitz and Laura L. Laloire, 1–6. Bielefeld: transcript Verlag.

Camus, Renaud. 2011. *Le Grand Replacement*. Neuilly-sur-Seine: Editions David Reinharc.

[34] Speeches by members of Fortress Europe in Dresden also ended abruptly with the departure of Festerling, with the exception of Tommy Robinson (PEGIDA UK), who was obviously loyal to Bachmann. He continued to make short appearances at PEGIDA events in Dresden, for instance on the second anniversary of the protest movement on 16.10.2016.

Decker, Frank, and Marcel Lewandowsky. 2017. Rechtspopulismus in Europa: Erscheinungsformen, Ursachen und Gegenstrategien. *Zeitschrift für Politik* 61: 21–38.

Ennser, Laurenz. 2012. The Homogeneity of West European Party Families. *Party Politics* 18: 151–171.

Farand, Cloe. 07.12.2015. Marion Maréchal-Le Pen: The Rising Star of France's Far-right Front National Party. *Independent*. Accessed 3 July 2017. http://www.independent.co.uk/news/world/europe/marion-mar-chal-le-pen-the-successful-face-of-france-far-right-front-national-party-a6762436.html

Federal Ministry of the Interior. 2017. Verfassungsschutzbericht 2016. *Bundesministerium des Inneren*. Accessed 3 July 2017. http://www.verfassungsschutz.de/embed/vsbericht-2016.pdf

Franzmann, Simon T. 2016. Calling the Ghost of Populism: The AfD's Strategic and Tactical Agendas until the EP Election 2014. *German Politics* 25: 457–479.

Gensing, Patrick. 2015. HoGeSa—Wie Hooligans rechte Brücken schlagen. *Bundeszentrale für politische Bildung*. Accessed 3 July 2017. http://www.bpb.de/politik/extremismus/rechtsextremismus/199362/hogesa-wie-hooligans-rechte-bruecken-schlagen

Götte, Karl-Wilhelm. 07.03.2015. Ideologischer Brückenschlag. *Süddeutsche Zeitung*: R11.

Green, Simon. 2013. Societal Transformation and Programmatic Change in the CDU. *German Politics* 22: 46–63.

Haak, Sebastian. 15.01.2015. Experte: Sügida war rechtsextreme Demonstration. *Thüringer Allgemeine*: 10.

Hensel, Alexander, Florian Finkbeiner, Philip Dudek, Julika Förster, Michael Freckmann, and Pauline Höhlich. 2017. *Die AfD vor der Bundestagswahl 2017. Vom Protest zur parlamentarischen Opposition*. Frankfurt a. M.: Otto-Brenner-Stiftung.

Hunger, Anna. 2016. Gut vernetzt—Der Kopp-Verlag und die schillernde rechte Publizistenszene. In *Strategien der extremen Rechten*, ed. Stephan Braun, Alexander Geisler, and Martin Gerster, 425–438. Wiesbaden: Springer.

Kellershohn, Helmut. 2015a. Das Institut für Staatspolitik und das jungkonservative Hegemonieprojekt. In *Strategien der extremen Rechten*, ed. Stephan Braun, Alexander Geisler, and Martin Gerster, 439–467. Wiesbaden: Springer Fachmedien Wiesbaden.

———. 2015b. Die jungkonservative Neue Rechte zwischen Realpolitik und politischem Existenzialismus. *Zeitschrift für Geschichtswissenschaft* 63: 720–740.

———. 2016. Risse im Gebälk. In *Die Alternative für Deutschland*, ed. Alexander Häusler, 181–200. Wiesbaden: Springer Fachmedien Wiesbaden.

Kiesel, Robert. 21.01.2015. Schulterschluss zwischen Islamkritikern und NPD. *Nordkurier*: 5.

Klaubert, David. 22.01.2015. Das sind die Köpfe hinter Legida. *Frankfurter Allgemeine Zeitung Online*. Accessed 3 July 2017. http://www.faz.net/aktu-ell/politik/inland/leipzig-das-sind-die-koepfe-hinter-legida-13384814.html

Köcher, Renate. 20.10.2016. Die AfD—Außenseiter mit Rückhalt. *Frankfurter Allgemeine Zeitung*: 8.

Lachmann, Günther. 11.12.2014. AfD sieht sich als natürlichen Pegida-Verbündeten. *Welt Online*. Accessed 3 July 2017. http://www.welt.de/poli-tik/deutschland/article135274592/AfD-sieht-sich-als-natuerlichen-Pegida-Verbuendeten.html

———. 08.01.2015. AfD-Chefin Petry sieht "Schnittmengen" mit Pegida. *Welt Online*. Accessed 3 July 2017. http://www.welt.de/politik/deutschland/article136170926/AfD-Chefin-Petry-sieht-Schnittmengen-mit-Pegida.html

Lang, Jürgen P. 2016. Biographisches Portrait: Jürgen Elsässer. In *Jahrbuch Extremismus und Demokratie*, ed. Uwe Backes, Alexander Gallus, and Eckhard Jesse, 225–241. Baden-Baden: Nomos.

Lewandowsky, Marcel. 2015. Eine rechtspopulistische Protestpartei? Die AfD in der öffentlichen und politikwissenschaftlichen Debatte. *Zeitschrift für Politikwissenschaft* 25: 119–134.

Lommel, Bernd. 2014. Erklärung der AfD-Fraktion im Stadtrat der Landeshauptstadt Dresden zu den Demonstrationen von PEGIDA. *AfD-Kreisverband Dresden*, November 20. Accessed 3 July 2017. http://afd-dd.de/erklaerung-der-afd-fraktion-im-stadtrat-der-landeshauptstadt-dresden-zu-den-demonstrationen-von-pegida

Meier, Albrecht, and Martin Niewendick. 09.12.2014. Kundgebung der Islam-Hasser in Dresden. Innenminister de Maizière: "Pegida ist eine Unverschämtheit". *Tagesspiegel Online*. Accessed 3 July 2017. http://www.tagesspiegel.de/politik/kundgebung-der-islam-hasser-in-dresden-innenminis-ter-de-maiziere-pegida-ist-eine-unverschaemtheit/11091188.html

Minkenberg, Michael. 2011. Die radikale Rechte in Europa heute. In *Die Dynamik der europäischen Rechten*, ed. Claudia Globisch, Agnieszka Pufelska, and Volker Weiß, 111–132. Wiesbaden: VS Verlag für Sozialwissenschaften.

Mohler, Armin. 1972. *Die konservative Revolution in Deutschland 1918–1932: Ein Handbuch*. Darmstadt: Wissenschaftliche Buchgesellschaft.

Mudde, Cas. 2007. *Populist Radical Right Parties in Europe*. Cambridge, UK: Cambridge University Press.

———, ed. 2017. *The Populist Radical Right. A Reader*. London: Routledge.

Neuerer, Dietmar. 11.12.2014. "Die AfD teilt viele Pegida-Forderungen". *Handelsblatt Online*. Accessed 3 July 2017. http://www.handelsblatt.com/politik/deutschland/bernd-lucke-die-afd-teilt-viele-pegida-forderun-gen/11107094.html

Pfeiffer, Thomas. 2016. Gegenöffentlichkeit und Aufbruch im Netz. Welche strat-egischen Funktionen erfüllen Websites und Angebote im Web 2.0 für den deutschen Rechtsextremismus? In *Strategien der extremen Rechten*, ed. Stephan Braun, Alexander Geisler, and Martin Gerster, 259–286. Wiesbaden: Springer.

Pleil, Ingolf, Hauke Heuer, and Andreas Friedrich. 25.11.2014. Erster "Bürgerdialog Asyl" verlief friedlich. *Dresdner Neueste Nachrichten*: 1.

Regional Branch of the NPD in Saxony. 05.01.2015. Die Dresdner Massenproteste gegen Überfremdung und Asylmißbrauch setzen klare politische Forderungen auf die Agenda. *NPD-Landesverband Sachsen*. Accessed 3 July 2017. https:// npd-sachsen.de/die-dresdner-massenproteste-gegen-ueberfremdung-und-asylmissbrauch-setzen-klare-politische-forderungen-auf-die-agenda

Saft, Gunnar. 30.01.2015. Ex-Pegida-Führer gründen neue Bewegung. *Sächsische Zeitung*: 1.

Sager, Tomas, and Jürgen Peters. 2008. Die PRO-Aktivitäten im Kontext der extremen Rechten. In *Rechtspopulismus als "Bürgerbewegung"*, ed. Alexander Häusler, 115–128. Wiesbaden: VS Verlag für Sozialwissenschaften.

Schimmer, Arne. 26.11.2014. Pressemitteilung: "Wir sind das Volk"—Mit der PEGIDA den Volkswillen auf die Straße tragen! *NPD-Landesverband Sachsen*. Accessed 3 July 2017. https://npd-sachsen.de/wir-sind-das-volk-mit-der-pegida-den-volkswillen-auf-die-strasse-tragen

Schmitt-Beck, Rüdiger. 2014. Euro-Kritik, Wirtschaftspessimismus und Einwanderungsskepsis: Hintergründe des Beinah-Wahlerfolges der Alternative für Deutschland (AfD) bei der Bundestagswahl 2013. *Zeitschrift für Parlamentsfragen* 45: 94–112.

———. 2017. The 'Alternative für Deutschland in the Electorate': Between Single-Issue and Right-Wing Populist Party. *German Politics* 26: 124–148.

Schroeder, Wolfgang, Bernhard Weßels, Christian Neusser, and Alexander Berzel. 2017. *Parlamentarische Praxis der AfD in deutschen Landesparlamenten*. Berlin: Wissenschaftszentrum Berlin für Sozialforschung.

Spanka, Eva, and Andreas Kahrs. 2014. Die Bewegung marschiert. Ruch Narodowy und Polens extreme Rechte. *Osteuropa* 64: 129–140.

Speit, Andreas. 2016. *Bürgerliche Scharfmacher. Deutschlands neue rechte Mitte— von AfD bis Pegida*. Zürich: Orell Füssli Verlag.

Strobl, Natascha, and Julian Bruns. 2016. Preparing for (Intellectual) Civil War. In *Trouble on the Far Right*, ed. Maik Fielitz and Laura L. Laloire, 1–6. Bielefeld: transcript Verlag.

Tagesspiegel. 17.01.2017. Höcke-Rede im Wortlaut. "Gemütszustand eines total besiegten Volkes". *Tagesspiegel Online*. Accessed 3 July 2017. http://www.tagesspiegel.de/politik/hoecke-rede-im-wortlaut-gemuetszustand-eines-total-besiegten-volkes/19273518-all.html

Vorländer, Hans, Maik Herold, and Steven Schäller. 2016. *PEGIDA. Entwicklung, Zusammensetzung und Deutung einer Empörungsbewegung*. Wiesbaden: Springer VS.

Weiß, Volker. 2011. *Deutschlands Neue Rechte. Angriff der Eliten—Von Spengler bis Sarrazin.* Paderborn: Ferdinand Schöningh.

Weiland, Severin. 19.12.2014. Eurokritiker: AfD-Vize Gauland verteidigt Pegida-Märsche. *Spiegel Online.* Accessed 3 July 2017. http://www.spiegel.de/politik/deutschland/afd-und-pegida-afd-vize-gauland-rechtfertigt-pegida-maersche-a-1009270.html

———. 17.04.2015. Flügelkämpfe bei Eurokritikern: AfD-Vize Henkel rechnet mit Pegida-Anhängern ab. *Spiegel Online.* Accessed 3 July 2017. http://www.spiegel.de/politik/deutschland/afdvize-hans-olaf-henkel-rechnet-mit-pegida-ab-a-1028984.html

Weller, Andreas. 21.04.2015. NPD unterstützt Pegida-Kandidatin in Dresden. *Sächsische Zeitung*: 1.

Wonka, Dieter, and Joachim Riecker. 17.12.2014. Reaktionen schwanken zwischen Gesprächsbereitschaft und Ablehnung. *Sächsische Zeitung*: 1.

CHAPTER 4

The PEGIDA Demonstrators: Characteristics and Motivations

At the beginning of the protests the socio-demographic characteristics and political motives of those taking part in the demonstrations of the Patriotic Europeans against the Islamisation of the Occident (PEGIDA) were initially unclear. This was due in no small part to a collective rejectionist attitude towards journalists on the part of the organisers and protesters. Thus, between October 2014 and January 2015, an extremely negative image became established in the media coverage. This was based primarily on the subjective impressions of media individuals, who had received treatment ranging from unfriendly to aggressive, and this image was then reinforced on a weekly basis with new video and audio recordings, which in some instances were disturbing. It was therefore assumed that the participants in the PEGIDA rallies came predominantly from those at the margins of society, that they had a low level of education and that they were motivated by openly xenophobic feelings of resentment as well as right-wing extremist ideas. In short, it was thought to be those who have been left behind, the notoriously antidemocratically-orientated who are overwhelmed by the changes in society or simply "clueless" fearful citizens, those who can still be encountered with startling frequency, despite the reunification and the development programme "Aufbau-Ost" in the

© The Author(s) 2018   73
H. Vorländer et al., *PEGIDA and New Right-Wing Populism in Germany*, New Perspectives in German Political Studies,
https://doi.org/10.1007/978-3-319-67495-7_4

new federal states.[1] When the first academic study of PEGIDA was presented to the public in mid-January 2015 parts of this image were called
into question (Vorländer et al. 2015). It became apparent from the findings, as well as the results of further empirical investigations, that many
PEGIDA protestors in fact came from a social middle class, were well-
educated, employed and had net incomes slightly above the average in
Saxony. Apparently, these people seemed to have no reservations about
joining protest rallies in which predominantly right-wing populist or even
xenophobic slogans were used. They also seemed prepared to express their
own concerns in public together with high-profile right-wing extremists
and people belonging to the hooligan scene.

The insights into the PEGIDA protesters, their socio-demographic
characteristics, their political opinions and motives can be drawn from the
findings of a number of studies. Between winter 2014 and spring 2016
participants at the PEGIDA demonstrations were regularly interviewed by
different teams of researchers with the help of standardised procedures.
These investigations were complemented by a systematic observation of
the corresponding rallies, the organisers and their communication on
social media platforms. The following studies of PEGIDA resulted, listed
here in chronological order based on when they first appeared:

- Asking "Who goes to PEGIDA and why?" a team led by Hans
  Vorländer, a political scientist at TU Dresden (TUD), conducted
  questionnaire-based face-to-face interviews with a total of 397 demonstrators at the PEGIDA events on 22.12.2014, 05.01.2015 and
  12.01.2015, and asked about socio-demographic characteristics and
  about the motivation to participate in PEGIDA. The interview participants were selected at random (Vorländer et al. 2015).
- A team, led by the sociologist Dieter Rucht, from the Berlin Institute
  for Social Movement Studies (ipb) handed out flyers at the PEGIDA
  event on 12.01.2015 with an invitation for people to participate in
  an online survey. Of the approximately 1800 participants of the
  demonstration who were spoken to, there were a total of 123 people
  who accepted the invitation and subsequently provided information
  via the internet (Rucht et al. 2015).

---

[1]Cf. here only Hebel and Reimann (16.12.2014), Lackerbauer (21.04.2015) as well as a
feature story on the ARD-magazine *Panorama* on 18.12.2014, in which a total of over
60 minutes of video material from interviews with PEGIDA demonstrators was collected
under the title "Contact attempt: 'The lying press' meets Pegida" (Panorama 18.12.2014).

- A team led by the political scientist Franz Walter from the Göttinger Institut für Demokratieforschung also handed out flyers with an invitation to participate in an online survey both on 12.01.2015 in Dresden as well as at subsequent PEGIDA events in Leipzig, Hanover, Braunschweig and Duisburg. In total 727 people responded. (Walter 19.01.2015; Geiges et al. 2015). On 30.11.2015 the Göttinger Institut then started an additional survey in which printed questionnaires to be returned by mail were distributed among the protesters. This enabled the analysis of a further 610 completed questionnaires (Finkbeiner et al. 31.01.2016).
- The Dresden political scientist Werner J. Patzelt and his team conducted questionnaire-based face-to-face interviews with PEGIDA demonstrators on Sunday, 25.01.2015. Here the selection of those spoken to was made on the basis of a quota plan. According to the sex and age distribution at PEGIDA events, as identified in the previous studies, the interviewers specifically selected certain participants at the demonstrations. Of those selected, 242 people took part in the interviews (Patzelt 2015). On 27.04.2015, on 04.05.2015 and on 18.01.2016 three additional rounds of interviews were conducted with demonstrators whereby the same approach was used, but with a greatly expanded questionnaire; the number of interviewees was 271, 434 and 386 respectively. The goal of the investigation was to clarify whether the make-up of the Dresden demonstrations had now changed (Patzelt and Eichardt 2015; Patzelt 2016).
- Finally, between December 2015 and April 2016, the Düsseldorf sociologist Karl-Heinz Reuband studied the PEGIDA demonstrators in Dresden in a total of three waves of research. On the basis of written postal surveys, he managed to receive and evaluate around 1000 completed questionnaires (Reuband 2017).

The results of these studies have been summarised and interpreted in several monographs.[2] In addition, there are further studies which looked at the social contexts of the PEGIDA demonstrations in Dresden between 2014 and 2016, as follows:

- On the basis of an existing contact database of inhabitants of Dresden the Professor of communication studies at TUD, Wolfgang Donsbach, also had 860 randomly chosen people answer questions about

[2] Geiges et al. 2015, Vorländer et al. 2016, Patzelt and Klose 2016.

PEGIDA via e-mail in mid-January 2015. Since only about 3 per cent of those asked revealed that they were PEGIDA participants, the study only provided indications as to "which attitudes increase the probability that someone agrees with the goals of Pegida or not" (Donsbach 23.01.2015; Schielicke et al. 2015).

- In June 2015 the Dresden sociologist Stefan Fehser conducted a representative telephone survey of the citizens of Dresden, the focus of which was the topics asylum, immigration and integration, but which also addressed PEGIDA. The key finding was that the protest movement and its goals were only supported by around 12 per cent of the 421 respondents (Fehser 2015).
- During the course of 2015 a team from the Göttinger Institut für Demokratieforschung also looked at the demonstrations against PEGIDA and analysed the socio-demographic profile and motivation of the participants (Marg et al. 2016).
- In 2016, within the framework of a biannual survey of extreme right wing attitudes in Germany (Leipzig "Mitte" study), respondents were also asked if they supported the goals of the PEGIDA movement. On this basis it was possible to gain further insights into the political orientation of the PEGIDA supporters in the population (Yendell et al. 2016).

For a description of PEGIDA participants, their socio-demographic profile and their motivation, it is a comparison of the data collected within the first months of PEGIDA's existence that has proven to be particularly fruitful: in other words, at a time when the protests were still constantly growing and able to mobilise well over 10,000 participants each week. In this initial phase of PEGIDA there was a disparate mix of discernibly different participating groups, concerns and protest motivations, which exemplarily reflected the potential of right-wing populist mobilisation phenomena.

A total of four teams of researchers studied PEGIDA in this initial phase (Fig. 4.1).[3] During the evaluation and interpretation of their quantitative

---

[3] Own compilation of information from Vorländer et al. (2015, p. 7), Rucht et al. (2015, pp. 8–9), Walter (19.01.2015), Patzelt (2015, p. 3ff.). The studies described here investigated PEGIDA in Dresden at its peak between December 2014 and the split of the organisation team at the end of January 2015. In order to ensure comparability, the presentation of the findings from Walter (19.01.2015) in Fig. 4.1 includes only the data related to Dresden. The researchers from Göttingen did, however, later supplement the data collected with additional surveys in other cities. The study was finally based on an online survey of 727 PEGIDA participants in total, from Dresden, Leipzig, Hanover, Duisburg and Braunschweig. According to the authors' statements approximately 17,500 people were approached. See Geiges et al. (2015, p. 61).

Study	Vorländer, Herold, Schäller (2015)	Rucht et al. (2015)	Walter (19.01.2015)	Patzelt (2015a)
Survey method	face-to-face interview (random sample)	online survey (systematic distribution of flyers)	online survey (systematic distribution of flyers)	face-to-face interview (quota sample)
Date of survey	22.12.2014, 05.01.2015, 12.01.2015	12.01.2015	12.01.2015	25.01.2015
People addressed	1106	1800	3500	492
Completed questionnaires	397	123	482	242
Response rate	35.9 %	6.8 %	13.8 %	49.2 %
Date of presentation of the results	14.01.2015	19.01.2015	19.01.2015	03.02.2015

Fig. 4.1 Overview: Empirical studies of PEGIDA in Dresden (Winter 2014/2015)

findings they were in addition able to make use of the knowledge gained from qualitative analyses which were conducted in parallel.[4] Despite the differing methodical approaches and degrees of success of the individual studies, their results are readily comparable. *Taken as a whole* they yield an overall picture which provides reliable, validated knowledge about the PEGIDA demonstrators in Dresden.[5]

[4] Vorländer, Herold and Schäller, and also Patzelt, carried out weekly observations of the demonstrations in Dresden between October 2014 and February 2015. The teams led by Walter and Rucht did the same on 12.01.2015. Furthermore, Geiges et al. (2015) were able to convince nearly 30 people to take part in group interviews. In addition, they, as well as Vorländer, Herold and Schäller, undertook a systematic evaluation of the coverage of PEGIDA in the national and international media and on social media.

[5] It was not possible to achieve representative results in the strict sense in any of the PEGIDA studies, since the population of the demonstrators was not determinable *a priori*. According to general experience in empirical survey research it is fair to assume that in all studies the results are slightly distorted towards the demonstrators who are more educated and more willing to provide information (a "middle-class bias"). This is especially true for both of the online surveys, which additionally presuppose that the participants have a certain degree of experience of using the internet (Diekmann 2014, pp. 422, 520ff.). In the case of the face-to-face interviews, in turn, one cannot exclude distortion in the response behaviour caused by the "social desirability" effect. Furthermore, when evaluating the results of the studies the respective response rates need to be taken into account. One popular interpretation, particularly among politically interested bloggers and activists, was that these, in some instances, low response rates should be taken as a reason to doubt the findings of the investigations in general. As K.-H. Reuband has shown, however, a criticism of this kind—at least in the case of the two face-to-face interviews with rates between 35 and 50 per cent—is

4.1   Socio-demographic Characteristics

With regard to the socio-demographic profile of the PEGIDA demonstrators the findings of the four studies mentioned were largely identical. As can be seen in Fig. 4.2,[6] the different samples all produced a nearly identical picture with regard to the sex, age, religious affiliation and origin of the demonstration participants surveyed. According to the results a clear majority of the PEGIDA demonstrators were male, between 30 and 60 years old, did not belong to any religion and came from Dresden or from the local area.

With regard to religious affiliation about 21 per cent of respondents indicated that they belonged to a Protestant religious community. Between 4 and 5 per cent professed the Catholic faith. A vast majority—nearly three-quarters—of the surveyed PEGIDA demonstrators, however, described themselves as not belonging to any particular religion or denomination.[7] Only a little over a third of the demonstrators who responded came from Dresden. A further, somewhat larger share, travelled to the PEGIDA demonstrations from other parts of Saxony—many from

---

misleading (Reuband 2015, pp. 135–136). On the one hand, it would be flawed to assume that there is an inevitable correlation between the response rate and distortion in the results (non-response bias)—for the relationship between the response rate and non-response bias cf. only Koch and Blohm (2015, p. 1ff.). On the other hand, in research using empirical surveys, response rates below 50 per cent tend to be the rule. Even with considerable technical and organisational effort and a significant investment of personnel, professional population surveys conducted face-to-face only reach similar rates (e.g. the German General Social Survey in 2012: approximately 38 per cent, cf. GESIS 2017), in the case of phone surveys the rate is often even lower. A detailed discussion of possible distortions in their PEGIDA survey can be found in Vorländer et al. (2015, p. 31ff.).

[6] Own compilation of data from Vorländer et al. (2015, p. 43ff.), Rucht et al. (2015, p. 11ff.), Walter (19.01.2015) and Patzelt (2015, p. 5f.). Rucht et al. (2015) did not ask about religious affiliation. In the case of Patzelt (2015) the surveyed participants were not asked about their religious affiliation or origin. In terms of religious affiliation Patzelt and Eichardt (2015, p. 12) determined in their two surveys in April and May that 78 per cent of respondents were non-denominational, 17 per cent evangelical, 4 per cent Catholic and about 1 per cent belonged to another religious community

[7] The results of the survey thereby provided a nearly precise depiction of the actual distribution of the religious affiliations in Saxony. According to data from the Federal Statistical Office of Germany, in Saxony 21 per cent of the population belong to an evangelical church or religious community, 4 per cent belong to the Catholic Church, and 75 per cent of the Saxon population are non-denominational or affiliated with another religion (Federal Statistical Office and the statistical offices of the Länder 2014, p. 42).

	Vorländer, Herold, Schäller (2015)	Rucht et al. (2015)	Walter (19.01.2015)	Patzelt (2015a)
Sex	- male: 74.6% - female: 24.9%	- male: 76.0% - female: 23.0%	- male: 81.5% - female: 18.5%	- male: 72.0% - female: 28.0%
Age	- average: 47.6 - 0-39: 34.7% - 40-59: 37.0% - above 59: 26.8%	- average: n/a - 0-39: 52.5% - 40-64: 42.5% - above 64: 5%	- average: n/a - 0-35: 27.1% - 36-65: 64.1 % - above 65: 8.7 %	- average: 46.4 - 0-40: 38% - 41-60: 43% - above 61: 19%
Religious Affiliation	- none: 71.8% - Catholic: 3.8% - Protestant: 21.2% - other: 2.3%		- none: 68.9% - Catholic: 4.9% - Protestant: 21.8% - other: 4.2%	
Origin	- Dresden: 39.9% - Saxony (without Dresden): 41.3%	- Dresden: 44.2% - surrounding area (within 50km): 41.7%	- Dresden: 37.8% - Saxony (without Dresden): 49.0%	

Fig. 4.2 The PEGIDA demonstrators in Dresden: Socio-demographic characteristics

locations in close proximity to the state capital. Only about one in every ten came from other eastern German federal states, about 6 per cent came from the former West German states.[8]

With regard to the employment, income and level of education of the PEGIDA demonstrators the studies unearthed findings which were unexpected. What was remarkable in the results shown in Fig. 4.3[9] was the exceptionally high number of people in regular employment. Only 2 per cent stated that they were unemployed or looking for work. Compared to the labour market statistics this is a figure well below the average. The unemployment rate in Saxony at the time of the surveys in December 2014 was 8.4 per cent, for Dresden it was 7.9 per cent.[10]

---

[8] In the Göttingen study (Walter 19.01.2015) 11.8 per cent came from other federal states, in the study by Vorländer et al. (2015) it was 15.8 per cent of those surveyed (of those: 9.4 per cent from the new and 6.4 per cent from the old federal states).

[9] Own compilation of information from Vorländer et al. (2015, p. 46f.), Rucht et al. (2015, p. 14) and Walter (19.01.2015)

[10] Cf. the numbers from the Federal Employment Agency (Agentur für Arbeit) at https://statistik.arbeitsagentur.de/Navigation/Statistik/Statistik-nach-Regionen/BA-Gebietsstruktur/Saxony-Nav.html (Accessed on 08.06.2017).

Employment situation of the interviewed PEGIDA demonstrators

Figures in percent

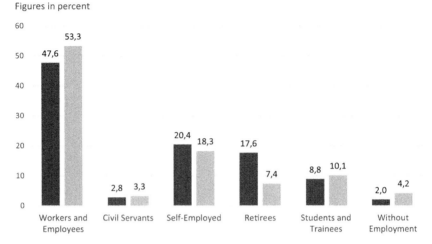

Fig. 4.3 Findings regarding the employment situation of the Dresden PEGIDA demonstrators

Also worthy of note was the average income distribution of those respondents interviewed at PEGIDA events (Fig. 4.4).[11] It more or less matched the average of the population of Saxony. According to data provided by the State Statistics Office in Saxony, in 2013 just 4.6 per cent of the population had a monthly net income of more than €2,500 at their disposal.

A look at the education level of respondents strengthened the finding that the majority of the PEGIDA demonstrators did not come from the socio-economic margins of society (Fig. 4.5). For instance, the rate of academics among the PEGIDA demonstrators, at around one third, was approximately twice as high as the average in the general population. This

[11] Own compilation of information from Vorländer et al. (2015, p. 48ff.) and Walter (19.01.2015). In the data collections undertaken by Rucht et al. (2015) and Patzelt (2015) there were no questions related to income. As part of their data collection in April and May, Patzelt and Eichardt (2015, p. 14) gave respondents the option to compare their gross monthly income with the Saxon average of €2,800. Here they could use a three-step scale to indicate whether their own gross income was "lower" (60 per cent), "average" (13 per cent) or "higher" (26 per cent)

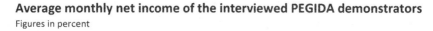

Average monthly net income of the interviewed PEGIDA demonstrators
Figures in percent

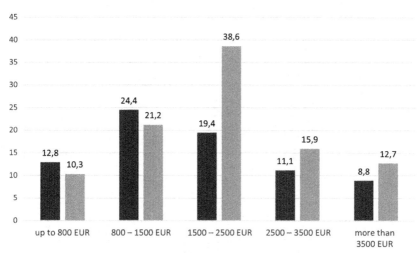

■ *Distribution in Vorländer et al.: N = 397; total less than 100%, remainder not specified.*

▨ *Distribution in Walter et al.: N = 321; total less than 100%, remainder: 'no own income'; The figures presented here are based on slightly different intervals: 'up to 900 EUR', ' 900–1500 EUR', '1500–2600 EUR', '2600–3600 EUR', 'more than 3600 EUR'.*

Fig. 4.4   Findings on the income of the Dresden PEGIDA demonstrators

finding may well—particularly in the case of the online surveys—have been influenced by certain distortion effects related to the respective data collection methods, but even when taking these effects into account it can still be assumed that in winter 2014/2015 the proportion of academics amongst the PEGIDA participants was greater than in the general population.

The findings outlined in Fig. 4.5[12] also clearly show that, alongside the academics, there were many PEGIDA demonstrators who held either a general qualification for university entrance (*Abitur*) or at least an intermediate-level qualification. Also common among the answers were the terms polytechnic secondary school (POS) and extended secondary school (EOS) since many of those surveyed had obtained the corresponding qualifications in the educational system of the former German Democratic Republic (GDR)—presumably often as a form of in-service training. Against this background one could assume that a number of the—on aver-

[12] Own compilation of data from Vorländer et al. (2015, p. 45f.), Rucht et al. (2015, p. 13), Walter (19.01.2015).

Level of education of the interviewed PEGIDA demonstrators

Figures in percent

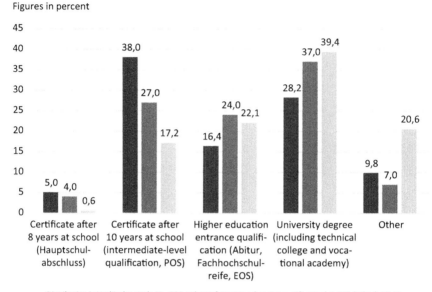

■ Distribution in Vorländer et al.: N = 397; other information: 'master certification': 8.6 %, 'other': 1.3 %; missing values: not specified.

■ Distribution in Rucht et al.: N = 123; other information: 'other': 7.0 %; missing values: not specified.

▫ Distribution in Walter et al.: N = 355; other information: 'vocational qualification': 20,0 %, 'still at school': 0,6 %; missing values: not specified.

Fig. 4.5   Findings on the education level of the Dresden PEGIDA demonstrators

age around 50 year old—academics held university qualifications in a scientific or technical field.

The reason for the overrepresentation of the better-educated amongst the protestors could, on the one hand, be linked to the known phenomenon that they as a group are in general more prepared to engage in political protest even in an unconventional form—through participation in demonstrations—than those with a poorer level of education. They see themselves as more capable of political activities, and have a greater belief that they can have an influence. And they normally also have the cognitive and social resources to do so (Reuband 2016, p. 172).[13] On the other hand, the socio-demographic profile of the PEGIDA participants was

[13] For fundamentals see Barnes et al. 1979.

consistent with findings made in previous years in other contexts. According to those findings, right-wing populist movements and parties have supporters not only at the socio-economic margins of society.

A look at the PEGIDA sympathisers in the total population reinforced this impression. Although it is well known that the tendency to support radical parties and positions is inversely proportional to socio-economic characteristics like income and level of education, it was ascertained that "social and collective economic deprivation [...] had no direct influence on the endorsement of the goals of PEGIDA" (Yendell et al. 2016, p. 151).

The insights into participants in the PEGIDA protests also corresponded with the socio-demographic structure of Alternative for Germany (AfD) voters. An evaluation of data from the Socio-Economic Panel (SOEP), for instance, revealed that in 2014 around 34 percent of AfD sympathisers belonged to the top 20 percent of the population in terms of wealth. Thus the socio-economic figures for AfD voters were about the same as for voters of the Christian Social Union in Bavaria (CSU) or the Greens (Bündnis90/Die Grünen), but far from the voter profile for the classical extreme right-wing parties like the National Democratic Party of Germany (NPD), whose supporters were recruited at a rate of over 31 per cent from the bottom fifth of the population in terms of income, and who often had a low level of education. In terms of concerns about immigration, however, supporters of the classical right-wing NPD and of the new right-wing populist AfD were quite similar (Fig. 4.6).[14]

Based on data for 2015, new studies have shown that in the course of a growing numbers of refugees and the emergence of PEGIDA not only the AfD's programmatic profile changed but also its electorate expanded. With the party's transformation from a club of opponents of Euro-bailout policy to a typical right-wing populist anti-immigration party, the number of AfD supporters grew in general, and especially in the socio-economic middle class. Accordingly, as Fig. 4.7[15] shows, 29 per cent of the party's supporters belonged to the middle 20 per cent of the population in terms of income, which was the highest figure among all parties.

A representative survey conducted by the opinion research institute Forsa confirmed this picture at the beginning of December 2016. According

---

[14] Own representation of the Cologne Institute for Economic Research's analysis of the data from the SOEP v31. The details about income that were provided refer to the year prior to the survey. See Bergmann et al. (2016, p. 2). The figures for NPD also include other small, right-wing extremist parties

[15] Cf. Bergmann et al. (2017, p. 62).

Concerns about immigration based on party preference 2014
Percentage of party supporters who are concerned about immigration

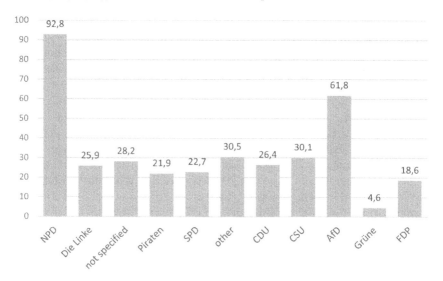

Fig. 4.6   Concerns about immigration according to party preference 2014

to its figures, just 28 per cent of AfD supporters need to get by with a household income of below €2000 per month—a considerably lower share than is the case with supporters of the Social Democratic Party of Germany (SPD) (32 per cent) and the left-wing party Die Linke (37 per cent).[16] Exit polls after the 2016 state elections in Saxony-Anhalt, Rhineland-Palatinate, Baden-Württemberg and Mecklenburg-Vorpommern also provided evidence that AfD voters have an income and level of education which is slightly above average. They also pointed to significant voter migration to the AfD, which can be attributed to the so-called "lower class" on the one hand, but on the other hand also to a conservative upper class.[17]

As was the case with the participants in the Dresden PEGIDA protests the electoral base of the right-wing populist AfD was also found to be an extremely heterogeneous group, recruited from all social classes, which

---

[16] Rütten (01.12.2016). According to the study the largest proportion of low-income earners (45 per cent) is to be found among the non-voters.

[17] See Niedermayer and Hofrichter 2016.

Income structure based on party preference in Germany 2015

Rates of party supporters according to different income groups in percent

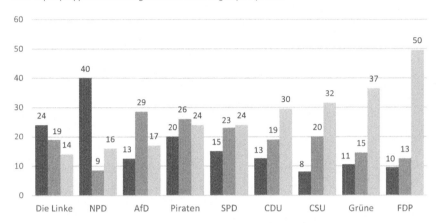

Fig. 4.7 Income structure based on party preference 2015

gained the party up to 25 per cent of the votes (Saxony-Anhalt) in the state elections in 2016. Accordingly, there were different, and in some cases strongly diverging, assumptions about the socio-demographic profile of the AfD supporters in circulation. These ranged from the theory of a party of the "precarity", whose supporters stand out due to a rather low income and a low level of education (Brähler et al. 2016; Welt Online 2016), to giving it the label as the party for the "helpless-feeling average earners" (Bergmann et al. 2017), right through to the characterisation of the AfD as the party for the "high-income earners and the educated" (Greive 2016).

In winter 2015/2016 in Dresden, by which time the PEGIDA protest marches had shrunk considerably in size, the participants were studied again. The result confirmed many of the previous year's findings. It did however find that there had been some changes in the socio-demographic profile of the participants in the demonstrations. In particular there was an increase in the average age of the demonstrators (Fig. 4.8).[18]

[18] Own representation of the comparative data from the Göttinger Institut für Demokratieforschung (2016, p. 17).

Age structure of PEGIDA demonstrators

Comparison of January and November 2015

Figures in percent

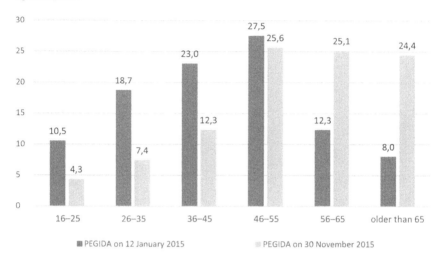

Fig. 4.8 Change in age structure of the Dresden PEGIDA demonstrators in 2015

There had, in turn, been a drop in the proportion of well-educated demonstrators. In November 2015 the share of respondents who indicated that they held a university qualification had gone down to just 24 per cent, a total of around 40 per cent had the university entrance qualification *Abitur*. As far as employment was concerned hardly any changes were found. The vast majority was still in full-time gainful employment either as employees or self-employed, and the proportion of pensioners had risen from under 20 to above 30 per cent. Only around 4 per cent of respondents described themselves as unemployed (Finkbeiner et al. 31.01.2016). Eventually, in a further study conducted in January 2016, only around 30 per cent of the nearly 400 interviewed PEGIDA participants possessed at least the *Abitur* as their highest educational qualification. Around 60 per cent stated a monthly income which was below the average for the Saxon population (Patzelt 2016). These changes matched, at least in part, a well-known dynamic—especially in other European contexts—of gradual socio-structural expansion of right-wing populist movements, according to which "the populist right always feeds off the middle class and the sociological centre in the beginning, but then grows quickly through workers, who for years have been dissatisfied with the social-democratic parties or the political left" (Spiegel Online 31.01.2016). PEGIDA was in fact able to successfully mobilise new groups of supporters in the course of the so-called refugee crisis, because almost 40 per cent of the demonstrators in Dresden on 30 November 2015 declared that they had only been participating in the protests for a few months. However, it is improbable that they were socially marginalised classes of the population because when asked to evaluate their personal situation almost half of the demonstrators indicated that it was good or very good, only around 12 per cent described it as bad (Finkbeiner 31.01.2016).

4.2   MOTIVES FOR THE PROTESTS

Yet what was the reason for participating in PEGIDA? The demonstration participants spoken to as part of the study conducted by Vorländer, Herold and Schäller were confronted with this open question and in the course of what were at times in-depth conversations they provided some noteworthy answers (Fig. 4.9).[19]

It was not Islam or a supposedly impending "Islamisation of the Occident", instead it was a dissatisfaction with politics expressed in various ways that was named as the main reason for participation in the PEGIDA demonstrations. Answers which could be grouped under "criticism of the media and the public" followed in second place; in third place were answers which can be classified as the articulation of prejudices and fundamental feelings of resentment towards immigrants and asylum seekers. Only 10.3 per cent of the respondents stated that they were protesting against violence motivated by religion or ideology. Only around a quarter of the interviewed PEGIDA demonstrators even referred to the topic of "Islam" in their often multi-faceted answers. This seemed remarkable, particularly because this motivation actually had given PEGIDA its name and was prominently represented as a slogan on the official banners of the protest marches.

The five groups of responses shown in Fig. 4.9 are, in each case, a grouping together of a set of similar responses: for instance, the group of responses "Dissatisfaction with policies" includes all the answers from the topic areas of "Dissatisfaction with asylum policy", "Dissatisfaction with

[19] See Vorländer et al. (2015, p. 57ff.). The basis for the groups of responses shown is the answer to the open question "What is your reason for participating in PEGIDA?"

Motivation of the PEGIDA demonstrators

Groups of responses

Figures in percent / share of the total number of all interviewed persons / multiple answers were possible

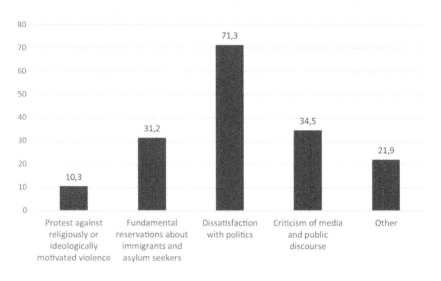

■ *Distribution in Vorländer et al.: N = 397.*

Fig. 4.9   Findings about the motivation of the Dresden PEGIDA demonstrators: groups of responses

foreign and security policy", and "Dissatisfaction with economic and social policy", among others. The most common response topics mentioned at this level are shown in Fig. 4.10.[20]

Here what was most frequently expressed—mostly in conjunction with other considerations—was a perceived distance between the general public and political decision-makers. About every fourth respondent also criticised the current asylum policy. Approximately one in five respondents protested against the, from their point of view, one-sided and distorted coverage of policies and political events in the media, or criticised specific regulations or institutions within the system of a representative party democracy in Germany, followed then (at 18.4 per cent) by a protest against a perceived defamation of PEGIDA in the media and in the public

[20] See Vorländer et al. (2015, p. 57ff.).

Motivation of the PEGIDA demonstrators

Most frequently mentioned subcategories of responses

Figures in percent / share of the total number of all interviewed persons / multiple answers were possible

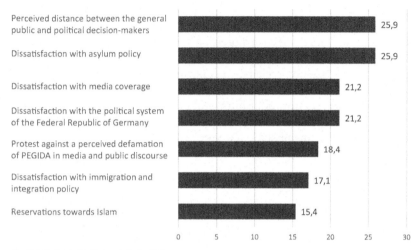

Fig. 4.10   Findings regarding the motivation of the Dresden PEGIDA demonstrators: response topics

discourse. Some 15.4 per cent articulated fundamental reservations towards Islam, considering it a "violent religion" and a "threatening culture", often referring to their own fears of estrangement and domination by foreign influences.[21] Overall the responses to this question expressed the perception of a vast gulf: a gulf between the mass media, published opinion and the political establishment on the one hand, and the everyday problems of the "general public", the "ordinary citizens" and the "will of the people" on the other. For a majority of participants, the PEGIDA rallies appeared to be an opportunity to express a deep sense

---

[21] On the basis of their online survey Rucht et al. (2015, p. 48ff.) accordingly named three dominant interpretations of the orientation of the Dresden PEGIDA demonstrators: "criticism of the asylum and immigration policy", "criticism of current government policy" and "dissatisfaction with the media and its coverage". These and other protest motives mentioned by the PEGIDA participants are described in more detail in Chap. 6. For the motivation of the PEGIDA demonstrators also cf. Herold and Schäller 2016.

of estrangement as well as resentment towards an influential political elite, which had not previously been expressed in public. The issue of immigration, refugee and asylum policy seems to have played more of a catalytic role. This must be seen, as should the question of how to deal with Islamist violence, not so much as the reason for the emergence of PEGIDA, but instead as the most current trigger. Nevertheless, the stimulation of emotions connected with such topics led to a reactivation of existing reservations towards asylum seekers, "economic refugees" and Muslims. This produced a consternation effect which contributed as strongly to PEGIDA's success in mobilising numbers as the coverage of the demonstrations in the media which ranged from critical to negative, often even being sweepingly dismissive (See Sect. 2.1 in Chap. 2).

4.3   POLITICAL ORIENTATION

In the course of an investigation into their political orientation the participants at PEGIDA events were first asked about their voting behaviour. The results on average indicated the actual voting in previous state and Bundestag elections: strong figures for the Christian Democratic Union of Germany (CDU), which has been dominant in Saxony since 1990, as well as the radical Left Party (Die Linke), which is typically strong in the East, are accompanied by weak ratings for the SPD and the Greens, which are both traditionally weak in Saxony. Contrary to publicly communicated expectations, the proportion of radical right NPD voters participating in the PEGIDA rallies turned out to be well below 5 per cent. The only thing disrupting this picture is the frequently named AfD (Fig. 4.11).[22]

The responses given to other questions indicate that the high numbers for AfD can be understood to a large extent to be "protest votes". For instance, a clear majority of the PEGIDA participants who were asked showed no sympathy for, affinity with, or attachment to any political party (Fig. 4.12).[23] This result even surpasses the already high percentage of non-voters in the last state

---

[22] Own compilation of data from Rucht et al. (2015, p. 21ff.) and Walter (19.01.2015).

[23] Own compilation of data from Vorländer et al. (2015, p. 51ff.) and Patzelt (2015, p. 23). The question as to the "feeling of attachment to a political party" amongst those interviewed was asked in this form only by Vorländer et al. (2015). Patzelt (2015) determined what he referred to as the "party tendency" of the respondents, by asking them which party they viewed as the most trustworthy ("Which party do you trust most at the moment?"). The answers to both questions are depicted together in Fig. 4.12, because they were both asked in pursuit of similar insights. An attachment to or trust in a party indicates the extent to which the parties are rooted in society and to a certain extent provides information about

Voting behaviour of the PEGIDA demonstrators

Figures in percent / referring to the federal election 2013

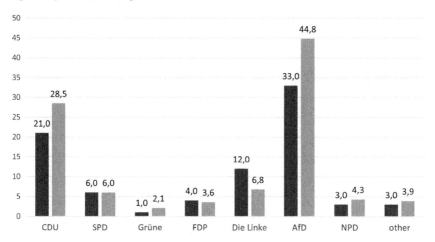

■ *Distribution in Rucht et al.: N = 123; additional category: 'I did not participate in that election': 17.0 %.*

▨ *Distribution in Walter et al.: N = 281.*

Fig. 4.11 Findings on the voting behaviour of the Dresden PEGIDA demonstrators

elections in Saxony in September 2014.[24] It shows that many PEGIDA activists, by their own admission, felt that the political choices on offer were of little use. Consequently, in the political discussion many interpretations assumed an obvious "disenchantment with politics or parties".

In this context, the question of where the PEGIDA participants placed themselves politically is also revealing. This is because it becomes clear here that an overwhelming majority saw themselves as part of the centre both politically and socially—in keeping with the chants often heard at the events "We are the people". However, as the self-assessment of the demonstrators presented in Fig. 4.13[25] illustrates, the one particular section of

the political socialisation of the respondents. Low levels of attachment and a low level of trust point to political homelessness or alienation.

[24] The voter turnout at the 2014 state election in Saxony was 49.1 per cent (State Statistical Office of the Free State of Saxony 2014).

[25] Own compilation of data from Rucht et al. (2015, p. 21f.) and Patzelt (2015, p. 7). The scales of the two studies differ slightly. In the study by Rucht et al. (2015) the respondents

Party affinity of the PEGIDA demonstrators

Figures in percent

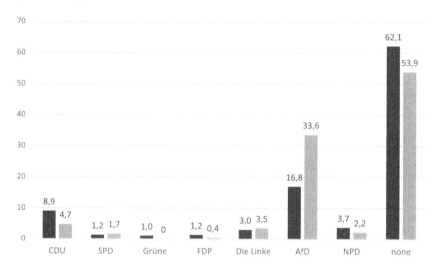

- ■ Distribution in Vorländer et al.: N = 397; missing values: not specified.
- ▨ Distribution in Patzelt et al.: N = 232.

Fig. 4.12 Findings on the feelings of attachment to a party among the Dresden PEGIDA demonstrators

"the people" which participated in PEGIDA rallies seemingly had a preference for positions more associated with the political right.[26]

On the whole, the studies of the PEGIDA participants revealed some remarkable things about the supporters of the protest movement.

were able to provide a self-assessment with the options "extreme left", "left", "centre", "right" and "extreme right" as well as "no position on this scale". The terms chosen by Patzelt (2015) were a little different ("completely left-wing", "left", "exactly in the centre", "right" and "completely right-wing"). He also opted not to offer a residual response option.

[26] One does need to take into account, however, that there is not necessarily a correlation between a possible extreme right-wing attitude of the respondents and the self-defined positioning on the left–right spectrum. Even respondents with "entrenched right-wing extremist attitudes" often do not consider themselves to be on the right, in fact, most even consider themselves to be on the left side of the political spectrum. Cf. Best et al. (2014, p. 82); Best and Salheiser (2012, p. 87ff.).

Political self-assessment of the PEGIDA demonstrators
Figures in percent

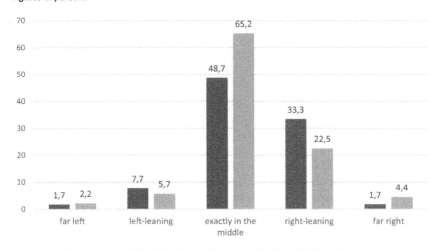

- Distribution in Rucht et al.: N = 117; missing values: not specified: 6.8 %; The figures here are based on a slightly differing designation: 'extreme left', 'left', 'middle', 'right', 'extreme right'.
- Distribution in Patzelt et al.: N = 227.

Fig. 4.13 Findings about the political self-assessment of the Dresden PEGIDA demonstrators

However, most of the results referred solely to Dresden and can only be seen to have a high informative value for the initial boom phase of the protests until the end of January 2015. The public appearance of the (for the most part not overly successful) PEGIDA offshoots in other large German cities already indicated a considerably more radical political agenda and group of participants. Although no studies exist, comparative observations of the demonstrations allow the assumption that in Bonn (BOGIDA), Berlin (BÄRGIDA), Munich (BAGIDA), Frankfurt a. M. (FRAGIDA) and elsewhere, the composition of the demonstrators did not match the more middle-class clientele that was able to be mobilised by PEGIDA in Dresden. In addition, it seems certain that many PEGIDA offshoots—in both the old and the new states—were either initiated or infiltrated by people who were known locally in their respective regions to be right-wing populists, hooligans or neo-Nazis. Even with regard to the somewhat successful offshoots in Leipzig (LEGIDA) and Chemnitz (PEGIDA Chemnitz/Erzgebirge), the suspected connections of the organisers to the neo-Nazi scene and the considerably lower number of participants suggest that the make-up of the demonstrators differed from that in Dresden (Klaubert 22.01.2015).

The composition of those attending PEGIDA events in Dresden also underwent a successive change over the course of 2015 and 2016. After the initial boom phase, which lasted until the split in the organisational team at the end of January 2015, the number of participants had stabilised at a comparatively low level. As early as in spring 2015, Patzelt and Eichardt were able to verify that this was coupled with a shift to the right, and a marked increase in the proportion of self-declared NPD voters.[27] This empirically proven "shift to the right" of the PEGIDA demonstrators was, however, attributed to the fact that "those demonstrators who remained loyal to Bachmann and his team were primarily those who were already politically more right-wing" (Patzelt and Eichardt 2015, p. 95). As those who were more moderate had increasingly withdrawn in resignation, the radicals had now become more visible.

In the course of 2015, which brought with it the height of the so-called refugee crisis in Germany, there was a discernible change in the mood of the demonstrators, which could be established by looking at their willingness to receive further refugees (Fig. 4.14).[28] A year earlier, around 73 per cent were in favour of doing so, but in January 2016 only about half of the respondents expressed a fundamental willingness.[29] As eventually established by Reuband (2017, p. 127), in winter 2015/2016 the political self-assessment of the participants had shifted. At the beginning of the PEGIDA protest 20 to 30 per cent of the respondents considered themselves "right-of-centre", and this had now become approximately 40 per cent.

---

[27] In the two data collections in April and May 2015 by Patzelt and Eichardt (2015, p. 23) in response to the question about voter behaviour at the 2013 Bundestag elections the NPD achieved figures of 11.1 per cent (27.04.2015) and 12.2 per cent (04.05.2015).

[28] Own representation of the findings from Patzelt 2016.

[29] A similar change in mood occurred after the temporary opening of the border in the summer of 2015 and after the mass sexual assaults on women committed mainly by refugees, immigrants and asylum seekers in Cologne and other German cities on New Year's Eve 2015. However, by now this change in mood had taken place in the entire German population.

Willingness to welcome refugees among PEGIDA demonstrators

Statement: "Germany should continue to receive persecuted asylum seekers and civil war refugees."
Figures in percent

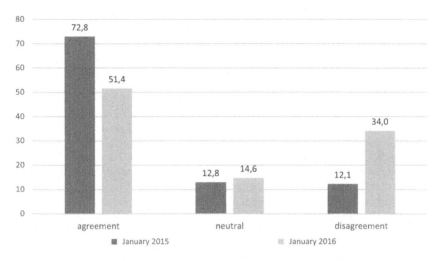

Fig. 4.14 Findings about the willingness to welcome refugees among PEGIDA demonstrators

REFERENCES

Barnes, Samuel H., Max Kaase, Klaus R. Allerbeck, Barbara Farah, Felix Heunks, Ronald M. Inglehart, Kent Jennings, Hans D. Klingemann, Allan Marsh, and Leopold Rosenmayr. 1979. *Political Action*. Beverly Hills and London: Sage Publishing.

Bergmann, Knut, Matthias Diermeier, and Judith Niehues. 2016. Die AfD—eine Partei der Besserverdienenden? *IW-Kurzberichte:* 19. Accessed 3 July 2017. https://www.iwkoeln.de/_storage/asset/280649/storage/master/file/9381123/download/IW-Kurzbericht_2016-19-AfD.pdf

———. 2017. Die AfD: Eine Partei der sich ausgeliefert fühlenden Durchschnittsverdiener. *Zeitschrift für Parlamentsfragen* 58 (1): 57–75.

Best, Heinrich, Steffen Niehoff, Axel Salheiser, and Katja Salomo. 2014. *Die Thüringer als Europäer. Ergebnisse des Thüringen-Monitors 2014.* Thüringer Staatskanzlei. Accessed 3 July 2017. http://www.thueringen.de/mam/th1/tsk/thuringen-monitor_2014.pdf

Best, Heinrich, and Axel Salheiser. 2012. *Thüringen International: Weltoffenheit, Zuwanderung, Akzeptanz. Ergebnisse des Thüringen-Monitors 2012.* Thüringer

Staatskanzlei. Accessed 3 July 2017. http://www.thueringen.de/mam/th1/tsk/thueringenmonitor_2012_mit_anhang.pdf

Brähler, Elmar, Johannes Kiess, and Oliver Decker. 2016. Politische Einstellungen und Parteipräferenz: Die Wähler/innen, Unentschiedene und Nichtwähler 2016. In *Die enthemmte Mitte. Autoritäre und rechtsextreme Einstellungen in Deutschland*, ed. Oliver Decker, Johannes Kiess, and Elmar Brähler, 67-94. Gießen: Psychosozial-Verlag.

Diekmann, Andreas. 2014. *Empirische Sozialforschung. Grundlagen, Methoden, Anwendungen*. Reinbek bei Hamburg: Rowohlt.

Donsbach, Wolfgang. 23.01.2015. Pressemitteilung: Welche Einstellungen führen zu PEGIDA? *TU Dresden*. Accessed 3 July 2017. http://tu-dresden.de/die_tu_dresden/fakultaeten/philosophische_fakultaet/ikw/news/2015/PM_Pegida_2015_01_23.pdf

Federal Statistical Office and the Statistical Offices of the Länder. 2014. *Zensus 2011. Bevölkerung nach Geschlecht, Alter, Staatsangehörigkeit*. Bad Ems: Statistische Ämter des Bundes und der Länder.

Fehser, Stefan. 2015. Eine gespaltene Stadt. Positionen der Dresdner Bevölkerung zum Thema Asyl. *TU Dresden*. Accessed 3 July 2017. http://www.kultur-buero-sachsen.de/images/PDF/Studie_Asyl_Dresden%202015.pdf

Finkbeiner, Florian, Julian Schenke, Katharina Trittel, Christopher Schmitz, and Stine Marg. 2016. Pegida. Aktuelle Forschungsergebnisse. *Göttinger Institut für Demokratieforschung*. Accessed 3 July 2017. http://www.demokratie-goettingen.de/blog/pegida-2016-studie

Geiges, Lars, Stine Marg, and Frank Walter. 2015. *PEGIDA. Die schmutzige Seite der Zivilgesellschaft?* Bielefeld: Transcript.

GESIS—Leibniz-Institut für Sozialwissenschaften. 2017. *Allgemeine Bevölkerungsumfrage der Sozialwissenschaften ALLBUS*. Accessed 3 July 2017. https://search.gesis.org/

Göttinger Institut für Demokratie-Forschung. 2016. *Büchse der Pandora? Pegida im Jahr 2016 und die Profanisierung rechtspopulistischer Positionen*. Göttinger Institut für Demokratie-Forschung. Accessed 3 July 2017. http://www.demokratie-goettingen.de/content/uploads/2016/10/Pegida2016_Göttinger_Demokratieforschung.pdf

Greive, Martin. 02.05.2016. Eine Partei der Besserverdiener. *Welt Kompakt*: 3.

Hebel, Christina, and Anna Reimann. 16.12.2014. Zitate von Pegida-Demonstranten. Die wirre Welt der Wohlstandsbürger. *Spiegel Online*. Accessed 3 July 2017. http://www.spiegel.de/politik/deutschland/pegida-in-dresden-die-kruden-aussagen-der-demonstranten-a-1008735.html

Herold, Maik, and Steven Schäller. 2016. Der neue Rechtspopulismus auf der Straße: Was motiviert die Wutbürger in Dresden? In *Politik in unsicheren Zeiten. Kriege, Krisen und neue Antagonismen*, ed. Karl-Rudolf Korte, 261–276. Baden-Baden: Nomos.

Klaubert, David. 22.01.2015. Das sind die Köpfe hinter Legida. *Frankfurter Allgemeine Zeitung Online*. Accessed 3 July 2017. http://www.faz.net/aktuell/politik/inland/leipzig-das-sind-die-koepfe-hinter-legida-13384814.html

Koch, Achim, and Michael Blohm. 2015. Nonresponse Bias. *GESIS—Leibniz-Institut für Sozialwissenschaften* (SDM Survey Guidelines). 10.15465/sdm-sg_004.

Lackerbauer, Simone. 21.04.2015. Pegida-Postings bei Facebook. Was der Nachbar denkt, aber nicht ausspricht. *Spiegel Online*. Accessed 3 July 2017. http://www.spiegel.de/unispiegel/wunderbar/pegida-facebook-postings-der-islamgegner-a-1027702.html

Marg, Stine, Katharina Trittel, Christopher Schmitz, Julia Kopp, and Franz Walter. 2016. *NoPegida. Die helle Seite der Zivilgesellschaft*. Bielefeld: Transcript.

Niedermayer, Oskar, and Jürgen Hofrichter. 2016. Die Wählerschaft der AfD: Wer ist sie, woher kommt sie und wie weit rechts steht sie? *Zeitschrift für Parlamentsfragen* 47 (2): 267–285.

Panorama. 18.12.2014. "Kontaktversuch: 'Lügenpresse' trifft Pegida". *ARD*. Accessed 3 July 2017. http://daserste.ndr.de/panorama/archiv/2014/Kontaktversuch-Luegenpresse-trifft-Pegida-,pegida136.html

Patzelt, Werner J. 2015. Was und wie denken PEGIDA-Demonstranten? Analyse der PEGIDA-Demonstranten am 25. Januar 2015, Dresden. Ein Forschungsbericht. *TU Dresden*. Accessed 3 July 2017. http://tu-dresden.de/die_tu_dresden/fakultaeten/philosophische_fakultaet/ifpw/polsys/for/pegida/patzelt-analyse-pegida-2015.pdf

———. 2016. "Rassisten, Extremisten, Vulgärdemokraten!" Hat sich PEGIDA radikalisiert? Januar 2015–Januar 2016: Ein Jahr PEGIDA im Vergleich. *TU Dresden*. Accessed 3 July 2017. https://tu-dresden.de/gsw/phil/powi/polsys/forschung/pegida/studie3-januar2016

Patzelt, Werner J., and Christian Eichardt. 2015. Drei Monate nach dem Knall: Was wurde aus PEGIDA? Dresden. *TU Dresden*. Accessed 3 July 2017. https://tu-dresden.de/die_tu_dresden/fakultaeten/philosophische_fakultaet/ifpw/polsys/for/pegida/patzelt-analyse-pegida-mai-2015.pdf

Patzelt, Werner J., and Joachim Klose. 2016. *Pegida. Warnsignale aus Dresden*. Dresden: Thelem Verlag.

Reuband, Karl-Heinz. 2015. Wer demonstriert in Dresden für Pegida? Ergebnisse empirischer Studien, methodische Grundlagen und offene Fragen. *Mitteilungen des Instituts für Deutsches und Internationales Parteienrecht und Parteienforschung* 21: 133–143.

———. 2016. Außenseiter oder Repräsentaten der Mehrheit? Selbst- und Fremdwahrnehmungen der Teilnehmer von PEGIDA-Kundgebungen. In *PEGIDA—Rechtspopulismus zwischen Fremdenangst und »Wende«-Enttäuschung?*, ed. Karl-Siegbert Rehberg, Franziska Kunz, and Tino Schlinzig, 165–187. Bielefeld: Transcript.

———. 2017. Die Dynamik des Pegida Protests. Der Einfluss von Ereignissen und bewegungsspezifischer Mobilisierung auf Teilnehmerzahlen und Teilnehmerzusammensetzung. *Mitteilungen des Instituts für Deutsches und Internationales Parteienrecht und Parteienforschung* 23: 112–130.

Rucht, Dieter, Priska Daphi, Piotr Kocyba, Michael Neuber, Jochen Roose, Franziska Scholl, Moritz Sommer, Wolfgang Stuppert, and Sabrina Zajak. 2015. *Protestforschung am Limit. Eine soziologische Annäherung an PEGIDA.* ipb Working Paper. Accessed 3 July 2017. https://protestinstitut.files.wordpress.com/2015/03/protestforschung-am-limit_ipb-working-paper_web.pdf

Rütten, Finn. 01.12.2016. Partei der Abgehängten? AfD-Wähler laut Umfrage nicht besonders arm. *Stern Online.* Accessed 3 July 2017. http://www.stern.de/politik/deutschland/afd-eine-partei-der-abgehaengten--neue-studie-widerspricht-7219754.html

Schielicke, Anna-Maria, Julia Hoffmann, and Wolfgang Donsbach. 2015. *Populism, Political Disenchantment and Media Criticism.* Paper presented at the Annual Conference of the International Association for Communication and Media Research, Montreal.

Spiegel Online. 31.01.2016. Studie über Pegida-Anhänger. Männlich, über 50, verheiratet, konfessionslos. *Spiegel Online.* Accessed 3 July 2017. http://www.spiegel.de/politik/deutschland/pegida-wer-geht-zu-den-demos-und-warum-gehen-sie-auf-die-strasse-a-1074028.html

State Statistical Office of the Free State of Saxony. 2014. Landtagswahl 2014. *Statistisches Landesamt des Freistaates Sachsen.* Accessed 3 July 2017. http://www.statistik.sachsen.de

Vorländer, Hans, Maik Herold, and Steven Schäller. 2015. *Pegida. Entwicklung, Zusammensetzung und Deutung einer Empörungsbewegung.* Wiesbaden: Springer Verlag.

———. 2016. *PEGIDA. Entwicklung, Zusammensetzung und Deutung einer Empörungsbewegung.* Wiesbaden: Springer VS.

Walter, Franz. 2015. Aktuelle Forschungsergebnisse zu den Pegida-Protesten. *Göttinger Institut für Demokratieforschung,* January 19. Accessed 3 July 2017. http://www.demokratie-goettingen.de/blog/studie-zu-pegida

Welt Online. 21.03.2016. AfD wandelt sich von Professoren- zur Prekariats-Partei. *Welt Online.* Accessed 3 July 2017. https://www.welt.de/politik/deutschland/article153514296/AfD-wandelt-sich-von-Professoren-zur-Prekariats-Partei.html

Yendell, Alexander, Oliver Decker, and Elmar Brähler. 2016. Wer unterstützt Pegida und was erklärt die Zustimmung zu den Zielen der Bewegung? In *Die enthemmte Mitte. Autoritäre und rechtsextreme Einstellungen in Deutschland,* ed. Oliver Decker, Johannes Kiess, and Elmar Brähler, 137–152. Gießen: Psychosozial-Verlag.

CHAPTER 5

Right-wing Populist Attitudes at PEGIDA: Findings and Interpretations

The findings presented in Chap. 4 come, for the most part, from the early phase of the protests in winter 2014/2015, when the Patriotic Europeans against the Islamisation of the Occident (PEGIDA)—which itself still had a relatively vague theme—was able to unify a large yet disparate group of supporters. The data thus essentially describe PEGIDA before the protests took on a clear right-wing populist profile and some of the leadership was changed, before attempts were made to network with like-minded European movements and parties, and before attention was eventually drawn to it due to slogans which displayed clearly racist and right-wing radical ideas. The extended group of supporters of the 'Patriotic Europeans', as shown in winter 2014/2015 and also to some extent again in autumn 2015, for the most part did not feel drawn to extreme right-wing statements but used the protest rallies in order to express their political dissatisfaction, anger and indignation, in particular their anger about the asylum and refugee policy. In this development phase the PEGIDA demonstrators provided an example of the very same milieu of society, in large part including elements of a bourgeois middle class, which has also been conspicuous in other European countries due to its support of right-wing populist parties. Hence, a comparative analysis of the findings about PEGIDA promises important insights into the social backgrounds of potential supporters of right-wing populist movements in general.

© The Author(s) 2018
H. Vorländer et al., *PEGIDA and New Right-Wing Populism in Germany*, New Perspectives in German Political Studies,
https://doi.org/10.1007/978-3-319-67495-7_5

For this purpose, the patterns of political and cultural attitudes which shape the perception of this milieu and which were also used to explain the rapid success of the PEGIDA protests need to be examined in detail: Islamophobia, right-wing extremism and xenophobia, but also ethnocentrism, dissatisfaction with democracy and alienation. These are the keywords according to which the following chapter is organised. What is known about the PEGIDA protestors can here be tied in with comprehensive research about the prevalence of different political views as well as the character of the political culture in Germany, especially in its eastern states. In particular the findings of the following long-term studies offer a comparative perspective:

- On the basis of a representative random sample, the so-called Leipzig Mitte Studies conducted face-to-face interviews asking about political attitude patterns in eastern and western Germany every second year since 2002. Alongside the use of questionnaires on authoritarianism, sexism, propensity for violence and social dominance orientation, the studies have also determined attitudes towards democracy and selected political institutions. At the centre of the long-term study is a questionnaire designed to determine the prevalence of extreme right-wing attitudes. It covers six dimensions, each with three questions (thus in total 18). On average between 2000 and 2500 respondents participated in each survey (the exception: in 2008 there were nearly 5000), the response rates ranged between 50 and 60 per cent, and most recently the rate was 49.4 per cent (cf.: Decker et al. 2016, p. 26).
- Since 2014, a representative series of interviews about the attitudes of the German population has also been conducted biennially on behalf of the Friedrich-Ebert-Stiftung by a research team from Bielefeld led by Andreas Zick. The particular focus of the survey, which is also referred to as a Mitte Study but is conducted with the help of computer-assisted telephone interviewing (CATI), is the fields of right-wing extremism and group-focused enmity (GFE, *Gruppenbezogene Menschenfeindlichkeit*) (cf. Zick and Klein 2014; Zick et al. 2016a).
- The newer Bielefeld Mitte Studies are rooted in the tradition of a similar long-term study, which comprised a series of surveys dealing with the "syndrome" of group-focused enmity in Germany, whereby a research team led by Wilhelm Heitmeyer and Andreas Zick

conducted annual surveys from 2002 to 2011 using computer-assisted telephone interviews (CATI). According to the researchers group-focused enmity is made up of 12 attitude patterns, including, for example, racism, Islamophobia and homophobia, but also the devaluation of homeless persons, disabled people and asylum seekers. In the first three surveys, from 2002 to 2004, a total of 3000 people were interviewed each year; in the later years 2000 people were interviewed. The interviewees were chosen at random from a representative sample of households (cf. most recently: Heitmeyer 2012a).

- The so-called Thuringia Monitor (*Thüringen-Monitor*) also examines political attitudes in the population. This study, which was commissioned by the Erfurt State Chancellery, is carried out by a research team led by the Jena-based sociologist Heinrich Best. Every year since 2000, on the basis of a random sample of eligible voters in Thuringia, 1000 people have been asked about fundamental political and social problems in telephone interviews (CATI). Until 2011 the survey series was led by the Jena-based political scientist Karl Schmitt (cf. most recently: Best et al. 2016).

- The study "Germany 2014. 25 Years of Peaceful Revolution and German Unity" (*Deutschland 2014. 25 Jahre Friedliche Revolution und Deutsche Einheit*), which was conducted by a research team led by Everhard Holtmann and Oscar W. Gabriel in 2014 on behalf of the Federal Government, took stock of the development of the political culture in Germany since reunification. Alongside the results of the study itself, a compilation of the findings from the most important empirical investigations into the political culture in Germany since 1990 is compared here (cf. Holtmann et al. 2015).

- Lastly, in November 2016 the Saxony Monitor *(Sachsen-Monitor)*, which was appearing for the first time in this form, provided current comparative figures on political attitudes in the population of Saxony. For this data collection, computer-assisted personal interviews (CAPI) were conducted with a representative sample of 1013 randomly chosen Saxons in August and September 2016. The interviews were carried out by the opinion research institute Infratest dimap on behalf of the Saxon State Government (cf. Infratest dimap 2016).

With regard to the PEGIDA data from 2015, it is in particular the 2014 editions of the Leipzig and Bielefeld Mitte Studies, as well as the

Thuringia Monitor, which promise numerous possibilities for comparison. While the Mitte Studies explicitly show survey results for the new *Bundesländer*, the Thuringia Monitor is a long-term study in a state which can be assumed to have certain historical and politico-cultural similarities with Saxony. It was not until mid-2016 that a similar study for Saxony became available in the form of the Saxony Monitor. In the following analysis some of the findings from the studies mentioned will be taken up and be considered in relation to the available insights into the composition of the PEGIDA demonstrations in winter 2014/2015.[1] Even though the methods of data collection in some instances differ in the individual studies, a comparison of the data forms an important basis for the interpretation and conceptual classification of PEGIDA.

5.1   ISLAMOPHOBIA

The demonstrations in Dresden and elsewhere in winter 2014/2015 occurred at a time when the keyword "Islamophobia" had just become prominent amongst a wider public through exposure in the media. As in other European countries in the past decade, attitudes which range from latent criticism of Islam through to manifest Islamophobia have also become established in the German population. These stances were underpinned not least by the almost daily news headlines about murdering attackers, angry rioters and holy warriors of Muslim faith, by reports about political trouble spots in predominantly Muslim regions like Syria, Afghanistan, Somalia, northern Nigeria, Iraq and elsewhere, by images of Islamist terrorist attacks in western cities, and further strengthened by reports about "parallel societies" made up of Muslim immigrants in large German and European cities. Against the background of this development recent research into political attitudes and political culture suggest that Islamophobia has by now become a central component of right-wing extremist and right-wing populist orientations (Zick et al. 2011, p. 30). The authors of the Leipzig Mitte Studies even claimed in 2015 that Islamophobia is "racism's new look": "Now the argumentation is (ostensibly) no longer along biological lines, instead the subject of discussion is the supposed backwardness of Islamic culture" (Decker et al. 2015a, p. 57; earlier, also similar Zick et al. 2011, p. 46ff.).

---

[1] An attempt is made to use comparative data which originate from the same time period as the findings regarding the PEGIDA participants.

	Germany (GFE 2009)	Germany (GFE 2010)	Germany (GFE 2011)	Germany (Mitte-B 2014)	Germany (Mitte-B 2016)
	CATI	CATI	CATI	CATI	CATI
Islamophobia					
Muslims should be prohibited from immigrating to Germany.	21,4	26,1	22,6	18,2	15,5
Due to the many Muslims here I sometimes feel like a foreigner in my own country.	32,2	38,9	30,2	31,5	34,7

Fig. 5.1 Agreement with Islamophobic statements in the German population 2009–2016

However, whether Islamophobic attitudes in Germany have in fact increased in recent years, is unclear. The sole long-term study that provides reliable data for this purpose, collected for years using the same analytical tool, is the study on group-focused enmity (GFE) by a Bielefeld research team led by Wilhelm Heitmeyer and Andreas Zick. Since 2014 their survey series has been continued on behalf of the Friedrich-Ebert-Stiftung under the title "Mitte Studies". If their findings over recent years are compared, one cannot see a clear trend. According to the data, Islamophobic attitudes are more likely to have remained at a constant level since 2009 (Fig. 5.1).[2]

Furthermore, it can be assumed that Islamophobia in Germany corresponds more or less to the European average (Zick et al. 2011, p. 71f.). With regard to the extent it exists one needs to differentiate between "criticism of Islam" on the one hand and "Islamophobia", based on hostile attitudes, on the other. For this purpose Decker et al. (2013) suggested

---

[2] Own compilation of the results from the survey series on group-focused enmity in Germany (GFE) and the Bielefeld Mitte Studies. The findings shown in this figure can be found in Heitmeyer 2012b, p. 38; Klein et al. 2014, p. 67 and Zick et al. 2016b, p. 44f. All the data collection took place with the help of computer-assisted telephone interviews (CATI). The percentages presented in the table are the aggregate proportion of the responses that indicated an explicit agreement with the relevant assertion on a four-step scale. The information in the table header refers to the year of data collection

	Germany-East (Mitte-Study 2012)	Germany-West (Mitte-Study 2012)	Germany-total (Mitte-Study 2012)
	Face-to-face	Face-to-face	Face-to-face
Islamophobia	41,3	35,0	36,2
Criticism of Islam	69,6	58,6	60,8

Fig. 5.2 Islamophobia and attitudes critical of Islam in eastern and western Germany

empirical clarification.[3] In their face-to-face survey in 2012, 50 to 60 per cent of the randomly chosen citizens agreed with individual Islamophobic statements. Those who clearly rejected such ideas reached figures of only around 15 to 25 per cent. Depending on the question, even as many as 60 to 75 per cent espoused positions critical of Islam. A summary of all the figures is shown in Fig. 5.2.[4]

Both Islamophobic attitudes and those critical of Islam proved to be much more widespread in the new Länder. In an evaluation of the survey data from the 2012 German General Social Survey (*Allbus/GGSS*) Yendell

---

[3] According to their view, agreement with the following statements was evaluated as being "critical of Islam": "The strict separation of Church and State is a western achievement, which would also be progress in Islamic-influenced countries", "Although some women voluntarily wear a headscarf, one should not overlook the fact that others are forced", "One should not give in to the strict separation of the sexes as prescribed in Islam, whether in the healthcare system or physical education", "We should support those liberal Muslims who distance themselves from a fundamentalist interpretation of Islam", "Universal human rights and certain legal norms should always take precedence over religious precepts". Agreement with the following statements was evaluated as being "Islamophobic": "The Islamic world is backwards and refuses to accept the new realities", "Islam is an archaic religion, unable to adapt to modern life", "I think that the proximity of Islam and terrorism is to be found within Islam itself and is created by aggressive aspects of the religion", "All criticism of the western world by representatives of Islam is exaggerated and unjustified", "Muslims and their religion are so different from us that it would be naïve to demand equal access to all positions within society" (Decker et al. 2012, p. 92).

[4] Own compilation of the data from Decker et al. (2012, p. 93). The percentages shown represent the proportion of respondents who "on average" agreed with *all* statements in the respective attitude category and thereby—according to the assessment of the authors of the Leipzig Mitte Study—are to be classified as "critical of Islam" or "Islamophobic" (Decker et al. 2012, p. 92)

(2016, p. 121) claimed that eastern Germans "disproportionately often hold the opinion that Muslims should be forbidden from migrating to Germany, that restrictions should be placed on practising Islam in Germany, that the presence of Muslims is a cause of conflict and furthermore that Islamic groups should be under government surveillance". In addition, it was found that Islamophobia was more common amongst men than women, and also more common amongst older respondents and those with a low level of education. Particularly noteworthy was that both Islamophobic orientations and those critical of Islam increased in line with higher income. These attitudes were by far most pronounced amongst those in the highest income brackets (Decker et al. 2012, pp. 93, 95).[5]

The theme of criticism of Islam or Islamophobia also plays a central role in the evaluation and explanation of PEGIDA. The critical phrase about the supposed "Islamisation of the Occident" was already displayed in the name of the demonstrations held in Dresden. Every week one could read slogans on banners and placards carried by the protesters such as "Peace treaty & constitution instead of Sharia & Jihad" or "Islam = carcinoma". Another memorable motif was a photo of Angela Merkel, to which a headscarf had been added, in order to warn against the creeping victory of Islamic culture in Germany.[6] Media representatives and politicians, on the other hand, described the PEGIDA rallies as "anti-Islam demonstrations", and the demonstrators as "Islam-haters" (Eichstädt 13.01.2015; Meier and Niewendick 09.12.2014). The numerous attempts to categorise what was happening in Dresden under the heading of "Islamophobia" were, however, confronted with an obvious contradiction: how can it be that in a city, in which according to estimates just 0.4 per cent of the population are of the Islamic faith, that there are protests against an impending Islamisation?[7]

In this context the so-called contact hypothesis was often discussed. Its premise is that the less often one has contact with members of certain groups of people seen as "foreign" in situations in day-to-day life, the

[5] The Bielefeld long-term study on group-focused enmity conducted until 2011 came to another conclusion. According to the survey results Islamophobia occurs more often in groups with low income (Heitmeyer 2012b, p. 33).

[6] Both observed on 12.01.2015.

[7] The figures for the share of Muslims in Dresden were brought into the discussion from different sides and were then repeatedly taken up by the media. However, the figures are only estimates, reliable calculations are not known. The share of Muslims in Saxony as a whole was stated to be 0.7 per cent (as of 2008) by the Saxon state agency for political education (cf. http://www.infoseiten.slpb.de/politik/sachsen/sachsen-allgemein/religion;   Accessed 15.06.2017).

greater the prejudices towards and rejection of these groups is. In the case of Islamophobia this would mean that a rejection of Muslims could be expected above all in those places where their share of the total population is lowest. This assumption could largely be confirmed using the findings of the Mitte Study from 2012 which calculated that only 10.3 per cent of those with Islamophobic attitudes indicated that they "had contact with foreigners at work, in their family or in their circle of friends" (Decker et al. 2012, p. 98).[8] With just 0.7 per cent Muslims one can expect pronounced Islamophobia for Saxony in particular. In their study in 2014, however, the researchers discovered some partly contradictory findings. They found that the rates of agreement for the section about "Islamophobia" were partly higher for western Germany than in the East.[9]

The fact that "Islamisation" was not the focus for the majority of PEGIDA demonstrators, in other words, that the Patriotic Europeans did not primarily take to the streets in Dresden to protest against an impending "Islamisation of the Occident", could already be established in the first empirical investigation into PEGIDA. Here, when asked about their reasons for participating in the PEGIDA demonstrations, only about every tenth respondent (10.3 per cent) indicated that they were protesting against "religious or ideologically motivated violence". A further 15.4 per cent showed resentment or reservations towards Muslims in particular,[10] which meant that just one in every four respondents gave answers indicating that the

[8] Whereas amongst those who had only made comments "critical of Islam", this was the case 89.7 per cent of the time (Decker et al. 2012, p. 99).

[9] Cf. Decker et al. (2015a, p. 58f.), see Fig. 5.4. Bavaria appears to be a special case because here strongly xenophobic attitudes were identified despite a relatively high proportion of foreigners at just below 10 per cent (Decker et al. 2015b, p. 75).

[10] The reservations expressed here referred not only to the rules of Islam regarding lifestyle, diet, clothing and social interaction in public, but also to a certain "mentality" which would not allow genuine integration of its followers into western societies, and instead would do the opposite by more or less blatantly counting on the gradual adaptation of life in Germany to cater for their preferences. The fear of an impending Islamisation was thus based primarily on the repeatedly expressed fear that the rules of Muslim culture would sooner or later become generally binding norms in Germany. It was alleged that, for fear of hurting the religious feelings of Muslims, politics, media and the general public were already prepared, even now, in a kind of pre-emptive obedience, to repeatedly give unjustified preferential treatment to Muslims. With keywords and anecdotes, like, for example the renaming of the Berlin Christmas markets to "Winterfest", the supposed ban on pork in kindergartens, the special rules for Muslims in swimming and sports classes, the "Sharia police" or the so-called "parallel societies" in German cities, an attempt was made to prove this claim (Vorländer et al. 2015, p. 70).

PEGIDA and the "Islamisation of the Occident"
Mention of the topic of Islam when giving reasons for participation in PEGIDA
Figures in percent / share of the total number of all interviewed persons

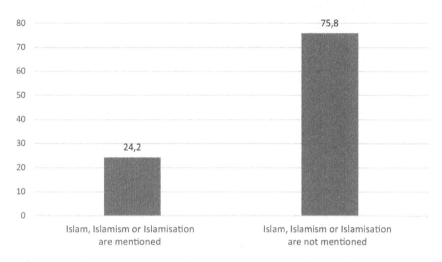

■ *Distribution in Vorländer et al.: n = 397.*

Fig. 5.3 Mention of the topic of Islam when giving reasons for participation in PEGIDA. Source: Vorländer et al. (2015, p. 72)

topic of "Islam, Islamism or Islamisation" played any kind of role. (Fig. 5.3).[11]

These findings were remarkable, firstly, because the fear of Islamisation had given PEGIDA its name, as is well known, and this motivation—and likewise the protest against religiously motivated violence—was prominently represented as a slogan on the official banners of the protest marches.[12] Secondly, the event on 12.01.2015, at which some of the interviews took place, was explicitly declared by the PEGIDA organisers to be a

[11] The basis was the open question as to the motivation for participation in PEGIDA in Dresden.

[12] Cf. the large banner, which was carried at the front of the protest march at every PEGIDA event. It read (occasionally in a slightly altered form): "Nonviolent and unified against religious wars on German soil". What was primarily meant was the threat of violence originating from Muslim compatriots.

	PEGIDA-Dresden (Rucht et al. 2015)	Saxony (Monitor 2016)	Germany-East (Mitte-L 2014)	Germany-West (Mitte-L 2014)	Germany-total (Mitte-L 2014)	Germany-total (Mitte-L 2016)
	Online	CAPI	Face-to-Face	Face-to-Face	Face-to-Face	Face-to-Face
Islamophobia						
Muslims should be prohibited from immigrating to Germany.	23,1	39	–	–	36,6	41,4
Due to the many Muslims here I sometimes feel like a foreigner in my own country.	46,0	–	33,9	45,4	43,0	50,0

Fig. 5.4   Islamophobia in Germany and among Dresden PEGIDA demonstrators in comparison

"funeral march" for the victims of the Islamist-motivated attacks on the French satirical magazine *Charlie Hebdo* and a Jewish supermarket in Paris on 07.01.2015 (Vorländer et al. 2015, p. 60).

According to this finding, which was confirmed by other studies, the topic of Islam or Islamisation was neither a central motivation for PEGIDA supporters, nor can it be assumed to be the main reason for the high degree of mobilisation. The data from Rucht et al. (2015), for instance, pointed to a similar tendency. Here too, the agreement levels with the statements presented actually indicated that Islamophobia was less pronounced than on average, even when looking at comparable eastern German figures from the Mitte Studies (Fig. 5.4).[13] According to the

[13] Own compilation of the findings from Rucht et al. (2015, p. 31), Decker et al. (2015a, p. 58f.), Infratest dimap (2016, p. 293) and Decker et al. (2016, p. 50). The years in the table header refer to the year in which the data were collected. The percentages presented in the table are the combined share of the responses indicating an explicit agreement with the relevant assertion on a four-stage scale. Specifically, in the Saxony Monitor those answers were "agree completely" and "tend to agree", in the Leipzig Mitte Study (Decker et al. 2015b, 2016) they were "fully agree" and "tend to agree". Where there is a dash either no data was collected or no information was provided for the respective category. The figures for PEGIDA, which were collected by Rucht et al. (2015), are only comparable with other findings to a limited extent. Although the same statements were presented, the respondents had a choice of four possible answers in the comparative studies on political culture, whereas in the case of Rucht et al. there were five because here an intermediate category ("partly agree/ partly disagree") was also offered. In order to make a comparison possible, despite these different scales, in Fig. 5.4, for the agreement among PEGIDA demonstrators according to

	PEGIDA-Dresden (Patzelt, 04.05.2015)	PEGIDA-Dresden (Patzelt, 18.01.2016)	Thuringia (Monitor 2016)	Germany (16.01.2015)
	face-to-face	face-to-face	CATI	CATI
Does Islam belong in Germany?				
Islam belongs in Germany! (Percentage of disagreement with this statement)	–	–	77	48
An Islam that is as peaceful as today's Christianity belongs in Germany! (Percentage of disagreement with this statement)	65,6	72,0	–	–
Muslims, who are as peaceful as most Germans, belong in Germany! (Percentage of disagreement with this statement)	33,8	43,9	–	–

Fig. 5.5   Disagreement with the assertion "Islam belongs in Germany"

findings, it appears that a stance critical of Islam is similarly or even more widespread in places where Muslims make up a greater share of the total population. Specifically feeling "foreign in one's own country because of the many Muslims" is more common in the West than in the East.

When specifically asked if Islam belongs in Germany, the PEGIDA participants again displayed quite ambivalent responses. On the one hand, two versions of this statement provided by Patzelt were rejected by more than half of the respondents; on the other hand, the extent of this rejection was at a level similar to the values previously calculated in several surveys of eastern Germany (Fig. 5.5).[14]

Rucht et al. (2015) an approximation was calculated by adding half the share of the "partly" responses to the aggregate share of the answers made up of both the response "agree completely" and "agree for the most part".

[14] Own compilation of the findings from Patzelt and Eichardt (2015, p. 51) and Patzelt and Klose (2016, p. 245). The survey data in the last column was collected by the opinion research institute Forschungsgruppe Wahlen. See Heute.de (16.01.2016), cf. for a similar survey Fröhlingsdorf (31.01.2015, p. 14). The years in the table header refer to when the data were collected. The percentages shown are the combined share of those answers that indicated an explicit *disagreement* with the respective assertions on a three- or five-step scale. Those answers were, in the case of Patzelt and Eichardt (survey on 04.05.2015) and also Patzelt and Klose (survey on 18.01.2016), "tend to disagree" and "do not agree at all". Wherever there is a dash no data were collected in the respective studies

	PEGIDA (December 2015) postal survey	PEGIDA (February 2016) postal survey	PEGIDA (April 2016) postal survey
Islamophobia			
Muslims should be prohibited from immigrating to Germany.	38	40	56
The construction of mosques should be prohibited in Germany.	67	72	86
I am afraid that the influence of Islam in Germany is becoming too strong.	87	88	95

Fig. 5.6   Islamophobia among PEGIDA participants in winter 2015/2016

By spring 2016, however—also against the backdrop of continued Islamist attacks in Western Europe—the attitudes towards Islam at PEGIDA events had progressively become more negative. The radicalisation of the rhetoric and the significant decline in the number of participants was also accompanied by an increase in Islamophobic feelings of resentment. By winter 2015/2016 around half of the demonstrators agreed with the statement "Muslims should be prohibited from migrating to Germany". A ban on building mosques in Germany was even wanted by around 70 to 80 per cent of PEGIDA demonstrators (Fig. 5.6).[15]

In the survey from April 2016, moreover, 84 per cent of PEGIDA participants were of the opinion that Islam as a whole—not only specific groups within Islam—constitutes a threat. In a survey of the total population a few months earlier, only 21 per cent had agreed with this statement (Reuband 2017, p. 121).

In view of the public behaviour, the speeches delivered, but also the attitudes of the participants, by spring 2016 PEGIDA had thus transformed into an openly Islamophobic protest movement. This uncovered

---

[15] Own compilation of the findings from Reuband (2017, p. 121). The percentages shown represent the share of answers for "fully agree". A comparison with data from the Bielefeld Mitte Study shown above in Fig. 5.1 is only possible to a limited extent because of different data collection methods. Unlike with written surveys, in telephone interviews one can assume that social desirability effects foster much more positive remarks about Muslims (cf. Reuband 2017, p. 121)

a stance which is also prominent in the overall population, especially in the old *Bundesländer* where a significantly higher proportion of citizens are Muslims. Whilst in the west of the Republic Islamophobic attitudes are mostly based on actual real-life experiences, and therefore more concrete conceptions of social fault lines possibly exist, in eastern Germany the prevailing form of Islamophobia and the one expressed at PEGIDA in Dresden is vaguer and largely characterised by abstract notions of an impending "cultural expropriation". The motivation repeatedly expressed by PEGIDA supporters, namely that they did not want "conditions" like in the "parallel societies" of large western German cities like Bremen, Duisburg or Berlin-Neukölln and therefore had to "nip things in the bud" early on, can be seen as symptomatic of this. These kinds of abstract reservations, projected onto Muslims, who are then representative for the rejection of everything "foreign", are likely to continue to grow in the future against the backdrop of the continued dominance of the topic of "Islam and violence" in the media. Latent Islamophobia must therefore be seen as part of an influential attitude pattern that is susceptible to political instrumentalisation and which exists not only in eastern Germany.

5.2   Right-wing Extremism

A further obvious concept for the classification of the PEGIDA protests is that of right-wing extremism. At the sight of thousands of people "marching" in the evening darkness, chanting slogans which were in part xenophobic, an interpretation along these lines was made shortly after the start of the demonstrations in autumn 2014, especially in media coverage. Parallels to the annual marches of neo-Nazis from all over Europe, which take place in the city every 13 February, the anniversary of the Allied bombing of Dresden, as well as to the xenophobic riots in eastern Germany at the beginning of the 1990s seemed obvious. As a "structurally conservative" *Bundesland*, Saxony was portrayed as being particularly receptive to right-wing trends and reference was made to the many years of the National Democratic Party's (NPD) representation in the Saxon State Parliament (cf. Sect. 6.1 in Chap. 6).[16]

In the debate in political science, *political extremism* is used as a collective term for anti-democratic aspirations. The concrete classification of specific orientations as "extreme" is made, as a rule, using the liberal-

---

[16] For the coverage of PEGIDA cf. Chap. 1.

democratic constitutional order of the Basic Law, its values and procedural rules as a benchmark. Additionally, there are more attitudes which characterise *right-wing extremism* in contrast to other types of extremism. According to a so-called *consensus definition* right-wing extremism is a political orientation pattern which is based on the conviction that people have a different value depending on certain characteristics such as nationality, hair colour or ethnic background. In turn, in the social and political realm, the concepts of order built on these perceptions of unequal value are characterised by anti-Semitic, xenophobic and social Darwinist convictions, a trivialisation of National Socialism, the endorsement of dictatorial forms of government, an exaggerated national sentiment as well as the elevation of the status of one's own country and the derogation of other countries.[17]

This definition, developed in 2001, has become the foundation for several empirical research series on the topic. It is used as the foundation for the Mitte Studies and also the Thuringia Monitor (Decker and Brähler 2006, p. 20; Best et al. 2014, p. 75).[18] Indicator statements across six dimensions were developed here to measure an *endorsement of dictatorships, nationalism/chauvinism, trivialisation of National Socialism, xenophobia, antisemitism* and *social Darwinism*. With the help of these statements a typical attitude pattern for right-wing extremism could be empirically established. In Fig. 5.7[19] the distribution of the approval ratings for these individual dimensions of right-wing extremism in Germany is shown based on Decker et al. (2016).

Here it appears that in the German population it is above all xenophobic and nationalistic attitudes that are prevalent. With approval ratings of between 14 and 23 per cent they reach a significantly higher level than the other dimensions. At the same time it also becomes apparent that eastern Germans do not universally exhibit more prominent orientations. With regard to antisemitism, nationalism/chauvinism and trivialisation of

---

[17] For the concepts of extremism and right-wing extremism cf. Backes (2001, p. 24), Kailitz (2004), Salzborn (2014), Pfahl-Traughber (1999, p. 11ff.). For the "consensus definition" of right-wing extremism cf. Decker and Brähler (2006, p. 20).

[18] Cf. also Stöss and Niedermayer (2008, p. 10).

[19] Own compilation of the findings from Decker et al. (2016, p. 43ff.). The figures refer to the share of "manifest" characteristics within the respective dimensions of the right-wing extremist attitude patterns, i.e. the percentage of the respondents who "on average agreed with all statements in a given dimension". For the precise calculation cf. Decker et al. (2015a, p. 46)

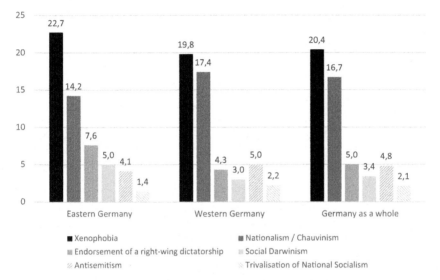

Right-wing extremist attitudes in Germany 2016
Prevalence of manifest attitudes in the individual dimensions
Figures in percent / share of the total population

Fig. 5.7   Patterns of manifestly right-wing extremist attitudes in Germany 2016

National Socialism for instance, consistently higher approval rates were obtained in the old *Bundesländer*. Even for xenophobia the approval ratings in eastern and western Germany differ only by a few percentage points. The findings of the Mitte Studies also show that "manifestly right-wing extremist orientations" have tended to be in decline in recent years specifically in eastern Germany and are now again approaching the figures for western Germany (Fig. 5.8).[20]

However, the methodical instruments for the measurement of right-wing extremism remain controversial among researchers. This is true for both the validity of the supposed indicator questions for individual attitude dimensions, and for their conceptual use with regard to the empirical definition of right-wing extremist attitudes (Jesse 2013). In particular,

[20] Own compilation of the findings from Decker et al. (2016, p. 48). The figures shown refer to "manifest right-wing extremist attitudes", i.e. the percentage of respondents who "on average agreed with all 18 statements in the questionnaire". For the precise calculation cf. Decker et al. (2015a, p. 56)

Manifestly right-wing extremist attitudes over time 2002–2016

Prevalence as a share of the total population
Figures in percent

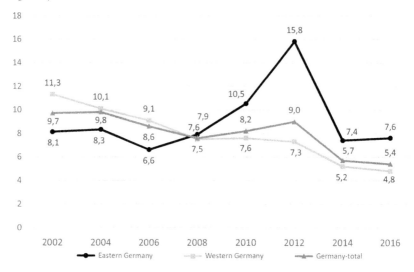

Fig. 5.8 Manifestly right-wing extremist attitudes over time 2002–2016

the question as to what response behaviour is the starting point from which one can attest to someone having a right-wing extremist attitude is answered differently in different studies.[21] With regard to this inconsistency and a certain arbitrariness of the labelling of the term right-wing extremism, the authors of the Thuringia Monitor have determined that

[21] For the data collected in the Thuringia Monitor a respondent was said to be right-wing extremist, when, having been asked ten specific attitude questions, he/she indicated "on average more approval than rejection". This was assumed to be the case if the total of all the answers produced a figure of more than 25 on a scale (maximum value = 40), whereby each question had four possible answers ranging from "reject completely" (value of 1) and "agree completely" (value of 4). If the total of all approval values was above three-quarters of the maximum value on the scale then the respondent was credited with having a "closed right-wing extremist world view" (Best und Salomo 2014, p. 11; Best et al. 2014, p. 75). The Leipzig Mitte Studies, in turn, speak of a "manifest right-wing extremist world view", if a respondent "on average" agreed with all 18 items in the questionnaire presented here, i.e. if the values for of all the responses added together resulted in a total of at least 64 (maximum value = 90), with the values for a response ranging from "reject completely" (value of 1) and "agree completely" (value of 5).

every *empirical* distinction between people with attitudes which are right-wing extremist and people whose attitudes are not right-wing extremist is "somewhat arbitrary", and that the attitude patterns studied should rather be viewed as a continuum (Best et al. 2014, p. 75). The political self-positioning of the respondents does not allow any great conclusions about possible existing right-wing extremist attitude patterns either, because as Best et al. (2014) have proven with the aid of their time series data, there does not appear to be, as one would otherwise have expected, a "connection between right-wing extremist attitudes and the positioning on the political left-right spectrum as determined by the respondents themselves".[22]

Against this background, one can assume that in the case of PEGIDA too, it cannot be unequivocally clarified as to what extent one needs to speak of right-wing extremism. The findings of the PEGIDA studies do, however, certainly allow the drawing of conclusions. Rucht et al. (2015) attempted to also use the indicator questions known from research into right-wing extremism for an (online) survey of PEGIDA supporters. As already indicated, the data resulting from this survey is subject to a high range of variation or probability of error due to the small sample size, with only 123 respondents, and the extremely poor response rate of a mere 6.8 per cent. Thus, the study can be seen to have only limited informative value. Nevertheless, one should not forgo a presentation of the results, as they do provide possible starting points for the interpretation of PEGIDA. A compilation with the most recent results of the *Mitte Studies* yields the picture shown in Fig. 5.9.[23]

---

[22] According to Best et al. (2014, p. 82) even a relative majority of the people with "entrenched right-wing extremist attitudes" position themselves on the left side of the political spectrum. Consequently, many of the supporters of the left-wing party Die Linke in eastern Germany specifically, who are seen as rather "structurally conservative", also represent political attitude patterns which are considered indicators for right-wing extremism in empirical attitude research. For the self-assessment of political positioning by the PEGIDA participants cf. Fig. 4.13 above.

[23] Own compilation of the findings from Rucht et al. (2015, p. 30), Decker et al. (2015a, p. 39ff.), Decker et al. (2016, p. 30ff.), Zick and Klein 2014, p. 36f. and Zick et al. 2016c, p. 124f. The years in the table header refer to the year in which the data were collected. The percentages shown are the combined share of those answers indicating an explicit agreement with the respective statement on a five-step scale. The specific answers were, in the case of Rucht et al. (2015), "agree completely" and "agree for the most part"; in the case of Decker et al. (2015a) and also Decker et al. (2016), "fully agree" and "agree for the most part". A dash indicates that no data were collected in the respective study. In the case of the online

	PEGIDA (2015)	Germany (Mitte-L 2014)			Germany (Mitte-B 2014)	Germany (Mitte-L 2016)			Germany (Mitte-B 2016)
	Online	Face-to-Face			CATI	Face-to-Face			CATI
		East	West	total	total	East	West	total	total
Endorsement of a right-wing dictatorship									
In the national interest, under certain circumstances, a dictatorship is a better form of government.	7,8	11,6	5,4	6,7	6,4	13,8	4,8	6,7	4,4
We should have a leader who governs Germany with a strong hand for the benefit of all.	4,3	12,4	8,4	9,2	11,4	12,8	10,0	10,6	12,2
Nationalism / Chauvinism									
We should finally regain the courage to have a strong national sentiment.	81,0	29,8	29,8	29,8	35,9	31,9	36,4	35,4	39,3
What our country needs today is for German interests abroad to be asserted firmly and energetically.	34,5	23,7	20,9	21,5	17,0	27,3	25,9	26,2	19,7
Trivialisation of National Socialism									
The crimes of National Socialism are exaggerated in historiography.	11,4	6,5	7,1	6,9	7,1	5,5	6,7	6,4	8,6
National Socialism also had its good sides.	5,2	8,6	9,4	9,3	10,1	7,3	8,7	8,4	11,0
Xenophobia									
Foreigners just come here to take advantage of our welfare state.	34,2	33,8	25,5	27,2	17,4	38,5	30,4	32,1	15,3
Germany has become overrun to a dangerous extent by the many foreigners.	41,4	31,5	26,5	27,5	17,7	35,2	33,5	33,8	18,1
Antisemitism									
Even today Jews have too much influence.	14,8	10,1	12,0	11,6	8,6	10,7	11,0	10,9	7,3

Fig. 5.9 Right-wing extremist attitude patterns in Germany and among Dresden PEGIDA demonstrators in comparison

According to these figures it was above all in the area of *xenophobia* that the approval rates amongst PEGIDA participants were high, even though these figures were within the range of those regularly found for the overall population in eastern Germany.[24] It is conspicuous in Fig. 5.9 that the levels of *endorsement for a right-wing authoritarian dictatorship* were also well below average for eastern German standards. According to this, there seemed to be a widespread, clear appreciation of democratic practices among the Dresden PEGIDA demonstrators—even though these may not focus on the established functioning mechanisms of the representative party democracy of the Basic Law, but instead on greatly simplified notions of (direct) democratic co-determination. At the same time, some relatively high rates of agreement with statements in the categories *trivialisation of National Socialism* and *antisemitism* indicate that numerous right-wing extremists were also among the demonstrators. This became increasingly obvious the more the movement became radicalised and lost protest participants during the course of 2015 and 2016. Here a core of the supporters, who stayed loyal to the protest marches even in times of low mobilisation and whose attitudes were considerably more right-wing, became more important. In May 2015, more than half of the participants of the demonstration who were asked agreed with the statement that "National Socialism was a dictatorship like any other". In January 2016, already 12.5 per cent had declared that "National Socialism also had its good sides" (Patzelt and Eichardt 2015, p. 81; Patzelt and Klose 2016, p. 176). On the other hand, the share of those who explicitly distanced themselves from right-wing extremist demonstrators, and who objected to being termed right-wing radical, remained high. The statement "It would be good if no right-wing radicals or right-wing extremists took part in PEGIDA demonstrations!" was met with 70.6 per cent approval among the PEGIDA demonstrators asked in May 2015, in January 2016 it was even 76.2 per cent (Patzelt and Klose 2016, p. 172).

survey data from Rucht et al. (2015) it is necessary to bear in mind that the response rate achieved was only 6.8 per cent. The figures used for PEGIDA in Fig. 5.9 thus accordingly have a comparatively limited informative value. Nevertheless they can provide certain indicators as to which attitude patterns played a motivational role for the PEGIDA demonstrators and should by no means "be seen as worthless and excluded from the debate" from the outset (Reuband 2015, p. 136)

[24] The exceptionally high approval rate for "We should finally regain the courage to have a strong national sentiment" in Rucht et al. (2015, pp. 29–30) must be viewed with caution in light of the potentially unreliable survey database.

In view of this, on the whole, very disparate picture, it nevertheless seems to make little sense to sweepingly classify the PEGIDA supporters as *right-wing extremist* (cf. Vorländer et al. 2016a, p. 80ff; 2016b). Though the demands, arguments and slogans expressed at the demonstrations were largely located on the right of the political spectrum, overall the term *extremism* still seems rather imprecise for a protest movement with supporters who were indeed conspicuous because of strong feelings of nationalistic and xenophobic resentment, but on the other hand could not be characterised as "antidemocratic", "approving of dictatorships" or even "neo-National Socialist". Instead, further information about the individual dimensions of right-wing extremist attitude patterns is needed for a classification—particularly in view of the clearly very pronounced approval figures within the realm of xenophobia among PEGIDA participants. This orientation was the one that dominated the public perception of the protests from the beginning.

5.3   Xenophobia

Against the backdrop of an influx of refugees, PEGIDA protests and the debates about the refugee and asylum policy, the number of acts of violence in Germany motivated by xenophobia increased significantly in 2014 and 2015. In 2015 there were 918 recorded acts of violence with a right-wing extremist motivation and a xenophobic background, including 756 assaults, 83 arsons and seven homicides—in comparison with 2014 these figures represented an increase of around 80 per cent. The regional focus of these xenophobically-motivated attacks was North Rhine-Westphalia, Berlin and, above all, Saxony. In 2015 Saxon towns and villages like Heidenau, Freital, Bautzen or Clausnitz became synonymous for a xenophobic, anti-refugee "dark" side of Germany. If all incidents of politically motivated right-wing violence are added together, then, in a comparison of the German *Länder*, Saxony, with its 201 recorded incidents, was behind only North Rhine-Westphalia, which led with 288 incidents. However, if these figures are seen relative to the size of the local population, a picture emerges of Saxony as a typical representative of a problem which extends to all the new *Bundesländer* (Fig. 5.10).[25]

---

[25] Cf. Federal Ministry of the Interior (2016, p. 25ff.). The information presented is based on own calculations on the basis of current population statistics

Politically motivated right-wing violence in Germany 2014–2015

Number of incidents according to Bundesland per million inhabitants
Figures in percent

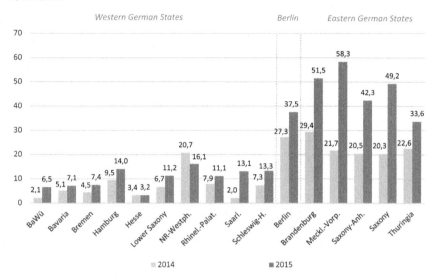

Fig. 5.10   Politically motivated right-wing violence 2014–2015

Against the backdrop of PEGIDA, the refugee crisis and the sharp rise in right-wing acts of violence, especially those motivated by xenophobia, in 2015 there was also a similarly substantial increase in violent acts with a left-wing extremist background. The number of such incidents increased by 62 per cent, whereby, here too, Saxony was a focal point (Fig. 5.11).[26]

Xenophobic incidents and politically motivated acts of violence need to be distinguished from the opinions and attitudes prevalent in the population. On the one hand, the findings of political culture research show that xenophobia is by far the most prominent component of the right-wing extremist attitude patterns in Germany (cf. Fig. 5.7 above). On the other hand, over the course of the past 15 years the figures have tended to stay constant or trended slightly downwards.[27] This can be clearly seen in the

[26] Cf. Federal Ministry of the Interior (2016, p. 31ff.). The information presented is based on own calculations on the basis of current population statistics

[27] For eastern Germany, Decker et al. (2016, p. 45) most recently recorded a particularly pronounced drop: from 38.7 per cent in 2012 to 22.7 per cent in 2016. For the period prior

Politically motivated left-wing violence in Germany 2014–2015

Number of incidents according to Bundesland per million inhabitants
Figures in percent

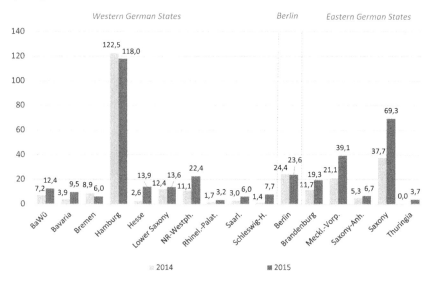

Fig. 5.11   Politically motivated left-wing violence 2014–2015

findings from the Mitte Studies (Decker et al. 2016, p. 45), but also the corresponding items, regularly analysed within the framework of the German General Social Survey (GGSS) (Fig. 5.12)[28] for the purpose of measuring xenophobic tendencies.

to 2012, conversely, steady increases were recorded in both eastern and western Germany (Decker et al. 2015a, pp. 46, 53). The decline was in reference to "manifestly xenophobic attitudes", in other words, the number of people who "on average" agreed with all the statements in the surveys in the category of xenophobia. Other time-based analyses also painted a similar picture, cf. only Holtmann et al. (2015, p. 163).

[28] Own calculation on the basis of the GGSS data from the years 2000 to 2016. Here the rate of agreement with the corresponding statements could be indicated on a seven-step scale. Presented in this figure are the average values of all responses given, recalculated and shown on a recoded scale from –3 ("do not agree at all") to +3 ("fully agree"). The wording of the question was: "This question is about foreigners living in Germany. On this list there are some sentences that you have heard before at some point. Please tell me for each sentence to what extent you agree. A value of 1 means that you 'do not agree at all', a value of 7 means that you 'fully agree'. You can use the values in between to grade your statement." In the years 2004 and 2008 data for the corresponding items was not collected. In the GGSS 2014, for the topic of "Immigration" different statements were presented to the respondents. Here

Average rates of agreement with xenophobic statements in Germany

Average value of all responses from "full agreement" (+3) to "complete disagreement" (-3)

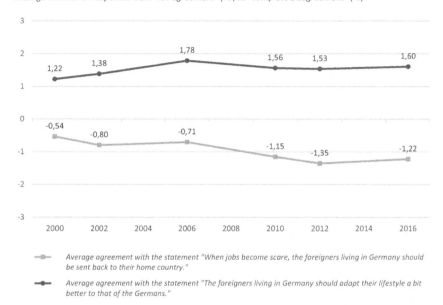

Average agreement with the statement "When jobs become scare, the foreigners living in Germany should be sent back to their home country."

Average agreement with the statement "The foreigners living in Germany should adapt their lifestyle a bit better to that of the Germans."

Fig. 5.12 Average rates of agreement with xenophobic statements in Germany (GGSS 2000–2012)

Although the high concentration of xenophobic incidents and the regional success of the PEGIDA protests point to Saxony, it also appears that there is no direct correspondence with the attitudes of the Saxon population. For instance, if one looks at the long-term average rates of agreement with xenophobic statements in Germany in Decker et al. (2015b), then the home territory of PEGIDA is more or less in the mid-field, at approximately the same level as Schleswig-Holstein or Lower Saxony (Fig. 5.13).[29]

the results were as follows: "Immigrants take jobs away from people who were born in Germany" = 23.0 per cent agreement; "Immigrants increase the crime rate" = 50.5 per cent agreement; "Immigrants enrich Germany through new ideas and cultures" = 66.4 per cent agreement; "The German culture is in general being undermined by immigrants" = 29.5 per cent agreement

[29] Own representation of the findings from Decker et al. (2015b, p. 75). Shown, in relation to the total population of the respective Länder, is the corresponding percentage of those

Xenophobic attitudes in Germany according to Bundesland
Long-term average rate of agreement with xenophobic statements (2002–2014)
Figures in percent

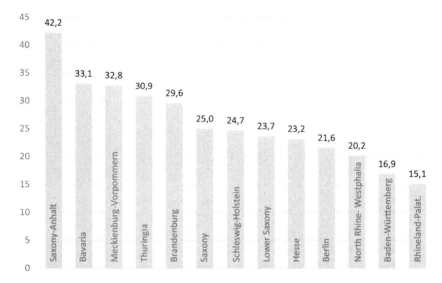

Fig. 5.13 Rates of agreement with xenophobic statements according to *Bundesland*

A representative survey of the populations of Dresden and Düsseldorf in 2014 even came to the conclusion that the measurements for xenophobia in the two cities were fairly even (Fig. 5.14).[30]

who were "on average in agreement" with all the xenophobic statements presented to them. The basis for the calculation was the data of all randomly chosen people surveyed since 2002, grouped according to their origin, and combined to form a so-called cumulative sample (N = 18,317). The results for the *Bundesländer* Bremen, Hamburg and Saarland are not included in the analysis of Decker et al. (2015b, p. 72f.) due to the sample size, namely below 500 cases, being insufficient. They are thus also missing in Fig. 5.13. If they were included then N = 19,080

[30] Own compilation of the data from Reuband (2015, p. 137). The years in the table header refer to the year in which the data were collected. The percentages shown represent the combined share of those answers which indicated an explicit agreement with the respective statement on a four-step scale, with the responses "agree fully/tend to agree". The data collection took place in Dresden and Düsseldorf and was carried out with the help of a standardised questionnaire sent by mail. Respondents were asked for the assessment of the living conditions of the population aged 18 and above with German citizenship. According to Reuband

	Dresden (Reuband 2014)	Düsseldorf (Reuband 2014)	Hamburg (Reuband 2011)
	postal survey	postal survey	postal survey
Xenophobic attitudes			
Too many foreigners live in Germany.	45	46	52
If there were fewer foreigners in Germany, there would be less crime.	48	43	52
Most asylum seekers abuse the right to asylum in Germany.	43	39	46
I like living in a city where people from different countries live.	69	83	74

Fig. 5.14 Xenophobic attitudes in Dresden, Düsseldorf and Hamburg in comparison (rates of agreement as a percentage)

On the basis of these findings, one must disagree with the assumption that Saxony or its state capital had provided a particularly ideal foundation for the emergence of PEGIDA because of a well above average concentration of xenophobic orientations in the population.

With regard to the demonstrations and the widespread xenophobic resentment among their participants there are also—at least for winter 2014/2015—largely consistent findings. The proportion of people with openly xenophobic attitudes among the Dresden demonstrators was estimated to be between 30 and 40 per cent.[31] The close to 400 interviews with PEGIDA demonstrators by Vorländer, Herold and Schäller already revealed that around a third (31.2 per cent) harboured fundamental feelings of resentment towards immigrants and asylum seekers. As Fig. 5.15[32]

the response rate was about 50 per cent (Reuband 2015, p. 137). For the prevalence of right-wing extremist attitude patterns in Dresden cf. also the study by Grau et al. (2010)

[31] In particular Vorländer et al. (2015, p. 57ff.) and Patzelt and Eichardt (2015, pp. 93–94), but also Rucht et al. (2015, p. 30) have shown that the prevalence of xenophobic orientations among PEGIDA participants can be assumed to be at about this level.

[32] The percentages shown in this figure represent the corresponding share of all 397 interviewees who gave each respective answer. They refer to the response category "Fundamental reservations about immigrants and asylum seekers", as presented in Fig. 4.9, and show the response category in detail. The figures in Fig. 5.15 thus complement the figure shown in Fig. 4.9 for the response category "Fundamental reservations", even if their exact total is not identical with 31.2 per cent due to multiple answers being possible.

Xenophobic feelings of resentment among PEGIDA demonstrators
The responses indicating "fundamental reservations" in detail
Figures in percent / share of the total number of all interviewed persons / multiple answers were possible

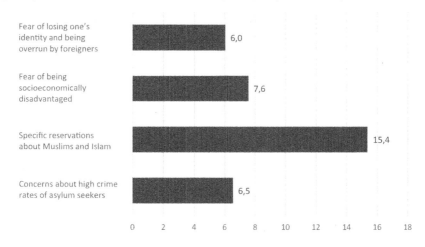

Fear of losing one's identity and being overrun by foreigners — 6,0

Fear of being socioeconomically disadvantaged — 7,6

Specific reservations about Muslims and Islam — 15,4

Concerns about high crime rates of asylum seekers — 6,5

■ Distribution in Vorländer, Herold, Schäller 2015; n = 397

Fig. 5.15 Xenophobic feelings of resentment among Dresden PEGIDA demonstrators. Source: Vorländer et al. (2015, p. 69)

shows, these reservations were directed towards Muslim immigrants and asylum seekers in particular.

The study by Rucht et al. from January 2015 confirmed these assessments. Its authors concluded from these rates of agreement, along with the impressions from their in situ demonstration observations on 12.01.2015, that PEGIDA was "in essence, about the expression of *group-focused enmity* and more pointedly, thinly veiled racism" (Rucht et al. 2015, p. 53). A comparative classification of the results, however, made it clear that this finding did not constitute a unique characteristic of PEGIDA participants, but corresponded more or less to the level of xenophobic orientations also regularly recorded elsewhere in Germany (above all in the new *Länder*) (cf. Fig. 5.9 above). The same was true for a critical, at times sweepingly derogatory, attitude towards asylum seekers (Fig. 5.16).[33]

---

[33] Own compilation of the findings from: Rucht et al. (2015, p. 31); Küpper et al. 2015, p. 33, 2016b, p. 44f.; Decker et al. 2015a, p. 58, 2016, p. 50. The years in the table header

	PEGIDA-Dresden (Rucht et al. 2015)	Germany (Mitte-L 2014)		Germany (Mitte-B 2014)	Germany (Mitte-L 2016)	Germany (Mitte-B 2016)
	Online	Face-to-Face		CATI	Face-to-Face	CATI
		East	total	total	total	total
Derogation of asylum seekers						
Most asylum seekers do not really fear being persecuted in their home country (agreement with this statement as a percentage).	66,2	–	55,3	42	59,9	41,0
When examining asylum applications, the state should be generous (rejection of this statement as a percentage).	86,5	84,7	76,0	62	80,9	71,6

Fig. 5.16 Derogation of asylum seekers in Germany and among Dresden PEGIDA demonstrators in comparison

Even a comparison with the results of the last survey looking at *group-focused enmity* from 2011 yielded a strong similarity between the rates of agreement for PEGIDA and for the general population. This is remarkable, all the more so considering that in light of escalating violence in geopolitical trouble spots (in particular in Syria) the number of asylum applications in Germany had risen sharply after 2011—they nearly quadrupled between 2011 and 2014.[34]

In turn, with the help of a factor analysis, Patzelt (2015, pp. 26–27) also determined that about a third of the 242 PEGIDA demonstrators he interviewed on 25.01.2015 were to be described as "right-wing nationalist xenophobes"—thus as people "who see themselves as very far to the right, and strongly feel that they are German patriots" and that they

refer to the year in which the data were collected. The percentages shown represent the respective share of responses that indicated explicit agreement with (top line) or rejection of (bottom line) the corresponding assertion on a four- or five-point scale. In the case of Rucht et al. (2015) those answers were "agree completely/agree for the most part" and "do not agree at all"/"largely disagree", in Decker et al. (2015a) "agree fully/agree for the most part" and "completely reject/ largely reject", and in Küpper et al. 2015 as well as Zick et al. (2016b) "agree fully"/"tend to agree" and "do not agree at all"/"tend to disagree". In the one field with a dash the figure is unknown. In the case of Rucht et al. a comparative value was calculated because of a different scale.

[34] Cf. the data on the website of the Federal Office for Migration and Refugees (BAMF) at http://www.bamf.de/DE/Infothek/Statistiken/Asylzahlen/asylzahlen-node.html (Accessed 15.06.2017).

	PEGIDA-Dresden (Jan. 2015)	PEGIDA-Dresden (May 2015)	PEGIDA-Dresden (Jan. 2016)	Germany (Heitmeyer 2011)
	Face-to-Face	Face-to-Face	Face-to-Face	CATI
Attitudes about immigration and asylum				
Germany should continue to accept asylum-seekers and civil war refugees.	72,8	65,5	51,4	–
Germany takes in too many civil war refugees.	30,3	33,1	51,4	–
Germany takes in too many asylum seekers.	67,1	82,5	89,8	–
Quite apart from asylum seekers and civil war refugees: There should simply be fewer foreigners in Germany.	–	42,2	45,4	47,1

Fig. 5.17 Rates of agreement with statements about the topic "Immigration and asylum" among Dresden PEGIDA demonstrators

thereby not only reject the intake of asylum seekers and refugees, but also " do not even consider a peaceful Islam to be suitable for Germany". In addition, in their surveys both Patzelt (2015) and Patzelt and Eichardt (2015) were able to gauge the positions of the surveyed PEGIDA participants on the topic of "Immigration, refugee and asylum policy" with the help of self-compiled attitude questions (Fig. 5.17).[35]

On the one hand, here it became apparent that even the high rates of agreement recorded among PEGIDA supporters for statements claiming that in Germany there are "too many foreigners in general" were roughly in line with the figures which the survey series on *group-focused enmity* had already calculated for the general population in Germany in 2011. On the other hand, it was remarkable that in the case of PEGIDA the rejection of

[35] Own presentation of the findings from Patzelt (2015, p. 19), Patzelt and Eichardt (2015, p. 58), Patzelt and Klose (2016, p. 257) and also Heitmeyer (2012b, p. 38). The information in the table header refers to the points in time when the respective data were collected. In the case of Patzelt (2015) and also Patzelt and Eichardt (2015) agreement was determined using a five-point scale. The percentages shown in this figure are the sums of the respective shares of responses for "very much agree" and "tend to agree". The rate of agreement from the study by Heitmeyer (2012b) relates to the assertion presented there, namely that "There are too many foreigners living in Germany". Here the level of agreement was determined using a four-point scale. Shown in this figure is the combined share of the answers "agree completely" and "tend to agree". A dash indicates that no data were collected in the respective study at the corresponding point in time.

that which is foreign was mainly expressed in a specific form—a form which adopted the distinction between politically persecuted civil war *refugees* and conventional *asylum seekers* and which was aimed primarily at the latter, especially since the local plans for their accommodation are to be seen as a key reason and catalyst for the emergence of the PEGIDA protests. Thus, hidden behind the term "asylum seeker" there was essentially the image of so-called "economic refugees", in other words people who were accused, for the sake of personal benefit, of wanting to benefit from the prosperity of Germany, despite making no contribution to the generation of wealth. Patzelt and Eichardt concluded from this that "the main problem that PEGIDA demonstrators have with foreigners" is related to the suspicion that they are "economic refugees". Notably, according to the authors, in many cases there was a belief that the overwhelming majority of asylum seekers had not really fled to Germany because of political persecution. Instead, many suspected that they were primarily seeking a better life in a material sense—with possible consequential costs for German social security funds and taxpayers (Patzelt and Eichardt 2015, p. 58).

It is questionable whether this can already be considered a form of social envy, because, as the survey series by Reuband (2017) in spring 2016 confirmed, the fear of negative social and economic effects, such as increased competition in the labour or housing market, played a comparatively subordinate role for the PEGIDA demonstrators.[36] Alongside the concern about the immediate costs of the intake of refugees, it was above all safety concerns and the anticipated cultural consequences of Muslim immigration, in particular the fear of losing one's own, culturally defined identity, that was driving people to the streets (Fig. 5.18).[37]

Although Patzelt and Eichardt determined in April and May 2015 at the PEGIDA events, which had by then shrunk significantly, that almost 43 per cent of the demonstrators agreed with the assertion that there are "too many foreigners in general in Germany", the authors stressed that among the demonstrators "a general and fundamental *xenophobia* could not really be established". The authors felt that although strong xenopho-

[36] Similar findings were made by Vorländer et al. (2015, p. 70).

[37] Own compilation of the findings from Reuband (2017, p. 122). The results of the three surveys presented there have been cumulated and weighted in Fig. 5.18 based on the information provided by Reuband (2017, p. 114). Thus, what is shown is the average proportion of the surveyed PEGIDA participants who in response to the question "What concerns do you have in connection with the refugees coming here?" responded to the respective assertions with "agree completely".

Concerns of the PEGIDA demonstrators related to the influx of refugees
Rates of agreement in percent (December 2015 – April 2016)

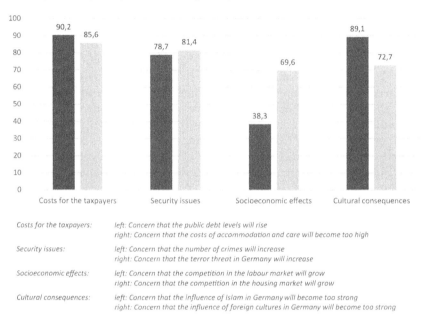

Costs for the taxpayers:	left: Concern that the public debt levels will rise
	right: Concern that the costs of accommodation and care will become too high
Security issues:	left: Concern that the number of crimes will increase
	right: Concern that the terror threat in Germany will increase
Socioeconomic effects:	left: Concern that the competition in the labour market will grow
	right: Concern that the competition in the housing market will grow
Cultural consequences:	left: Concern that the influence of Islam in Germany will become too strong
	right: Concern that the influence of foreign cultures in Germany will become too strong

Fig. 5.18 Concerns of the PEGIDA demonstrators related to the influx of refugees

bic feelings of resentment could indeed be observed, it was not therefore a reason to "attribute to *all* the PEGIDA-goers a *groundless*, simply group-focused and thereby *racist* form of xenophobia in the sense of 'group-focused enmity'" (Patzelt and Eichardt 2015, p. 59, emphasis in original). As a matter of fact, in both spring 2015 and January 2016 approximately three-quarters of all demonstrators interviewed were of the opinion that right-wing radicals or right-wing extremists had no business being at PEGIDA protests (Patzelt and Klose 2016, p. 172).

Karl-Heinz Reuband (2017, p. 128f.) arrived at a similar conclusion. According to him it would be "too simple" to look at the attitude patterns identified at PEGIDA and "simply equate them with generalised xenophobia and racism and attribute them to the majority of the demonstrators". Even in spring 2016, long after PEGIDA had become radicalised and marginalised, still approximately two-thirds of the protesters (67 per cent) expressed "sympathy for the people fleeing the civil war in Syria", 62 per cent indicated that they were ashamed because of the violent attacks on accommodation for refugees, 64 per cent "were either opposed to demonstrating in front of planned or existing refugee accommodation themselves, or in general". As many as 80 per cent were even in favour of receiving further asylum seekers. The PEGIDA supporters were certainly not "regular citizens" with regard to their xenophobic attitudes, yet they did not differ as much from the general population as was often assumed.

5.4   ETHNOCENTRISM

High levels of approval for assertions in the categories *xenophobia* and *nationalism/chauvinism*, without at the same time showing evident sympathies for positions in the categories of *antisemitism, affinity for dictatorships* and *trivialisation of National Socialism* point to an attitude pattern which is known in political culture research as *ethnocentrism* and which as a theoretical concept has already been in use for more than a century in cultural anthropology and social psychology. William G. Sumner defined ethnocentrism as far back as 1906 as "a technical term" for a view "in which one's own group is the center of everything, and all others are scaled and rated with reference to it" (Sumner 2007, p. 13). In contemporary scientific discourse the term is now used with at least two different connotations. On the one hand *ethnocentrism* is deemed to be a particularly pronounced form of orientation towards the values, customs, interests and characteristics of groups or community contexts which are often defined by region or based on a shared "homeland"—an orientation, which as a rule is connected with strengthened feelings of belonging and solidarity towards this collective framework and also a directly resulting lower opinion of everything "foreign". On the other hand, an attitude pattern of this kind is described as a precursor to or a subtype of right-wing extremist attitudes. Ethnocentrism encompasses a strongly pronounced thinking in the categories of "we" (in-groups) versus "the others" (out-groups), "whereby the standards of one's own group decide how people perceive and evaluate the world. Here, as a rule, in-groups are viewed more positively compared to out-groups, which can strain the relationship between groups and possibly lead to an open conflict or to social discrimination of members of out-groups" (Fritsche et al. 2013, p. 162f.; Kessler and Fritsche 2011).

Apart from this theoretical definition of ethnocentrism there is also an empirically based concept, which is used, for instance, in Best et al. (2014). After analyses of large amounts of time series data on right-wing extremist attitudes, the research group came to the conclusion that the previously assumed six-dimensional structure (xenophobia, chauvinism, NS-trivialisation, affinity for dictatorships, antisemitism and social Darwinism) used to establish right-wing extremist attitudes empirically could not be valid because the individual items in the data do not enable the identification of a direct link and thus do not indicate a uniformly identifiable attitude pattern.[38] Instead, on the basis of the insights gained it was possible to "differentiate two groups of attitude questions, each containing items which have a greater association with each other than with the questions from the other groups". Basically, according to Best et al. (2014, p. 78), there are two identifiable dimensions of right-wing or right-wing extremist notions of inequality: *ethnocentrism* is a combination of those items which are seen as indicators for xenophobia and nationalism/chauvinism, whereas the remaining items represent a sort of *neo-National Socialist ideology*.[39] In terms of these two empirically distinguishable attitude patterns, in the data for Thuringia a picture emerges in which a large part of the population (over time always between 30 and 50 per cent) displays ethnocentric attitudes, but a considerably lower proportion (approximately 7–11 per cent) neo-National Socialist attitudes (Fig. 5.19).[40]

For Germany as a whole the general spread of ethnocentric orientations can be estimated using the data from the Leipzig Mitte Study. On the basis of their cumulative sample from the period 2002–2014 the preva-

---

[38] It had become apparent, for instance, that respondents who agreed with an assertion on the topic of social Darwinism, would not therefore with a high degree of probability also affirm other indicators of right-wing extremist views (Best et al. 2014, p. 77ff.). Furthermore, according to the researchers, problems had become evident in the question category affinity for dictatorship. The result of validity checks here was that the hitherto used questions needed to be seen not only as an indicator for affinity with a right-wing dictatorship, but also as an indicator for approval of left-wing authoritarian dictatorships. Even the question of a "dictatorship in the national interest" was said to be approved of equally by both rightist and leftist respondents (Best et al. 2014, p. 81).

[39] For Best et al. (2016, p. 96) this reorientation of the measurement methodology resulted in the proportion of "those with right-wing extremist attitudes" in the population as a whole having to be revised upwards in some cases, to 16 per cent most recently for Thuringia in 2016.

[40] In the compilation in Best et al. (2014) the data are missing for 2009.

Right-wing attitude patterns in Thuringia 2001-2016

Prevalence of support for ethnocentric and neo-National Socialist statements

Figures in percent

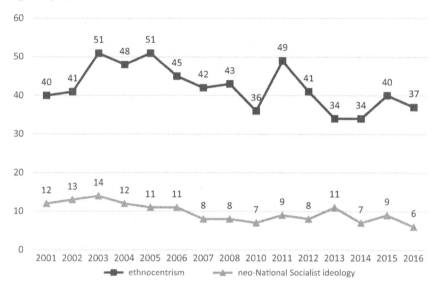

Fig. 5.19 Support for ethnocentrism and NS-ideology in the population of Thuringia 2001–2016. Source: Best et al. (2014, p. 77), own representation

lence of individual orientations can be grouped according to *Bundesland* and the results compared (Figs. 5.20 and 5.21).[41,42]

Looking at the ethnocentric attitude profile there are two things in particular that stand out. Firstly, the findings of the Mitte Studies reinforce

---

[41] Own presentation of the findings from Decker et al. (2015b, p. 71ff.). Shown, in relation to the total population of the respective *Länder*, is the corresponding percentage of those who were "on average in agreement" with all the respective xenophobic or nationalist/ chauvinist statements presented to them. Basis: cumulative sample 2002–2014, *N* = 18,317. Due to the number of cases being insufficient, namely below 500, the results from the *Länder* Bremen, Hamburg and Saarland were not taken into account in the evaluation in Decker et al. (2015b) and are consequently missing in Figs. 5.20 and 5.21 (Decker et al. 2015b, p. 72f.). If they had been included then *N* = 19,080.

[42] Own representation of the findings from Decker et al. (2015b, p. 71ff.), cf. preceding figure note for detail.

Ethnocentric attitudes according to Bundesland

Average agreement with statements from the individual topic areas in detail

Figures in percent

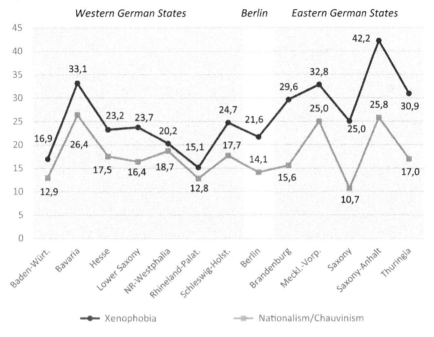

Fig. 5.20 Agreement with statements in the topic areas of "xenophobia" and "nationalism/chauvinism" according to *Bundesland*

the theory of Best et al. (2014) that attitudes of this kind are widespread in the German population, especially in the new *Länder*. As such, Thuringia is not a special case. Secondly, however, it became evident that this is also the case for the former West German states. In particular Bavaria, but also Schleswig-Holstein, even reached the otherwise higher overall level of the new *Länder*. In Bavaria the figures obtained for "xenophobia" and "nationalism/chauvinism" are even higher than in almost all the eastern German *Länder* (Decker et al. 2015b, p. 73).

Neo-National Socialist attitudes according to Bundesland

Average agreement with statements from the individual topic areas in detail

Figures in percent

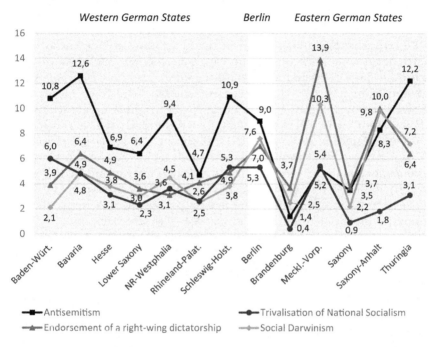

Fig. 5.21 Agreement with statements from the categories Antisemitism, Trivialisation of National Socialism, Endorsement of a right-wing authoritarian dictatorship and Social Darwinism according to *Bundesland*

With regard to neo-National Socialist attitude patterns, on the other hand, the result (as seen with the figures from the Thuringia Monitor in Fig. 5.21) is a much lower overall level of approval. Here the statements about the "Endorsement of a right-wing authoritarian dictatorship" and "Social Darwinism" were met with approval on average more in the East, whereas assertions on the topics of "Antisemitism" and the

"Trivialisation of National Socialism" more in the West (Decker et al. 2015a, pp. 46, 52ff.). This illustrates the trend that had already been detected in previous years, namely that in the old *Bundesländer* the figures for certain dimensions of right-wing extremist attitudes are considerably higher than the level in the new *Bundesländer*. However, it seemed somewhat surprising, especially against the backdrop of PEGIDA, that Saxony displayed, if anything, noticeably below average rates of agreement in comparison with the other new *Bundesländer*, as shown in Figs. 5.20 and 5.21. With regard to "Xenophobia" Saxony is at approximately the same level as Schleswig-Holstein, Hesse and Lower Saxony, in terms of "Endorsement of a right-wing authoritarian dictatorship" it is below the average in western Germany, and in the case of "Antisemitism", "Social Darwinism" and "Trivialisation of National Socialism" even well below the level of the western German *Bundesländer*. In the category "Nationalism/chauvinism" Saxony even recorded the lowest approval rates in the whole of Germany. It is unclear to what extent these findings regarding the prevailing orientations in the population are compatible with the fact that, from a national perspective, in 2015 Saxony became a hotspot for xenophobic violence. To determine this it will be necessary to wait for the future findings of the Saxony Monitor survey series, which only commenced in 2016.

The ethnocentrism, which is also strongly present in Saxony, can however be compared with the findings from the Thuringia Monitor and empirically evaluated. Its main concentration in the population up to now (aside from the so-called "left behind antidemocrats" has been in two milieus in particular. On the one hand, there are those people who Best et al. (2014, p. 84ff.) term "the prototypical losers of the reunification". They say that this section of the population is characterised by experiences of, in some cases, severe economic deprivation, yet it nevertheless remains firmly committed to the idea of democracy and still has the will to participate in political life. On the other hand, it is claimed that ethnocentric attitude patterns were an integral part of a classically (eastern German) conservative milieu. The members of this group had not endured significant disadvantages or failures, neither economically nor socially. On the contrary, they had a "positive final balance" with regard to German reunification. They are said to nevertheless have attitudes which are more strongly authoritarian than other

	PEGIDA (January 2015)	PEGIDA (May 2015)	PEGIDA (January 2016)	Germany (GGSS 2014)
	Face-to-Face	Face-to-Face	Face-to-Face	CAPI
Attitudes towards patriotism				
I consider myself a German patriot!	76,2	82,8	82,0	87,3
I consider myself a European patriot!	73,2	50,3	–	65,6

Fig. 5.22 Agreement among Dresden PEGIDA demonstrators with statements about "Patriotism"

sections of the population and in their voting behaviour mainly lean towards the Christian Democratic Union of Germany (CDU).[43]

Looking at PEGIDA, one would initially assume that a similar picture would emerge for Saxony—and that is to say, both with regard to the prevalence of ethnocentric attitude patterns, and also with regard to their distribution in individual sections of the population. In both the Dresden organisational team and among the demonstrators in Dresden, the groups described in the Thuringia Monitor, namely "typical losers of the reunification" and "eastern German conservatives", were to be found in large numbers. On top of the openly xenophobic orientations described in Sect. 5.3 in Chap. 5, which were identified in about 30 to 40 per cent of the demonstrators, other attitude patterns among PEGIDA participants which were very pronounced were above all patriotic, nationalistic or even chauvinistic. In the interviews conducted by Patzelt and Eichhardt (2015), for instance, more than three-quarters of respondents claimed to be a "German patriot" (Fig. 5.22).[44]

[43] The Thuringia-based researchers do not however see an "extremism of the centre" because neo-National Socialist attitudes were observed predominantly amongst those in economically precarious situations, thus more at the social margins of society (Best and Salomo 2014, p. 77ff.).

[44] Own representation of the findings from Patzelt (2015, p. 21), Patzelt and Eichardt (2015, p. 70), Patzelt and Klose (2016, p. 237) as well as from the Allbus (GESIS 2017). The information in the table header refers to the point in time at which the corresponding data was collected. In the case of Patzelt (2015), Patzelt and Eichardt (2015) as well as Patzelt and Klose (2016) agreement was determined with the help of a five-point scale. The percentages shown in this figure are the sums of the respective shares of responses for "very much agree" and "tend to agree". The figure given in the Allbus 2014 was calculated using a four-step scale and relates to the following question: "To what extent do you feel attached

With regard to the question as to whether the Patriotic Europeans also felt like "Europeans", changes in the rates of agreement with the assertions between January and May 2015 point to possible changes in the make-up of the participants. Apparently, after the split of the PEGIDA organisational team and the decline in the number of participants in spring 2015, more and more of the "Patriotic Europeans" stayed at home, and allowed those "patriots" to come to the fore who felt that they were above all "patriotic Germans". A comparison with the response behaviour for similar questions asked within the framework of the German General Social Survey (GGSS) 2014, however, shows here too that the figures calculated for PEGIDA in Dresden were completely in line with the national average.

Shared nationally, locally and culturally patriotic convictions were, to an extent, a kind of "breeding ground" for the right-wing populist protest, which enabled a mobilisation that extended well into the middle class. As a kind of common denominator these patriotic feelings constituted a pre-requisite, then allowing young and old, well-educated and socially weak, radical and bourgeois demonstrators to demonstrate at PEGIDA with and beside each other. Additionally, the fears expressed at PEGIDA of an "Islamisation", of "being overrun by foreigners" and of "paternalism on the part of foreign or alienated political and media elites" were only con-ceivable against the backdrop of pronounced nationally patriotic orienta-tions, which operated with emotional ties (to a "homeland") and emphasis on privileges for the "indigenous population" (Heitmeyer 2012b). This impression could already be gained at first sight because of the numerous German flags carried at all the demonstrations. It was further reinforced by placards being carried with slogans like "Preserve homeland and iden-tity, stop asylum fraud" (08.12.2014), "Our country, our values" (05.01.2015) or "Stop excessive immigration! We want a safe, social, German homeland" (12.01.2015). In addition, many of the PEGIDA participants carried signs with regionally patriotic greetings like "Blankenstein sends greetings to Pegida" (01.12.2014), "The Vogtland sends its greetings" (15.12.2014) or "Zschopau Erzgebirge: We want to be German and free!" (in dialect in the original German: *Zschopau Erzgebirge: Deitsch on frei wolln mr sei!*, 12.01.2015). This served to show

to … Germany/Europe?" (items V642/V643). The percentages shown represent the com-bined share of the answers "very strongly attached" and "strongly attached".

that the supposedly vulnerable "Occident" in the thoughts of the demonstrators primarily extended to Saxony and their own home region.[45]

As has been shown, the PEGIDA supporters on the streets largely revealed an attitude pattern characterised by orientations which go from strongly nationally patriotic to latently xenophobic, but overall the supporters cannot be considered right-wing extremist, because of a lack of increased levels of agreement in all the other characteristics of right-wing extremism. Moreover, in winter 2014/2015 the manifestations of these patterns at PEGIDA were within the scope of what is regularly established for the general population—above all in the new *Länder*. If the findings about the sociographic composition, the political outlook and motives of the PEGIDA demonstrators are incorporated here then the protests can also be considered to be proof for the theory that attitude patterns of this kind enjoy broad support even in parts of a social middle class. Consequently, the phenomenon that became visible in winter 2014/2015 at PEGIDA marches on the streets of Germany can be referred to as "middle class ethnocentrism" because it is also prevalent in that section of society.[46] One could sum up by saying that PEGIDA, with its resentful messages and slogans, used this ethnocentrism consciously and with temporary success in the face of various crises and threatening scenarios. The protest movement thereby made publicly apparent the continued relevance of this, in many respects problematic, yet still influential attitude pattern, which in the more cosmopolitan-orientated democratic discourse of the twenty-first century normally only has limited media resonance. It also highlighted a reservoir, the political mobilisation of which has already brought votes and political success for right-wing populist parties in other European cities. In Germany in the course of the PEGIDA demonstrations, as is well known, the AfD appeared on the scene to make political capital from the protests on the streets.

[45] For the signs, banners and slogans at the PEGIDA demonstrations cf. in more detail Sect. 1.3 in Chap. 1.

[46] On the basis of their empirical surveys, in 2006 the authors of the Leipzig Mitte Studies already established the more sweeping concept of a "right-wing extremism of the centre", arguing that the term "right-wing extremism" was misleading "because it describes the problem solely as a marginal phenomenon". Right-wing extremist attitudes were said to be just as typical for the centre of society (Decker and Brähler 2008, p. 6; Decker and Brähler 2006, p. 55). This theory, however, was taken as grounds to express, at times severe, criticism of the methodological approach, the political orientation and in particular the conclusions of the Mitte Studies (Backes 2013; Jesse 2013; Schroeder 21.10.2010).

5.5   ATTITUDES TOWARDS POLITICS, DEMOCRACY AND THE MEDIA

An important criterion for the categorisation and interpretation of PEGIDA is also provided by its demonstrators' aggressive criticism of "the politicians", "the media" and "the political system" of the Federal Republic, expressed with slogans like "Traitors to the people" (*Volksverräter*) and "Lying press" (*Lügenpresse*). In the eyes of the organisers this criticism was even to be regarded as the central thrust of the protest movement.[47] All studies unanimously established that the PEGIDA participants in winter 2014/2015 were indeed strongly motivated by fundamental feelings of resentment towards a political and opinion-forming elite. Already in the study by Vorländer et al. (2015, p. 59) 71.2 per cent of the demonstrators interviewed stated that they were dissatisfied with policies and politicians, more than a third (34.5 per cent) expressed that their "dissatisfaction with the media and the general public" was a motivation for their protests (cf. Fig. 4.9). These two answer categories represented the most frequently mentioned motivations. In the study by Vorländer et al. (2015, p. 62f.) they were most frequently expressed as "a general perception of distance between the people and politicians" (25.9 per cent), as fundamental criticism of the representative democracy of the Federal Republic—in particular with regard to the role of the parties as well as in view of the absence of direct democratic co-determination on a national level (21.2 per cent). When asked about specific policy areas, the respondents most frequently expressed their displeasure at the asylum policy (25.9 per cent) and the immigration and integration policies (17.1 per cent). Topics such as foreign affairs, security, economic or social policy tended to play more of a subordinate role.

This finding can initially be put into a wider context. It is somewhat in contrast to the results of other research—in some cases long survey series—on political culture dealing with the development of democracy in Germany. A study by Holtmann et al. (2015, p. 191), for instance, showed that over the course of time up until 2014, the beginning of the PEGIDA protests, satisfaction with democracy had increased if anything, both with

---

[47] The organisers of the PEGIDA demonstrations repeatedly made it clear that, from their point of view, the protest should not be directed towards refugees and asylum seekers, instead it should mainly be directed towards the failing political and media elite. The background to these statements was violent protests, which had been indirectly associated with PEGIDA, against planned preliminary reception centres for asylum seekers.

Support for democracy in eastern and western Germany 1991–2014

Compilation of the results of various representative surveys

Figures in percent

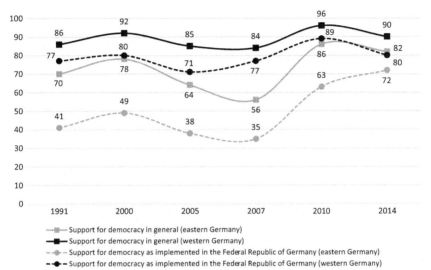

- ━■━ Support for democracy in general (eastern Germany)
- ━■━ Support for democracy in general (western Germany)
- ━◆━ Support for democracy as implemented in the Federal Republic of Germany (eastern Germany)
- ━◆━ Support for democracy as implemented in the Federal Republic of Germany (western Germany)

Fig. 5.23   Support for democracy in eastern and western Germany

regard to democracy as an abstract idea, and also in terms of its concrete implementation in the Federal Republic (Fig. 5.23).[48]

As far as the appraisal of parties and politicians is concerned, however, studies repeatedly point to what is perceived to be inadequate "closeness to the public", insufficient feedback related to the genuine wishes and opinions of citizens (responsivity) as well as a relatively low degree of confidence in parties and politicians. Holtmann et al. (2015, p. 148ff.) state that in particular eastern Germans are here "consistently

[48] Own representation of the compilation in Holtmann et al. (2015, p. 191). The support was determined using a three-step scale. The percentages shown in this figure refer to the answer "Democracy is the best form of government" in response to the question "Do you believe that democracy is the best form of government, or in your opinion is there a form of government that is better?" and also the answer "The democracy we have in the Federal Republic of Germany is the best form of government" in response to the question "And do you believe that the democracy we have in the Federal Republic of Germany is the best form of government or is there a form of government that is better?"

Preferences for direct and representative democracy 1991–2014

Compilation of the results of various representative surveys
Figures in percent

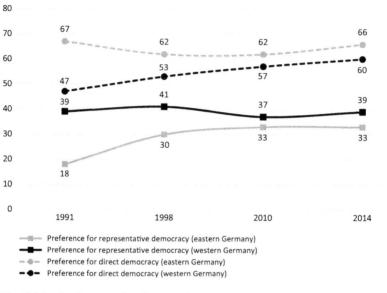

Fig. 5.24 Preferences for direct and representative democracy models in eastern and western Germany

more sceptical, more critical and more distanced" than the general population. The phenomenon that comes to light here is a preference for "direct" as opposed to representative democracy models, often expressed schematically and using generalisations. As an attitude component this preference has been stable in the German population for decades, with more or less consistently high differences in both eastern and western Germany (Fig. 5.24).[49]

[49] Own representation of the compilation in Holtmann et al. (2015, p. 192). The approval was determined by offering three alternative responses. The respondents were able to choose between the responses "I am for a representative democracy, in other words, I am for the people electing the parliament and then the parliament making the political decisions and also taking responsibility for those decisions" and "I am for a direct democracy, in other words I am for as many decisions as possible being made directly by the citizens and binding for all in referenda", as well as "don't know" (not shown).

	PEGIDA (Jan. 2015)	PEGIDA (Mai 2015)	PEGIDA (Nov.2015)	PEGIDA (Jan. 2016)	Saxony (2016)	Germany-East (Mitte 2016)	Germany-total (Mitte 2016)
	Online	Face-to-Face	postal survey	Face-to-Face	CAPI	Face-to-Face	Face-to-Face
Satisfaction with democracy							
Satisfaction with democracy as an idea in general	78,1	74,0	63,4	–	83	94,2	94,2
Satisfaction with democracy regarding the way it works in practice in the Federal Republic of Germany	5,5	3,0	1,3	2,6	51	44,3	54,1

Fig. 5.25   Satisfaction with democracy among Dresden PEGIDA demonstrators

Corresponding questions about satisfaction with democracy were also put to the Dresden PEGIDA participants. There were high levels of support for the idea of democracy. However, with regard to the specific example of a democratic order as practised in the Federal Republic, with its political system characterised by parliamentary representation, the respondents judged things quite differently. Here a dissatisfaction on the part of the PEGIDA participants emerged which differed strikingly even from the typically low figures established for eastern Germany (Fig. 5.25).[50]

[50] Own compilation of the findings on PEGIDA from Walter (19.01.2015: figures for January 2015), Patzelt and Eichardt (2015, pp. 74, 76: figures for May 2015), Finkbeiner et al. (31.01.2016: figures for November 2015) and Patzelt and Klose (2016, p. 188: figures for January 2016). The comparative figures come from Infratest dimap (2016, p.19) and from Decker et al. (2016, p. 52f.). The wording of the questions about satisfaction with democracy in the various studies was at times different and data were collected using a three- or five-step scale. The percentages shown in Fig. 5.25 represent the sum of the possible responses that indicate explicit agreement. In the case of Walter (19.01.2015) the specific questions were: "How satisfied are you with democracy... as an idea in general" and "How satisfied are you with democracy... as it works in the Federal Republic of Germany?" Patzelt and Eichardt (2015) and also Patzelt and Klose (2016) asked about "a general attitude towards democracy". Of the two possible answers the figures shown here are those for "Democracy tends to be something advantageous". With regard to "satisfaction with democracy as it works in Germany" the figure refers to "satisfied", which is the relevant answer out of the three possible responses provided. In the Saxony Monitor (Infratest dimap 2016) it

This result was also confirmed by Vorländer et al. (2015, p. 62ff.), because when respondents were asked about their motivation for protesting more than a fifth (21.2 per cent) named dissatisfaction with the political system of the Federal Republic as a reason for participating in PEGIDA. As a first step those representing this position often sweepingly referred to "the policies", "the politicians" or "the system", but then also criticised rather specific aspects—such as the obligation for parliamentarians to obey a party whip as well as the absence of possibilities for citizens to exercise direct political influence through participatory instruments on a national level. In autumn 2015 even more than 90 per cent of the demonstrators who were asked were of the opinion that the political system in the Federal Republic needs more such "direct democratic" elements (Finkbeiner et al. 31.01.2016, p. 33). This stance was also expressed in a striking distrust of the political institutions. Just a fraction of the PEGIDA participants indicated that they trusted political institutions like the Federal Chancellor (4.4 per cent), the Federal Government (3.2 per cent), the Bundestag (3.5 per cent), the Federal President (6.6 per cent), the parties (0.9 per cent) or the European Union (4.4 per cent)—figures which once again were clearly below that of the total population.[51] Trust in intermediary entities– such as parties and the media—was particularly low. A clear majority of the surveyed PEGIDA participants neither showed any kind of attachment to a political party nor sympathy or an affinity for one (cf. Fig. 4.12 above).

Against the backdrop of the ideas expressed at PEGIDA events about the incorrect implementation and inadequate "effectivity" of democratic decisions it seems plausible to assume that PEGIDA supporters were also open to more strongly authoritarian-orientated political models. Consequently, their attitudes towards democracy were also frequently

---

was asked: "Do you consider democracy to be a good form of government in general or a not so good form of government?" and "Looking at the way democracy works in practice in the Federal Republic of Germany are you overall very satisfied, quite satisfied, quite dissatisfied or very dissatisfied?" In the Mitte Study by Decker et al. (2016) respondents were asked general questions as to their "satisfaction with democracy as an idea" and "with democracy as it works in the Federal Republic of Germany".

[51] Walter (19.01.2015). The percentages represent the respective proportion of people who expressed their level of confidence in the corresponding institution on a five-step scale with the responses "a lot" or "utmost". For the German population's confidence in the political institutions of the Federal Republic cf. the survey series GGSS (GESIS 2017).

associated with the forms of upbringing and socialisation in the former German Democratic Republic (GDR). Making use of Horkheimer and Adorno (1952) the authors of the Leipzig Mitte Studies have, for example, painted the picture of a "post-authoritarian destructive character type" and thereby attempted a social psychological explanation of the prevalence of right-wing extremist, xenophobic and anti-democratic attitudes in the eastern German population.[52] According to the results from empirical attitude research, authoritarian attitudes are indeed still widespread in the population (Decker et al. 2016, p. 56), but an "authoritarian legacy" from the GDR past—as an "overhang" of attitudes which range from being critical to being dismissive of the representative democracy of the Basic Law—can barely be detected any more. The study Deutschland 2014, commissioned by the Federal government, came to the conclusion "that the initial post-reunification differences between the East and the West when it came to attitudes towards democracy [...] have become considerably smaller" (Holtmann et al. 2015, p. 200). This, according to Everhard Holtmann, Oscar W. Gabriel and their co-authors, applies not only to the steadily growing proportion of the population that has grown up after 1990, but also for the older generations that were socialised in the GDR-system. Other surveys have established that identification with the Grundgesetz, in particular with regard to its guaranteed values of freedom and the rule of law, is by now also strongly pronounced in eastern Germany (Vorländer 2009, p. 15).[53]

In the case of PEGIDA, however, it became apparent that it is still a long way away from applying to everyone. Even though the vast majority of the Dresden demonstrators rejected the return to a more strongly authoritarian system, the surveys of the demonstrators did reveal that here there were widespread notions of democracy which were certainly still guided by experiences from GDR times. The opinions, motivations and demands expressed by the protestors reflected in this context a highly simplified and technocratic concept of democracy. It was connected with a job profile for those in positions of political responsibility that worked according to the simple scheme "we ask and order—you answer and deliver". There often seemed to be a limited

---

[52] The argument is that experiences of arbitrary violence during childhood express themselves later in the form of violence against marginalised groups and those who are weaker (Decker et al. 2014, pp. 9–10).

[53] Here more than two-thirds of the respondents in eastern Germany and even about three-quarters of the respondents in western Germany declared that they were "proud" of the *Grundgesetz*.

awareness of the fact that processes of democratic opinion-forming and decision-making are complex, time-consuming and require a strong willingness to compromise. Instead, on the one hand, concepts of democracy were revealed that were shaped by own life experiences in different political systems and possibly borrowed from the simplifying schemes of Marxist-Leninist ideologemes as well as the "submissions system" (*Eingabewesen*) known from GDR times.[54] On the other hand, the notions expressed at PEGIDA events were also characterised by the technical intelligence of academics educated in engineering and natural sciences, who—often also socialised in the former GDR—evaluated political processes above all according to the stringent dualisms of "right and wrong", "cause and effect" or "problem and solution".

As far as the content of the specific criticism of policies expressed by the PEGIDA demonstrators was concerned, it was above all shaped by recent experiences with the immigration, refugee and asylum policies. Complaints were made about unclear issues to do with decision-making, financing and jurisdiction, about decisions made at short notice which were described as being "without any alternative"[55] as well as about a lack of communication and insufficient involvement of local citizens (Vorländer et al. 2015, p. 64). In this context the demonstrators identified a full-blown "fear of contact" on the part of the competent state and local politicians, who by then had often refused conversations about the topic area "asylum and refugees", because from their point of view there was little to be gained from discussions which would be highly conflictual, laden with emotions and with often uncontrollable dynamics. In this way a necessary wider public debate had possibly been thwarted for too long, which had fuelled the need to protest even more. With regard to the criticisms of this kind raised by 33.8 per cent of the respondents in total in the study by Vorländer, Herold and Schäller, a breakdown by age seems sensible. In Fig. 5.26[56] this is shown together with the existing xenophobic feelings of resentment and their frequency.

[54] The term *Eingabewesen* refers to the practice known from the GDR of sending a pleading letter to the state or party secretary assumed to be responsible in the event of problems and then hoping for extraordinary decisions or arbitrary acts of mercy. Of course, this notion presupposed a certain undermining of rule-of-law structures so that the usual procedures in a specific individual case could be circumvented by people with the relevant powers to do so.

[55] This referred to Chancellor Angela Merkel who justified important political decisions and agendas like the bailout of banks or Germany's nuclear phase-out by declaring them to be logical, rational and "without any alternative" (*alternativlos*).

[56] Shown is the respective share, as a percentage, of all people in an age group who answered the open question as to their motivation for participating in a PEGIDA demonstration by expressing "Criticism of the immigration, integration or asylum policy" or "Fundamental reservations towards immigrants and asylum seekers". Cf. the group of

Criticism of immigration policy and feelings of resentment by age group
Figures in percent

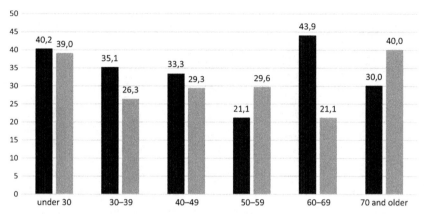

Shares of those who mentioned a "Dissatisfaction with immigration, integration or asylum policy" within different age groups; N = 397.

Shares of those who mentioned "Fundamental reservations against immigrants and asylum-seekers" within different age groups; N = 397.

Fig. 5.26   Criticism of policy and feelings of resentment in the area of immigration, integration and asylum policy among Dresden PEGIDA demonstrators by age group. Source: Own survey (Vorländer et al. 2015)

It was found that criticism of the current immigration, integration and asylum policy was strongest amongst the 60 to 69 year olds and also amongst those under 30. With regard to reservations towards refugees, immigrants or asylum seekers possibly being expressed at the same time, however, the first named age group was the very group for which the lowest frequency was found. This kind of sentiment was instead expressed most by the two outermost age groups (i.e. by those under 30 and those over 70). A breakdown according to the average monthly net income of the respondents, however, gave the picture shown in Fig. 5.27.[57] Based

responses "Fundamental reservations" in Fig. 4.9. The group of responses "Criticism of the immigration, integration or asylum policy" presented in Fig. 5.26 combines all the forms of criticism of immigration policy, integration policy, refugee policy and asylum policy that were expressed. However, here no significant correlations can be derived on the basis of the underlying data. This also applies to Figs. 5.27 to 5.29, which follow.

[57] Shown is the respective percentage share of all people in an income group, who in response to the open question as to their motivation for participating in a PEGIDA demonstration answered by expressing "Criticism of the immigration, integration or asylum policy"

Criticism of immigration policy and feelings of resentment by income group
Figures in percent

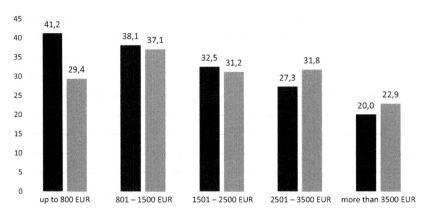

■ Shares of those who mentioned a "Dissatisfaction with immigration, integration or asylum policy" within different income groups; N = 397.

▨ Shares of those who mentioned "Fundamental reservations against immigrants and asylum-seekers" within different income groups; N = 397.

Fig. 5.27 Criticism of policy and feelings of resentment in the area of immigration, integration and asylum policy among Dresden PEGIDA demonstrators according to income group. Source: Own survey (Vorländer et al. 2015)

on the data it seemed that with regard to asylum policy the impression of powerlessness was a noticeable reason for protest, in particular in the lower income groups, suggesting that in this group fears of being socially disadvantaged compared to the "foreigners" also played a role.

The, at times aggressively expressed, criticism of the representative decision-making procedures of constitutional democracy at PEGIDA demonstrations was directed not only at policies or the existing form of democracy, but also at the institutions, procedures and players involved in the forming of public opinion. Many journalists who were at the PEGIDA rallies experienced this directly.[58] The criticism of "the media" and the structure of the public discourse were expressed both in general and also

or "Fundamental reservations towards immigrants and asylum seekers". Cf. the previous figure note.

[58] Cf. only the attempts to disrupt the live coverage of a ZDF news team in Dresden on 12.01.2015 made by Stéphane Simon, a PEGIDA speaker for a time (Thurau 12.01.2015).

with reference to specific policy areas—in Vorländer et al. (2015) more than a third (34.5 percent) of respondents did so (cf. Fig. 4.9 above). Completely in keeping with the vilifying slogan "Lying press" scores were settled with the work of journalists being criticised in an often severe and generalising manner. Those responsible in newsrooms were, according to the portrayal indicated by many respondents, "conceited, selfish and arrogant, had lost all contact with 'reality in Germany' and were instead following their own political agenda". Against this background claims were often made of a close interconnection between the political and media elites, independent journalism was called into question and especially public sector broadcasters were accused of being corrupted by "the system"—a view which was compressed into the term "system media". Within the scope of the resulting distortion of the coverage, according to the opinion of many PEGIDA participants who were asked, the political actions of the government are put in an artificially favourable light (as currently with the issues of asylum policy, the integration of Muslim immigrants or the war in Ukraine), and the media agenda is filled with pseudo problems ensuring that the genuine concerns of the "ordinary citizen" are no longer taken up in political discourse (Vorländer et al. 2015, p. 65ff.).[59]

A breakdown of the findings from Vorländer et al. (2015) according to income groups and level of education suggest that this criticism of a biased media was prevalent in particular among the more highly educated and wealthier PEGIDA participants (Figs. 5.28 and 5.29).[60,61] To all appearances it was thus not the "underprivileged" and "poorly educated" demonstrators, but in fact also the well-off and well-informed readers and viewers of the news, who were complaining about a lack of representation of their political views and politico-cultural attitudes in the mass media.

Added to this was the media coverage about PEGIDA itself. It caused a vast majority of the demonstrators to themselves feel like victims of distorted and biased reporting. In the survey by Patzelt and Eichardt (2015, p. 40), for instance, only 5.0 per cent of the respondents were of the opin-

---

[59] Media analyses have indeed come to the conclusion that media coverage of German policy during the refugee crisis was one-sided and rather uncritical (cf. Haller 2017).

[60] Shown for each income group is the respective percentage share of people who made statements critical of the media in response to an open question about their motivation for participation in a PEGIDA demonstration. Cf. the group of responses "Media" in Fig. 4.9.

[61] Shown here are the highest educational qualification and the respective percentage share of people who made statements critical of the media in response to an open question about their motivation for participation in a PEGIDA demonstration. Cf. the group of responses "Media" in Fig. 4.9.

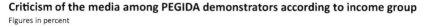

Criticism of the media among PEGIDA demonstrators according to income group
Figures in percent

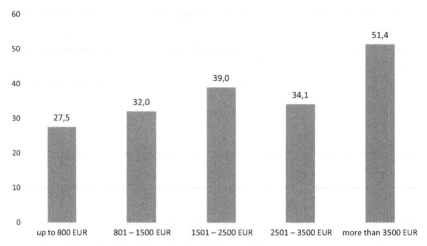

▩ *Shares of those who criticised the media and public discourse in the respective income group; N = 397.*

Fig. 5.28 Criticism of the media and public discourse among Dresden PEGIDA demonstrators according to income group. Source: Own survey (Vorländer et al. 2015)

ion that the media representation was balanced (Fig. 5.30),[62] in Vorländer et al. (2015, p. 66) nearly a fifth of respondents (18.4 per cent) named such a perceived "defamation" of the Dresden demonstrators in the media as an immediate reason for their own participation in PEGIDA.

With this, the PEGIDA demonstrators mirrored a mistrust of the media which is widespread in the German population. In response to the question as to whether they would personally endorse the PEGIDA slogan "Lying press", in Decker et al. (2016, p. 63) well over half of the representatively surveyed German respondents expressed at least partial agreement (Fig. 5.31).[63]

This finding of an, at times, aggressively expressed criticism of the media is not new and it can by all means be seen to be part of a general

---

[62] Own representation of the findings from Patzelt and Klose (2016, p. 199).

[63] Own representation of the findings in Decker et al. (2016, p. 63). The specific question asked was: "When you think of newspapers, radio and television in Germany, would you personally speak of the 'lying press'?"

Criticism of media among PEGIDA demonstrators according to level of education
Figures in percent

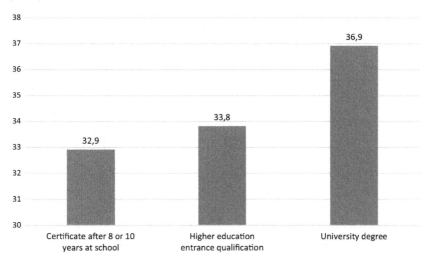

Shares of those who criticised the media and public discourse in the respective level of education; N = 397.

Fig. 5.29 Criticism of the media and public discourse among Dresden PEGIDA demonstrators according to educational qualification. Source: Own survey (Vorländer et al. 2015)

development. It seems that in the age of Facebook, Twitter and the like, there is no longer "an understanding, which had long existed, that the media are something like a protection force for the citizens and for democracy as a whole" (Hamann 26.06.2015, p. 8f.). Instead, media representatives and journalists appear to have long since become an "inherent part of the very elite which is regarded with general suspicion", the order of the day for journalists now includes "readers in the mood for a lynching", "cyberbullying", "sudden onslaughts of criticism", "orgies of outrage" and even death threats—as a rule initiated by people who hide behind the cover of an alias on the internet. As a "fifth power" the internet in particular has had an effect which was unforeseen, because here "serious research and conspiracy theories spread at the same rate and lay the same claim to truth". Accordingly, a representative survey conducted by the weekly newspaper *Die Zeit* showed that across Germany 60 per cent of respondents had "little" or "no trust at all" in reporting in the media. The most frequent accusations included suspected misinformation and manipulation

Appraisal of the media coverage of PEGIDA in the population
Agreement with the statement: "The media coverage of PEGIDA is balanced"
Figures in percent

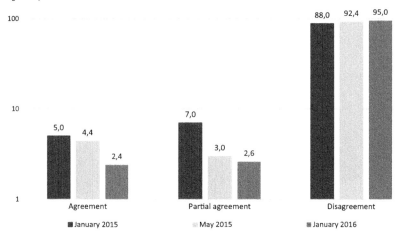

Fig. 5.30　Appraisal of the media coverage of PEGIDA

Agreement in the German population with the PEGIDA accusation of the lying press
Figures in percent

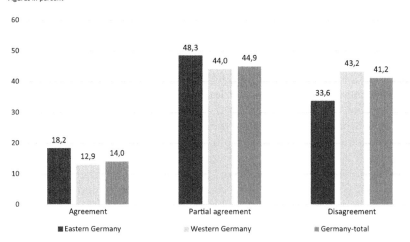

Fig. 5.31　Agreement in the German population with the PEGIDA accusation of the lying press

(27 per cent), the allegation of bias (20 per cent), poor research (15 per cent) and also a suspected lack of independence (10 per cent)—all allegations, which could also be in heard in this form at PEGIDA events.[64]

5.6   POPULISM

The attitudes towards politics, democracy and media which were observed in the PEGIDA movement indicate the phenomenon of populism, for which there are numerous definitions. Beyond attempts to describe a coherent and complete doctrine with an essentialistic determination of certain characteristics, an assessment now prevails which understands populism in terms of heuristic descriptive semantics as a set of features that come together differently according to the context. Regardless of whether populism is thereby seen as an ideology, a mentality or a strategy for the acquisition, exercise and retention of power,[65] the central axis of populistic phenomena is constituted by a distinction between "the elite" and the "people" as two homogenous and antagonistic groups. "People", which is highlighted as being positive, conveys on the one hand the polemic contrast of "below" and "above", appeals for the political primacy of "the many" over "the few" and emphasises the imagined collective singular of an identity-building community. On the other hand, the term "people" acts above all also as a cipher for the romanticising utopia and higher dignity of a realm of the self-evident (Edmund Husserl).[66] The distinction between "the" people and "the" elite can be made in various dimensions: *spatially*, as the contrast between a (corrupt) centre of power and an

[64] Source: Infratest Dimap, survey period 04–06.05.2015. Cf. https://www.infratest-dimap.de/umfragen-analysen/bundesweit/umfragen/aktuell/wenig-vertrauen-in-medien-berichterstattung/ (Accessed 3.07.2017).

[65] Cf. Priester (2012, p. 3f.), Vorländer (2011, p. 188). In the sense of a strategy, populism is defined as "a mass movement led by an outsider or maverick seeking to gain or maintain power by using anti-establishment appeals and plebiscitarian linkages" (Barr 2009, p. 44). As a construct, on the other hand, the term means "an ideology that considers society to be ultimately separated into two homogeneous and antagonistic groups, 'the pure people' versus 'the corrupt elite', and which argues that politics should be an expression of the *volonté générale* (general will) of the people" (Mudde 2004, p. 543). However, such attempts at a definition with intent to generalise—even in the case of those declared to be minimal definitions—quickly reach their empirical limits. For common definitions of populism in the media cf. Bale et al. (2011).

[66] In German this is mainly expressed by the term *Lebenswelt* (lifeworld). Cf. also the term "heartland" used by Taggart (2004, p. 274ff.).

(unspoilt) periphery, *temporally*, to distinguish between the original source of political power and the criticised forms of its misuse, *mentally*, as the exposure of the misguided intellectualism of the social knowledge elite through common sense, *morally*, as the condemnation of the corruption, self-referentiality and arrogance of the elite against the backdrop of a popular sense of truth and justice which does not require justification, *culturally*, as the positive emphasis on an unquestionable real life tradition which is however threatened by social processes of change, and lastly, *politically*, as a confrontation of the agents of economic, social or cultural paternalism with an original idea of freedom (cf. Priester 2011, p. 196, 2012, p. 5f.).

Almost all these populistic topoi were also present in PEGIDA, in speeches made, and in the statements of the demonstrators—for instance the belief that "common sense" rooted in actual real-life experiences (in everyday life, at work, in the family, in clubs or associations, etc.) is superior to the artificial reflective knowledge of the elite. In personalised form this primacy was expressed by terms such as "the average citizen", "the man in the street", "the working population" or the "common people". With typifications of this sort the PEGIDA supporters polemicised against the, in their perception, corrupt political functionary elite, the aloof influencers of moods in the media or the snooty "eggheads" in the ivory towers of science.[67] Simple lines of argument, crude generalisations and language coloured by dialect were in this context not coded as features of backwardness, educational disadvantage and social periphery, but as a sign of being down-to-earth and a display of "true proximity to the people".[68] The hostility towards elites expressed in a number of ways was generalised in the self-staging as the actual representation of the people, in a general scepticism towards intermediary structures of political opinion and interest formation (in particular parties) as well as in the call for an unfiltered articulation of political will through instruments of direct democracy.[69]

---

[67] Cf. the observation protocols of the 1st and 2nd dialogue forums "Together in Saxony" which took place on 29.01.2015 and 10.03.2015.

[68] When conducting the face-to-face interviews, Vorländer et al. (2015, p. 26) found that the establishment of contact with PEGIDA participants proved to be more successful when more colloquial language was chosen on the part of the interviewer, where possible using dialect.

[69] Cf. Sect. 5.5 above. Evidence of populist criticism of the elite is also provided by Lutz Bachmann's speeches, which tried to concentrate the rejection of the politico-cultural elite and turn it into a positive sense of community: "As one could see again brilliantly last night, […] policy experts and political scientists are experiencing a boom at the moment—and to

Against this background a more precise characterisation of the form of populism observed among PEGIDA participants makes sense. A first possible conceptual delimitation was provided by the distinction between protest and identity populism as per Pierre-André Taguieff.[70] While protest populism, as a monothematic public opposition movement that engages in concrete actions (like demonstrations, blockades, occupations, *inter alia*), is usually directed against certain political projects as well as the political-economic concentration of power suspected to be behind them, identity populism, which is predominant today, stresses a certain identity understood in a traditionalistic way and tends to indirectly engage in the debasement of "the other" with the radicalisation and essentialisation of one's own cultural affiliation. PEGIDA too should be classified as a typical example of such *identity populism*. In addition, the form of populism observed in PEGIDA was also characterised by a certain *latency*. Experience shows that populism is more about the action of certain leaders, who as "people's tribunes" manage to orchestrate the immediacy of the concerns and wishes of "the people" and thus to successfully instrumentalise these concerns and wishes. This political action is then referred to (usually with negative connotations) as "populist". As however shown, not only by PEGIDA, populist phenomena and ideologemes can also achieve effective public support, without being more or less "ignited" by figures acting demagogically.[71] If the concept of populism is turned around, then in this "passive" sense for the Dresden PEGIDA demonstrators the picture emerges of a political mentality in which defensive reactions to perceived threats to one's own cultural identity have reinforced existing conservative to ethnocentric orientations. The simultaneous complaint about political powerlessness and

recite their views en masse and as the crowning achievement of their studies to present all of us as losers with fears of social descent. [Calls of "Boo!" in the crowd] I am of the opinion that these very people are scared, scared that you all notice that you are not the losers, but that you discover your power, that people in the whole of Germany and Europe combine and become winners, [Calls of "Yes!", cheers, clapping], by you showing them who the source of all the power is [long chants of "We are the people"]. Let them chat in their talk shows, let them discuss in their political discussion groups and let them rack their brains about what they are doing wrong. They won't understand anyway. They have long since lost contact with the base and betrayed their voters [cheers and applause]." Transcript of the speech made by Lutz Bachmann on 15.12.2014.

[70] Cf. in reference to Pierre-André Taguieff: Priester (2012, p. 6f.).

[71] Although it cannot be denied that the leading figures in the PEGIDA movement had a certain charismatic effect, overall they were characterised more by a sober, not overly charismatic, manner.

insignificance fuelled these attitudes and gave them political momentum. The concept of populism in terms of heuristic descriptive semantics here identifies a particular *form* of predisposition to politico-cultural attitude patterns in the population—a predisposition which ensures that nationalistic, regional-patriotic, xenophobic orientations or those related to the strong emphasis on privileges for the long-established regional native population gain a momentum of their own in certain situations and are expressed as an eruption of public indignation, but can then just as quickly return to latency.[72] The particular *willingness*, fomented by concrete grounds, to also take this mistrust to the streets as open criticism and to emphasise it by the symbolic occupation of public space, may provide part of the answer as to why PEGIDA emerged in Saxony of all places.

In connection with the xenophobic or Islamophobic feelings of resentment that were identified, with regard to PEGIDA the term *right-wing populism* was also relevant. In discussion about the theory of democracy, populism is mainly seen to be in an antagonistic relationship with representative democracy and the values of pluralism on which it is based. In this context populists are to be understood as anti-pluralists, who present themselves as the moral identical embodiment of a people they imagine to be homogenous (Müller 2016, p. 18ff.; Plotke 1997, p. 28). Unlike left-wing populists, whose concept of community tends to be more open, right-wing populists operate with an exclusionary concept of the people that focuses on culture and ethnos. This anti-pluralistic stance results in frequently observed hostility towards the so-called intermediary institutions of constitutional democracies on the part of the populists (Mouffe 2013; Urbinati 2015). Where populists come to power they interfere with the system of institutional barriers step by step, for example by weakening the constitutional jurisdiction as in Hungary and Poland, or they exert influence on the media landscape through a rigid regulatory or licensing policy. On the other hand, if populist actors are not yet in power they construct an antagonistic relationship between themselves and the established political and social institutions. The intermediary function of these institutions in the democratic process is reinterpreted as a method of control used by the elite in order to keep the political power away from "the people". Fierce attacks are thus directed against the so-called "old parties", against "do-gooder cartels" in the trade unions and churches, and

---

[72] Following Ionescu and Gellner (1969), Karin Priester (2011, p. 196) here speaks of a "populist moment".

also against the role of democracy-forming institutions, such as schools, universities and the media (Müller 2016, p. 70ff.; Schäller 2016, p. 229f.). Not only do right-wing populists promise their supporters the abolition of this intermediary relationship between the people and political power, they also strive to make direct contact with their supporters, "the people".[73]

In empirical research on political attitudes, attempts have been made for a number of years to identify the concept of right-wing populism as a specific orientation pattern and to operationalise it by means of certain indicator statements. Klein and Heitmeyer (2012, p. 91ff.), for instance, have defined a right-wing populist orientation as a correlation context of various, but in particular, authoritarian, anti-Semitic, xenophobic and (increasingly important) Islamophobic attitudes.[74] Similarly, the author team of the Bielefeld Mitte Studies identified *group-focused enmity* as a central criterion of a right-wing populistic orientation (Küpper et al. 2015, p. 26f.). According to the theory, this is expressed "by the derogation and exclusion of cultural, ethnic and religious minorities", but also "by the rejection of the equality of homosexuals and women". Further features are said to be "right-wing, aggressive authoritarianism, which can be described as a law and order attitude", and also mistrust of democracy, nationalism and anger. A differentiation from "hard right-wing extremism" is said to be possible primarily through the much greater acceptance of violence there. On the basis of this operationalisation, these orientations—with the exception of Islamophobia—were trending downwards between 2003 and 2011 in Germany. Yet, on the other hand, in particular amongst those who according to empirical definition could be confirmed to have a "right-wing populist attitude", an increased willingness to take part in political events or demonstrations was identified (Klein and Heitmeyer 2012, pp. 94, 99). This estimation was confirmed in more recent studies. Zick (2017) showed that even after 2011 the proportion of the population with right-wing populist attitudes in Germany has not grown, but that a

---

[73] In the case of PEGIDA this can be observed in the self-made counter-public on social media, with which the organisers made themselves largely independent from the intermediary, classifying media institutions when communicating with their supporters (Cf. Sect. 1.4 in Chap. 1).

[74] In the Bielefeld series of studies on *group-focused enmity*, the term used for the group of people who agree with xenophobic, anti-Semitic, authoritarian and also Islamophobic statements is "right-wing populist potential" as the group is seen to be made up of possible supporters of a right-wing populist movement (Heitmeyer 2011, p.11; Klein and Heitmeyer 2012, p. 91ff.; Schaefer et al. 2002, p. 103).

certain radicalisation and increased willingness of these people to participate in protest events and demonstrations can be observed.

The emergence of right-wing populist attitudes and political phenomena in modern democracies is also attributed to the growing of a specific feeling of estrangement, in which sections of the population have got the impression that they have lost any connection to a class of apparently autistic acting functionaries in politics, media and society. Long-term developments like the processes of globalisation, specialisation and international integration could also be responsible here, as could extraordinary events, like the global *financial crisis* in 2008 or the *refugee crisis* in 2015, which dramatically showed the limits of nation states' control. In their data collection in 2010 the authors of the long-term study of *group-focused enmity* had, for instance, established that the statement "People like me have no influence on what the government does anyway" was affirmed most of all by those people who saw themselves threatened by a crisis. Among this group the proportion of those who agreed was 73.5 per cent, for others it was only 54.6 per cent (Heitmeyer 2011, p. 27).[75] It follows that in the political sphere a perception of an "emptying" of democracy has been increasingly observed, in other words a loss of confidence in politics coupled with a simultaneous increase in perceived powerlessness.[76] At the end of 2011, the authors of the GFE Study predicted that these were initial warning signals, because this could result in susceptibility to attempted populist mobilisations. They indicated that, especially in the case of people with a right-wing populist orientation, political alienation has increased significantly since 2007, recognisable for instance by approval rates of as high as 92.2 per cent for the statement "People like me have no influence on what the government does anyway". Here again, it could be observed that the willingness of these "estranged" people to take part in protest events like demonstrations had increased dramatically during the investigation period: from 29.7 per cent in 2009 to 41.9 per cent in 2011 (Heitmeyer 2011, pp. 12ff., 17).

On the other hand, however, attitudes in the population that are critical of the elite seem to have been sinking for years. In 2016 only about 60 per

[75] For the connection between right-wing populism, feelings of being disadvantaged, and criticism of democracy cf. Klein et al. (2009, pp. 93–112).

[76] For the concept of the emptying of democracy cf. Heitmeyer and Mansel (2003).

cent of all Germans felt they could attribute functional shortcomings to the political parties or accuse the politicians of -rom the survey series on *group-focused enmity* in 2003 that figure was still well above 80 per cent (Fig. 5.32).[77]

In the surveys of PEGIDA demonstrators the perception of a great distance between "the people" and "politicians" nevertheless stood out in a striking way. Here impressions of a "lack of contact with reality" and "aloofness" of those in positions of political responsibility came together with vague ideas about the "true" will of the citizens or the people being unable to come to the fore in the representative system of the current democracy, instead being suppressed by special interests and lobby groups (Vorländer et al. 2015, p. 63). It was striking that, for the most part, the criticism directed at the political procedures, decisions and decision-makers as well as the actors and mechanisms of published opinion, neither

	Germany (GMF 2003)	Germany (GMF 2008)	Germany (Mitte-B 2014)	Germany (Mitte-B 2016)
	CATI	CATI	CATI	CATI
Criticism of democracy as a criticism of the elite				
The democratic parties discuss everything to death and do not solve the problems.	89,3	74,1	73,1	58,3
Politicians circumvent existing laws when it is to their advantage.	89,7	–	75	63,5
Politicians believe they have more rights than ordinary citizens.	89,5	82,1	75,6	63,3
Ultimately, the economy decides in our country and not politics.	83,4	80,3	74,6	–

Fig. 5.32 Attitudes critical of the elite in the German population

[77] Sources of the data: Heitmeyer and Mansel (2003, p. 43); Zick and Klein (2014, p. 89f.); Küpper et al. (2015, p. 33); Zick et al. (2016c, p. 117). Sources of the findings: about PEGIDA: (a) Patzelt and Klose (2016, p. 194); (b) Rucht et al. (2015, p. 27); about the PEGIDA sympathisers in the population: Infratest Dimap (06.01.2015); about Germany 2014: Küpper et al. (2015, p. 37); (c) these data come from Infratest Dimap (06.01.2015) and were collected at the beginning of January 2015; about Saxony 2016: Infratest dimap (2016, p. 25); about Germany 2016: Decker (2016, p. 54); Zick et al. (2016c, p. 120). The percentages shown represent the combined share of all answers which indicated an explicit agreement with the respective statements.

	PEGIDA-demonstrators (Jan. 2015)	PEGIDA-sympathisers (Jan. 2015)	PEGIDA-demonstrators (Jan. 2016)	Germany-population (2014)	Saxony-population (2016)	Germany-population (2016)
Feelings of political alienation						
I feel represented by our politicians and parties.	2,1 [a)]	–	1,8	–	–	–
People like me have no influence on what the government does anyway.	68,9 [b)]	85	–	64 [c)]	71	72,7
I consider it pointless to be politically active.	–	–	–	–	–	60,0
The interests of the citizens are not sufficiently taken into account by the politicians.	–	12	–	21 [c)]	–	–
In Germany one cannot say anything critical about foreigners without immediately being called a racist.	–	–	–	58	–	54,9
In Germany one can no longer freely express an opinion without getting in trouble.	–	–	–	28	–	28,0

Fig. 5.33 Feelings of political alienation among Dresden PEGIDA demonstrators

targeted concrete ideas about necessary changes nor alternative political models, instead it rather expressed a diffuse collective state of mind. This state of mind was able to be identified as a general feeling of political powerlessness, a feeling of "not being heard" or "not being taken seriously", thus as a form of political alienation. In the surveys by Patzelt, for example, on a regular basis only about 2.0 per cent of the PEGIDA supporters who were surveyed were prepared to agree with the statement that one feels represented by "our politicians and parties", over 90 per cent strongly disputed this (Patzelt and Klose 2016, p. 194). In the study by Rucht et al. (2015, p. 27) almost 70 per cent of the surveyed PEGIDA participants indicated that they had no influence whatsoever on government policy. The figures from a survey conducted by the opinion research institute Infratest dimap among PEGIDA sympathisers in the population at the beginning of January 2015 were even higher (Fig. 5.33).

These high values were remarkable. The comparative data in Fig. 5.33 also reveal that in the German population there truly is a widespread feeling of being domineered over by political, social and media elites. In 2016 a large proportion of Germans were of the opinion that one could "no longer freely express one's opinion without getting in trouble"—in

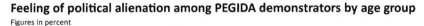

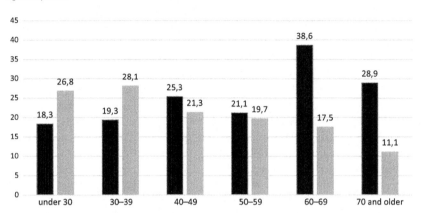

■ *Shares of those who mentioned a "general distance" between politicians and the people in individual age groups;*
   N = 397.

▨ *Shares of those who mentioned a "dissatisfaction with the political system of the Federal Republic" in individual*
   age groups; N = 397.

Fig. 5.34   Feeling of political alienation among Dresden PEGIDA demonstrators according to age group

particular about foreigners—or "immediately being called a racist". The widespread feeling among PEGIDA participants that there is distance between the people on the one side, and the political and media elites on the other, can be broken down according to the age group of those interviewed using the data from Vorländer et al. (2015) (Fig. 5.34).[78]

It was, above all, the over 60-year-old interviewees who expressed an impression of a great distance between members of the public and politicians. This is probably the generation which, when German reunification occurred, at between 35 and 45 years old, had already established a life for themselves and already achieved some success, and which would have had the most difficulty coping with a professional, political and social reorientation after

---

[78] Source: Own survey (Vorländer et al. 2015). Shown for each age group is the respective percentage share of people who answered the open question as to their motivation for participating in a PEGIDA demonstration by expressing a "general perception of distance between the people and politicians" or a "dissatisfaction with the political system". Cf. the answer categories concerning dissatisfaction with politics in Fig. 4.10. However, no significant correlations can be derived on the basis of the underlying data. This also applies to Fig. 5.35 which follows.

1989. It is also the generation which—in comparison with their West German peers—should now actually look back on a long and successful employment history and—having reached correspondingly influential positions—should be leading the public debate in their home regions. The fact that a great number of 55- to 70-year-old former East Germans were unable to do so because of numerous interruptions in their lives, could help to explain an inner attitude which is still very reserved when it comes to the political culture of the new Federal Republic, its discursive routines, and its rules of the game in the media. As far as criticism of Germany's political system is concerned, however, this was less pronounced in the older age groups, instead it was greatest specifically among those younger PEGIDA demonstrators who were not socialised in the GDR.

What comes to light in a breakdown according to income groups is also noteworthy. It can be seen here that criticism of the system and a feeling of alienation were strongly pronounced in particular among the interviewees with higher incomes (Fig. 5.35).[79]

Feeling of political alienation among PEGIDA demonstrators by income group
Figures in percent

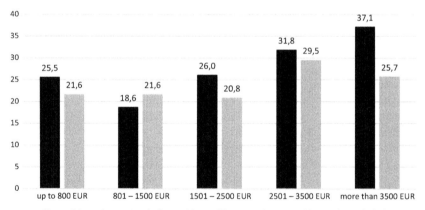

■ Shares of those who mentioned a "general distance" between politicians and the people in individual income groups; N = 397.

▨ Shares of those who mentioned a "dissatisfaction with the political system of the Federal Republic" in individual income groups; N = 397.

Fig. 5.35 Feelings of political alienation among Dresden PEGIDA demonstrators according to income group

[79] Source: See previous figure note. Cf. also Canovan (1981), Vorländer (2011, p. 187ff.), Vorländer et al. (2016a, p. 145ff.).

This indicates that a group of well-educated and well-paid high achievers were also among those who felt politically powerless and saw themselves as divorced from important decisions. A similarity here to the findings of the Bielefeld GFE Studies is striking here, for the researchers there had also observed that, since 2009, there had been a significant rise in right-wing populistic attitudes, above all in the higher income groups (Heitmeyer 2010, p. 29).

In general the role of populist tendencies, movements or parties in a democratic order is to be seen as mixed. On the one hand, they can be interpreted as a danger for democracy or as a symptom of its ongoing degeneration because they tend to relate to the principles of representation, finding compromises and separation of powers in a pathological way. On the other hand, however, populist protest also helps to make something visible. It displays deeper social and political lines of conflict which are yet to attract any attention. In this sense the PEGIDA demonstrations also had a direct impact on the political agenda in Germany. Furthermore, populist movements can also promote the inclusion of sections of the population which were previously marginalised and which feel excluded, force the responsivity of the political elite and thus increase the representativity of the political system. Their waves of outrage which flare up are then to be understood as a kind of "rejuvenation of democracy"—as a call to deliver on the promise of popular participation. In this sense, the PEGIDA demonstrations were also a moment of direct participation, of the kind which invigorates representative structures and breathes new life into a democracy which has lost all dynamism. They were to be understood as a chance to "politically [activate] sections of the population, which were apathetic and passive—even if the price was the mobilisation of anger, indignation and other 'passions'".[80] It is doubtful, however, whether the politicisation and polarisation triggered by PEGIDA and the AfD in Germany will actually have this kind of effect since right-wing populist trends are not only a symptom but also an intensifier of a crisis of representative democracy.

[80] Priester (2012, p. 6).

REFERENCES

Backes, Uwe. 2001. Gestalt und Bedeutung des intellektuellen Rechtsextremismus in Deutschland. *Aus Politik und Zeitgeschichte* 46: 24–30.

Backes, Uwe. 2013. Rechtsextremismus in der Mitte der Gesellschaft? Paradoxie und triste Banalität eines Gemeinplatzes alarmistischer Zeitdiagnostik. In *Rechtsextremismus zwischen "Mitte der Gesellschaft" und Gegenkultur. Tagungsband zur Fachtagung des Verfassungsschutzes der Länder Sachsen und Brandenburg am 28. Januar 2013 in Dresden,* ed. Landesamt für Verfassungsschutz Sachsen, 29–42. Dresden: Initial Werbung & Verlag.

Bale, Tim, Stijn van Kessel, and Paul Taggart. 2011. Thrown Around with Abandon? Popular Understandings of Populism as Conveyed by the Print Media. A UK Case Study. *Acta Politica* 46 (2): 111–131.

Barr, Robert R. 2009. Populists, Outsiders and Anti-Establishment Politics. *Party Politics* 15 (1): 29–48.

Best, Heinrich, Steffen Niehoff, Axel Salheiser, and Katja Salomo. 2014. *Die Thüringer als Europäer. Ergebnisse des Thüringen-Monitors 2014.* Thüringer Staatskanzlei Online. Accessed 3 July 2017. http://www.thueringen.de/mam/th1/tsk/thuringen-monitor_2014.pdf

Best, Heinrich, Steffen Niehoff, Axel Salheiser, and Lars Vogel. 2016. *Gemischte Gefühle: Thüringen nach der "Flüchtlingskrise". Ergebnisse des Thüringen-Monitors 2016.* Thüringer Staatskanzlei Online. Accessed 3 July 2017. http://www.thueringen.de/mam/th1/tsk/thuringen-monitor_2016_mit_anhang.pdf

Best, Heinrich, and Katja Salomo. 2014. *Güte und Reichweite der Messung des Rechtsextremismus im Thüringen Monitor 2000–2014.* Thüringer Staatskanzlei Online. Accessed 3 July 2017. http://www.thueringen.de/mam/th1/tsk/thuringen-monitor_gute_und_reichweite_der_messung_des_rechtsextremismus.pdf

Canovan, Margaret. 1981. *Populism.* New York: Harcourt Brace Jovanovich.

Decker, Oliver, and Elmar Brähler. 2006. *Vom Rand zur Mitte. Rechtsextreme Einstellungen und Einflussfaktoren in Deutschland.* Berlin: Friedrich-Ebert-Stiftung.

———. 2008. *Bewegung in der Mitte. Rechtsextreme Einstellungen in Deutschland mit einem Vergleich von 2002 bis 2008 und der Bundesländer.* Berlin: Friedrich-Ebert-Stiftung.

Decker, Oliver, Johannes Kiess, and Elmar Brähler. 2013. *Rechtsextremismus der Mitte. Eine sozialpsychologische Gegenwartsdiagnose.* Gießen: Psychosozial-Verlag.

———. 2014. *Die stabilisierte Mitte. Rechtsextreme Einstellungen in Deutschland 2014.* Universität Leipzig. Accessed 3 July 2017. http://www.qucosa.de/fileadmin/data/qucosa/documents/14490/Mitte_Leipzig_Internet.pdf

———. 2015a. Die Untersuchung 2014—Starke Wirtschaft, gefestigte Mitte. In *Rechtsextremismus der Mitte und sekundärer Autoritarismus,* ed. Oliver Decker, Johannes Kiess, and Elmar Brähler, 35–69. Gießen: Psychosozial-Verlag.

————. 2015b. Rechtsextreme Einstellungen in den Bundesländern. In *Rechtsextremismus der Mitte und sekundärer Autoritarismus*, ed. Oliver Decker, Johannes Kiess, and Elmar Brähler, 71–80. Gießen: Psychosozial-Verlag.

Decker, Oliver, Johannes Kiess, Eva Eggers, and Elmar Brähler. 2016. Die "Mitte"-Studie 2016: Methode, Ergebnisse und Langzeitverlauf. In *Die Enthemmte Mitte. Autoritäre und rechtsextreme Einstellung in Deutschland*, ed. Oliver Decker, Johannes Kiess, and Elmar Brähler, 23–66. Gießen: Psychosozial-Verlag.

Decker, Oliver, Benjamin Schilling, Johannes Kiess, and Elmar Brähler. 2012. Islamfeindschaft und Islamkritik. In *Die Mitte im Umbruch. Rechtsextreme Einstellungen in Deutschland 2012*, ed. Oliver Decker, Johannes Kiess, and Elmar Brähler, 86–101. Berlin: Dietz.

Eichstädt, Sven. 13.01.2015. Anti-Islam-Demo: Pegida-Anhänger ignorieren Strategieschwenk ihrer Spitze. *Welt Online*. Accessed 3 July 2017. http://www.welt.de/politik/deutschland/article136303424/Pegida-Anhaenger-ignorieren-Strategieschwenk-ihrer-Spitze.html

Federal Ministry of the Interior. 2016. Verfassungsschutzbericht 2015. *Bundesministerium des Inneren*. Accessed 3 July 2017. https://www.verfassungsschutz.de/embed/vsbericht-2015.pdf

Finkbeiner, Florian, Julian Schenke, Katharina Trittel, Christopher Schmitz, and Stine Marg. 2016. Pegida. Aktuelle Forschungsergebnisse. *Göttinger Institut für Demokratieforschung*. Accessed 3 July 2017. http://www.demokratie-goettingen.de/blog/pegida-2016-studie

Fritsche, Immo, Janine Deppe, and Oliver Decker. 2013. Außer Kontrolle? Ethnozentrische Reaktionen und gruppenbasierte Kontrolle. In *Rechtsextremismus der Mitte. Eine sozialpsychologische Gegenwartsdiagnose*, ed. Oliver Decker, Johannes Kiess, and Elmar Brähler. Gießen: Psychosozial-Verlag.

Fröhlingsdorf, Michael. 31.01.2015. Ablehnung im Osten deutlich höher. *Der Spiegel*: 14.

GESIS—Leibniz-Institut für Sozialwissenschaften. 2017. *Allgemeine Bevölkerungsumfrage der Sozialwissenschaften ALLBUS*. Accessed 3 July 2017. https://search.gesis.org/

Grau, Andreas, Sylja Wandschneider, and Julia Marth. 2010. Gruppenbezogene Menschenfeindlichkeit und bürgerschaftliches Engagement gegen Rechtsextremismus in Dresden. In *Rechtsextreme Strukturen, Gruppenbezogene Menschenfeindlichkeit und bürgerschaftliches Engagement gegen Rechtsextremismus in der Landeshauptstadt Dresden*, ed. Wilhelm Heitmeyer. Accessed 3 July 2017. https://www.dresden.de/media/pdf/auslaender/studie_rechtsextremismus_110524.pdf.

Haller, Michael. 2017. *Die "Flüchtlingskrise" in den Medien. Tagesaktueller Journalismus zwischen Meinung und Information*. Frankfurt a. M: Otto Brenner Stiftung.

Hamann, Götz. 26.06.2015. Wer vertraut uns noch? *Zeit Online*. Accessed 3 July 2017. http://www.zeit.de/2015/26/journalismus-medienkritik-luegenpresse-vertrauen-ukraine-krise

Heitmeyer, Wilhelm. 2010. Disparate Entwicklungen in Krisenzeiten, Entsolidarisierung und Gruppenbezogene Menschenfeindlichkeit. In *Deutsche Zustände. Folge 9*, ed. Wilhelm Heitmeyer, 13–33. Frankfurt a.m.: Suhrkamp.

———. 2011. Deutsche Zustände. Das entsicherte Jahrzehnt. Presseinformation zur Präsentation der Langzeituntersuchung Gruppenbezogene Menschenfeindlichkeit. *Universität Bielefeld*. Accessed 3 July 2017. https://www.uni-bielefeld.de/ikg/Handout_Fassung_Montag_1212.pdf

———, ed. 2012a. *Deutsche Zustände. Folge 10*. Frankfurt a. M.: Suhrkamp.

———. 2012b. Gruppenbezogene Menschenfeindlichkeit (GMF) in einem entsicherten Jahrzehnt. In *Deutsche Zustände, Folge 10*, ed. Wilhelm Heitmeyer, 15–41. Frankfurt a. M.: Suhrkamp.

Heitmeyer, Wilhelm, and Jürgen Mansel. 2003. Entleerung der Demokratie. Die unübersichtlichen Folgen sind weitreichend. In *Deutsche Zustände. Folge 2*, ed. Wilhelm Heitmeyer, 35–60. Frankfurt a. M.: Suhrkamp.

Heute.de. 16.01.2016. "Islam gehört zu Deutschland": Nation gespalten. *ARD*. Accessed 3 July 2017. http://www.heute.de/islam-gehoert-zu-deutschland-nation-gespalten-nur-17-prozent-finden-pegida-gut-36757200.html

Holtmann, Everhard, Oscar W. Gabriel, Jürgen Maier, Michaela Maier, Tobias Jaeck, and Melanie Leidecker. 2015. *Deutschland 2014. 25 Jahre Friedliche Revolution und Deutsche Einheit: Ergebnisse eines Forschungsprojekts*. Bundesministerium für Wirtschaft und Energie. Accessed 3 July 2017. https://www.bmwi.de/Redaktion/DE/Publikationen/Studien/deutschland-2014-25-jahre-friedliche-revolution-und-deutsche-einheit.html

Horkheimer, Max, and Theodor W. Adorno. 1952. Vorurteil und Charakter. In *Theodor W. Adorno—Gesammelte Schriften*, ed. Rolf Tiedemann, Bd. 9.2, 360–373. Frankfurt a.M.: Suhrkamp.

Infratest Dimap. 2016. Sachsen Monitor 2016. Ergebnisbericht. *Infratest Dimap*. Accessed 3 July 2017. https://www.staatsregierung.sachsen.de/download/staatsregierung/Ergebnisbericht_Sachsen-Monitor_2016.pdf

Ionescu, Ghita, and Ernest Gellner. 1969. *Populism: Its Meanings and National Characteristics*. London: Weidenfeld and Nicolson.

Jesse, Eckhard. 2013. Mitte und Extremismus. Eine Kritik an den "Mitte"-Studien einer Leipziger Forschergruppe. In *Jahrbuch Extremismus & Demokratie*, ed. Uwe Backes, Alexander Gallus, and Eckhard Jesse, vol. 25, 13–35. Baden-Baden: Nomos.

Kailitz, Steffen. 2004. *Politischer Extremismus in der Bundesrepublik Deutschland: Eine Einführung*. Wiesbaden: VS Verlag für Sozialwissenschaften.

Kessler, Thomas, and Immo Fritsche. 2011. Ethnocentrism. In *The encyclopaedia of peace psychology*, ed. Daniel J. Christie, 425–429. Malden: Wiley-Blackwell.

Klein, Anna, Eva Groß, and Andreas Zick. 2014. Menschenfeindliche Zustände. In *Fragile Mitte, Feindselige Zustände. Rechtsextreme Einstellungen in Deutschland 2014*, ed. Andreas Zick and Anna Klein, 61–84. Bonn: Dietz Verlag.
Klein, Anna, and Wilhelm Heitmeyer. 2012. Demokratie auf dem rechten Weg? Entwicklungen rechtspopulistischer Orientierungen und politischen Verhaltens in den letzten zehn Jahren. In *Deutsche Zustände. Folge 10*, ed. Wilhelm Heitmeyer, 87–104. Frankfurt a. M.: Suhrkamp.
Klein, Anna, Beate Küpper, and Andreas Zick. 2009. Rechtspopulismus im vereinigten Deutschland als Ergebnis von Benachteiligungsgefühlen und Demokratiekritik. In *Deutsche Zustände. Folge 7*, ed. Wilhelm Heitmeyer, 93–112. Frankfurt a. M.: Suhrkamp.
Küpper, Beate, Andreas Zick, and Daniela Krause. 2015. PEGIDA in den Köpfen—Wie rechtspopulistisch ist Deutschland? In *Wut, Verachtung, Ablehnung. Rechtspopulismus in Deutschland*, ed. Andras Zick and Beate Küpper, 21–43. Berlin: Dietz.
Meier, Albrecht, and Martin Niewendick. 09.12.2015. Kundgebung der Islam-Hasser in Dresden. Innenminister de Maizière: "Pegida ist eine Unverschämtheit". *Tagesspiegel Online*. Accessed 3 July 2017. http://www.tagesspiegel.de/politik/kundgebung-der-islam-hasser-in-dresden-innenminister-de-maiziere-pegida-ist-eine-unverschaemtheit/11091188.html
Mouffe, Chantal. 2013. *Agonistics: Thinking the World Politically*. London: Verso.
Mudde, Cas. 2004. The Populist Zeitgeist. *Government and Opposition* 39 (3): 541–563.
Müller, Jan-Werner. 2016. *Was ist Populismus?* Berlin: Suhrkamp.
Patzelt, Werner J. 2015. Was und wie denken PEGIDA-Demonstranten? Analyse der PEGIDA-Demonstranten am 25. Januar 2015, Dresden. Ein Forschungsbericht. *TU Dresden*. Accessed 3 July 2017. http://tu-dresden.de/die_tu_dresden/fakultaeten/philosophische_fakultaet/ifpw/polsys/for/pegida/patzelt-analyse-pegida-2015.pdf
Patzelt, Werner J., and Christian Eichardt. 2015. Drei Monate nach dem Knall: Was wurde aus PEGIDA? Dresden. *TU Dresden*. Accessed 3 July 2017. https://tu-dresden.de/die_tu_dresden/fakultaeten/philosophische_fakultaet/ifpw/polsys/for/pegida/patzelt-analyse-pegida-mai-2015.pdf
Patzelt, Werner J., and Joachim Klose. 2016. *Pegida. Warnsignale aus Dresden*. Dresden: Thelem Verlag.
Pfahl-Traughber, Armin. 1999. *Rechtsextremismus in der Bundesrepublik*. München: Beck.
Plotke, David. 1997. Representation is Democracy. *Constellations* 4: 19–34.
Priester, Karin. 2011. Definitionen und Typologien des Populismus. *Soziale Welt* 62: 185–198.
———. 2012. Wesensmerkmale des Populismus. *Aus Politik und Zeitgeschichte* 62 (5–6): 3–9.

Reuband, Karl-Heinz. 2015. Wer demonstriert in Dresden für Pegida? Ergebnisse empirischer Studien, methodische Grundlagen und offene Fragen. *Mitteilungen des Instituts für Deutsches und Internationales Parteienrecht und Parteienforschung* 21: 133–143.

———. 2017. Die Dynamik des Pegida Protests. Der Einfluss von Ereignissen und bewegungsspezifischer Mobilisierung auf Teilnehmerzahlen und Teilnehmerzusammensetzung. *Mitteilungen des Instituts für Deutsches und Internationales Parteienrecht und Parteienforschung* 23: 112–130.

Rucht, Dieter, Priska Daphi, Piotr Kocyba, Michael Neuber, Jochen Roose, Franziska Scholl, Moritz Sommer, Wolfgang Stuppert, and Sabrina Zajak. 2015. *Protestforschung am Limit. Eine soziologische Annäherung an PEGIDA.* ipb Working Paper. Accessed 3 July 2017. https://protestinstitut.files.wordpress.com/2015/03/protestforschung-am-limit_ipb-working-paper_web.pdf

Salzborn, Samuel. 2014. *Rechtsextremismus: Erscheinungsformen und Erklärungsansätze.* Baden-Baden: Nomos.

Schaefer, Dagmar, Jürgen Mansel, and Wilhelm Heitmeyer. 2002. Rechtspopulistisches Potential. Die "saubere" Mitte als Problem. In *Deutsche Zustände. Folge 1*, ed. Wilhelm Heitmeyer, 123–135. Frankfurt a. M.: Suhrkamp.

Schäller, Steven. 2016. Begriffe und Befunde: Populismus in der politikwissenschaftlichen Forschung. Kommentar zu Jan-Werner Müllers Essay "Was ist Populismus?". *Zeitschrift für Politische Theorie* 7 (2): 221–231.

Schroeder, Klaus. 21.10.2010. Überall Chauvinisten. *Tagesspiegel Online.* Accessed 3 July 2017. http://www.tagesspiegel.de/meinung/andere-meinung/gastkommentar-ueberall-chauvinisten/1962532.html

Stöss, Richard, and Oskar Niedermayer. 2008. Rechtsextreme Einstellungen in Berlin und Brandenburg 2000–2008 sowie in Gesamtdeutschland 2005 und 2008. *FU Berlin.* Accessed 3 July 2017. http://www.polsoz.fu-berlin.de/polwiss/forschung/systeme/empsoz/forschung/media/rex_00_08.pdf

Sumner, Wiliam G. 2007. *Folkways: A Study of Mores, Manners, Customs and Morals.* New York: Cosimo.

Taggart, Paul. 2004. Populism and Representative Politics in Contemporary Europe. *Journal of Political Ideologies* 9 (3): 269–288.

Thurau, Carsten. 12.01.2015. Live-Bericht von der Pegida-Demonstration. *Heute Journal.* Accessed 3 July 2017. https://www.youtube.com/watch?v=3VXH9b64Ca8

Urbinati, Nadia. 2015. A Revolt against Intermediary Bodies. *Constellations* 22: 477–486.

Vorländer, Hans. 2009. Die Deutschen und ihre Verfassung. *Aus Parlament und Zeitgeschichte* 18–19: 8–18.

———. 2011. The good, the bad, and the ugly. Über das Verhältnis von Populismus und Demokratie—Eine Skizze. *Totalitarismus und Demokratie* 8: 187–194.

Vorländer, Hans, Maik Herold, and Steven Schäller. 2015. *Wer geht zu PEGIDA und warum? Eine empirische Untersuchung von PEGIDA-Demonstranten in Dresden.* Dresden: Zentrum für Verfassungs- und Demokratieforschung.
———. 2016a. *Pegida. Entwicklung, Zusammensetzung und Deutung einer Empörungsbewegung.* Wiesbaden: Springer Verlag.
———. 2016b. PEGIDA—eine rechtsextremistische Bewegung? In *Extremismus in Sachsen. Eine kritische Bestandsaufnahme,* ed. Gert Pickel and Oliver Decker, 109–118. Leipzig: Edition Leipzig.
Walter, Franz. 2015. Aktuelle Forschungsergebnisse zu den Pegida-Protesten. *Göttinger Institut für Demokratieforschung,* January 19. Accessed 3 July 2017. http://www.demokratie-goettingen.de/blog/studie-zu-pegida
Yendell, Alexander. 2016. Islamfeindlichkeit und negative Haltungen gegenüber Muslimen, dort wo kaum Muslime leben—einige Fakten und Erklärungsversuche. In *Extremismus in Sachsen,* ed. Gert Pickel and Oliver Decker, 119–129. Leipzig: Edition Leipzig.
Zick, Andreas. 2017. Zwischen Elitenkritik und Menschenfeindlichkeit—Rechtspopulistische Orientierungen in der (bundesrepublikanischen) Bevölkerung. In *Populismus und Extremismus in Europa: Gesellschaftswissenschaftliche und sozialpsychologische Perspektiven,* ed. Winfried Brömmel, Helmut König, and Manfred Sicking, 119–147. Bielefeld: Transcript.
Zick, Andreas, and Anna Klein. 2014. *Fragile Mitte, Feindselige Zustände. Rechtsextreme Einstellungen in Deutschland 2014.* Bonn: Dietz Verlag.
Zick, Andreas, Daniela Krause, Wilhelm Berghan, and Beate Küpper. 2016a. Gruppenbezogene Menschenfeindlichkeit in Deutschland 2002–2016. In *Gespaltene Mitte, Feindselige Zustände. Rechtsextreme Einstellungen in Deutschland 2016,* ed. Andreas Zick, Beate Küpper, and Daniela Krause, 33–81. Bonn: Dietz Verlag.
Zick, Andreas, Daniela Krause, and Beate Küpper. 2016b. Rechtspopulistische und rechtsextreme Einstellungen in Deutschland. In *Gespaltene Mitte, Feindselige Zustände. Rechtsextreme Einstellungen in Deutschland 2016,* ed. Andreas Zick, Beate Küpper, and Daniela Krause, 111–142. Bonn: Dietz Verlag.
Zick, Andreas, Beate Küpper, and Andreas Hövermann. 2011. *Die Abwertung der Anderen. Eine Zustandsbeschreibung zu Intoleranz, Vorurteilen und Diskriminierung.* Berlin: Friedrich-Ebert-Stiftung.
———. 2016c. *Gespaltene Mitte—Feindselige Zustände.* Berlin: Dietz.

CHAPTER 6

Right-Wing Populism in Germany: Classification and Explanation

The profound feeling of political and social alienation that was characteristic of the supporters of the Patriotic Europeans against the Islamisation of the Occident (PEGIDA) is not new, and has also been observed for some time in other Western democracies. In the case of the United States, for instance, it has been proven that a feeling of being "disrespected" and "overlooked" is present in part of the population there too, together with the perception of a latent paternalism with regard to one's own lifestyle choices by those better off or by elites who feel morally superior. This feeling has a long history even beyond current issues like immigration policy, political correctness or criticism of globalisation. It is here that lines of social conflict, which can also be described geographically, become visible in terms of differences in the political culture between the cosmopolitan coastal regions in the East and West and areas more influenced by religion in the interior of the country, between the industrial North and the agricultural South as well as in general between urban and rural regions.[1]

Among the PEGIDA supporters the feeling of a latent political and moral paternalism by media-political elites also referred to specific political-cultural lines of conflict, so that the German protest marches were initially compared with the American Tea Party movement. In

[1] Cf. Cramer (2016) as well as Packer (2013).

© The Author(s) 2018
H. Vorländer et al., *PEGIDA and New Right-Wing Populism in Germany*, New Perspectives in German Political Studies,
https://doi.org/10.1007/978-3-319-67495-7_6

January 2015 the *New York Times*, for instance, wrote the following about PEGIDA: "Many of the supporters' grievances are similar to those of the early Tea Party movement in the United States, though their goals for government could not be more different: Tea Party supporters want less government, while PEGIDA supporters are calling for more government involvement in their lives. Both, though, share a disenchantment with their elected leaders and the political system."[2] In both cases a right-wing populist movement born of indignation was able to tie in with existing social and political lines of conflict on various levels. In this sense, PEGIDA knew how to exploit the special mentality of the south-easternmost *Bundesland* Saxony. It revealed a remarkable difference between eastern and western German patterns of attitude and interpretation, and referred to long-term and globally relevant political, cultural and socio-economic processes of change. Each one of these various levels became the starting point of attempts to classify and explain the protest movement.

6.1   SAXON PECULIARITIES

In light of the exceptional strength and longevity of the PEGIDA protests in Saxony, the first question that arose was why the right-wing populist protest movement emerged there of all places, in other words to what extent the movement resonated within a special environment offered by the *Bundesland* Saxony. Many speculations about this question have been made and discussed in the media by journalists, intellectuals and political activists—often with considerable polemics. In this discussion it was common practice to hold all the citizens of Dresden collectively responsible for PEGIDA, or all Saxons, or even all eastern Germans. In light of the protest demonstrations the Saxons were yet again accused of obvious democratic deficits, Saxony was decried as a "brown Bundesland" and Dresden was portrayed as "Germany's xenophobia capital", in which "contempt for humanity" and "racism" had "become normal".[3] Many reports and comments about PEGIDA used the common clichés of dim-witted and intolerant Saxons and, in reference to Dresden, talk quickly turned to the

---

[2] Cf. Eddy (25.01.2015). In fact, PEGIDA's call for more government commitment mainly referred to a stricter control of immigration.

[3] Cf. with evidence of the quotations Reuband (2016, p. 166).

"Valley of the Clueless".[4] An attempt was also made to apportion some of the blame for PEGIDA to the local Christian Democratic Union of Germany (CDU), which has governed in Saxony since 1990, as it was seen to downplay right-wing extremist activities, thereby promoting an environment in which right-wing populism could thrive.[5] Especially in light of recent xenophobic incidents as well as an initially failed attempt to arrest a suspected Islamist terrorist and his subsequent suicide in prison in Leipzig on 12.10.2016, there was repeated talk of "special conditions in Saxony" or even of a "failed Free State" (referring to the full name Free State of Saxony).[6]

Empirical findings were, however, unable to confirm the theory of Saxony playing a special role. Although Saxony exhibits strongly right-wing extremist structures, in empirical studies—most recently in the Saxony Monitor (*Sachsen-Monitor*) 2016—the prevalence of xenophobic, nationalistic and neo-National Socialistic orientations in the population of Saxony could always be seen as typical of the new federal states, even though it is considerably higher than in large parts of western Germany (Fig. 6.1).[7,8]

---

[4] Cf. Sect. 2.1 in Chap. 2 above. "Valley of the Clueless" (Tal der Ahnungslosen) was, in common parlance of the former German Democratic Republic (GDR), a controversial designation for those regions of the country in which one could not receive West German television channels and radio stations, and whose inhabitants were therefore reliant on the information from the GDR state media. This area also included parts of eastern Saxony, in particular the Elbe valley around Dresden. Kern and Hainmüller (2009) have however shown that the decoupling from the West German media's news and entertainment options probably led less to political naivety or a willingness to adapt in the population, but rather to greater dissatisfaction with the GDR system.

[5] A memorable quote from the former Prime Minister of Saxony and CDU chairman Kurt Biedenkopf lingers as paradigmatic for this trivialisation. He declared in the year 2000 that the Saxons' background made them "immune" to right-wing extremism (Sächsische Zeitung 28.09.2000).

[6] Bartsch (29.02.2016), Gathmann (14.10.2016).

[7] The picture is similar for the prevalence of negative attitudes towards Muslims in Saxony cf. the data in Yendell (2016, p. 121).

[8] Own compilation of the findings from 2016's Saxony Monitor (Infratest Dimap 2016b, p. 29ff.), Thuringia Monitor (Best et al. 2016, p. 92), Leipzig Mitte Study (Mitte-L: Decker et al. 2016, p. 30ff.) and Bielefeld Mitte Study (Mitte-B: Zick et al. 2016, p. 124ff.). When comparing the values it is not only the different methods of data collection (specified in the table header), which need to be taken into account, but also the scales, which in some instances are different. Although the same statements were presented, the respondents in both of the Monitor studies had only four possible answers, but in the Mitte Studies there were five possible answers, because here an intermediate category ("partly agree/partly

| | Saxony (2016) | Thuringia (2016) | Germany-total (Mitte-L 2016) | Germany-total (Mitte-B 2016) |
	CAPI	CATI	Face-to-Face	CATI
Endorsement of a right-wing dictatorship				
In the national interest, under certain circumstances, a dictatorship is a better form of government.	11	16	15,5	8,1
Nationalism / Chauvinism				
What our country needs today is for German interests abroad to be asserted firmly and energetically.	53	60	40,6	29,3
Xenophobia				
Germany has become overrun to a dangerous extent by the many foreigners.	58	51	47,8	24,6
My personal environment has become overrun to a dangerous extent by the many foreigners.	17	7	–	–
Antisemitism				
The Jews simply have something special and peculiar about them and are not really campatible with us.	13	8,0	18,8	8,9
Jews today are trying to take advantage of the fact that they were victims during the Nazi era.	25	–	–	25,6
Social Darwinism				
Germans are in fact naturally superior to other peoples.	18	–	22,4	11,6
As in nature, in society it should always be a case of the survival of the fittest.	9	12	18,1	12,7
There is valuable and less valuable human life.	9	21	16,4	10,2
Trivialisation of National Socialism				
The crimes of National Socialism are eggagerated in historiography.	18	–	14,3	10,6

Fig. 6.1 Agreement with ethnocentric and neo-National Socialist statements in Saxony in comparison

A survey with over 3000 respondents from the European Social Survey came to the same conclusion with regard to the widespread attitudes towards outsiders and foreigners. Here too, the figures for Saxony were within the typical scope of the other eastern German Länder (Fig. 6.2).[9]

Even the sharp rise in politically motivated acts of violence "from the right-wing" in 2015 represents—measured in terms of Saxony's population—only an average (though high) figure for eastern Germany.[10] Furthermore, empirical findings show that in comparison with other large cities (even western German ones) the Saxon state capital and home of PEGIDA Dresden does not have an above-average concentration of xenophobic orientations in the population (Cf. Figs. 5.13 and 5.14 above as well as Reuband 2015, p. 137). Analyses of the concentration of xenophobic incidents in certain regions of Saxony or the local areas where right-wing populist internet communication is concentrated also suggest that the regional differences within Saxony are far larger than those between Saxony and

disagree") was also available. In order to make the findings still comparable the agreement figures from the Mitte Studies, as presented in Fig. 6.1, are an approximation calculated by adding half the share of the "partly" responses to the combined total share of the answers for "agree completely" and "agree for the most part". The percentages shown in both the Monitor studies, on the other hand, are the aggregate share of those answers which indicated explicit agreement with the corresponding assertions on a four-step scale. Where there is a dash, no data were collected in the respective study. In the case of the statement "The Jews simply have something special and peculiar about them and are not really compatible with us", when evaluating the figure from the Thuringia Monitor (8 per cent agreement) one must take into consideration the fact that here a conspicuously high additional 9 per cent was accounted for by the residual category "I don't know"/not specified.

[9] The prepared data from the European Social Survey can be found in Reuband (2017, p. 104). The data collection was carried out between August 2014 and January 2015. The percentages shown are the aggregate share of those answers which indicated explicit agreement with the corresponding assertion on a five-point scale. In terms of "Acceptance of Muslim immigration" respondents were asked "to what extent Germany [...] should allow immigration of Muslims from other countries". The possible answers provided were: "allow many to come and live here", "allow some", "allow a few", and "allow no-one". The percentage shown here is the sum of the share for the first two answers mentioned. In the case of "Preferential treatment of immigrants over locals" respondents were asked whether the treatment "by the government and the country of immigrants who only recently came to Germany as compared to people [...] who were born in Germany", was "a lot better", "a little better", "the same", "a little worse" or "a lot worse". Shown here is the share made up of the sum of the first two answers

[10] Cf. Fig. 5.10 above. The *Bundesland* ranks even behind Saxony-Anhalt and Mecklenburg-Vorpommern (cf. Federal Ministry of the Interior 2016, p. 30).

	Germany		Eastern Germany by state				
	western	eastern	Saxony	Branden-burg	Meckl.-Vorpomm.	Saxony-Anhalt	Thuringia
Attitudes towards immigrants in Germany by state							
When considering asylum applications the state should be generous.	41	27	26	21	32	28	28
Muslims should be allowed to come to Germany and to live here.	72	50	58	50	48	43	43
It is better for a country if almost all ist inhabitants share the same customs and traditions.	25	39	34	30	44	45	45
Immigrants receive preferential treatment compared to locals.	24	37	35	46	37	41	30

Fig. 6.2   Attitudes towards immigrants in Germany by state

other *Bundesländer* (Reuband 2017, p. 105).[11] Furthermore, the protest against PEGIDA was not as unsuccessful as the media coverage or a first glance at the number of participators at PEGIDA and NO-PEGIDA demonstrations would suggest. For one thing, the absolute numbers of participants at the counter-demonstrations in Dresden exceeded those in other cities in Germany at all times, and apart from that, surveys suggest that over time more inhabitants of Dresden took part in anti-PEGIDA demonstrations than in PEGIDA-demonstrations (Reuband 2016, p. 166). Consequently, it does not seem possible to explain the emergence of PEGIDA in Dresden with attitude patterns in the population; instead it must be attributable to other factors. Further specific regional characteristics may have played a role here.

In Saxony, for instance, one can observe a particularly pronounced form of disenchantment with politics and political parties, which can be seen in the context of a long-term development. The CDU, which has

[11] For the regional focal points of xenophobic acts of violence in Saxony cf. Quent (2016, p. 76). In addition, Lühmann et al. (2017) have provided a recent case study on xenophobic hotspots in Saxony and Thuringia; for analysis of the internet communication cf. Pleul and Scharf (2016).

governed since 1990 in Saxony, had lost more than half of its absolute voter numbers by 2014—a loss which none of the other parties have been able to gain from. The group which has profited the most is that of the non-voters, as well as a growing potential on the right-wing fringe. The share of non-voters rose during the most recent state elections in Saxony in September 2014 to over 50 per cent.[12] Developments of this kind apply to eastern Germany in general, but are concentrated in a special way in Saxony, which is by far the most populous of the new federal states.

In addition, one must state that Saxony has an interpretive culture and a political mentality characterised by a strong self-awareness and sense of tradition, which allows existing ethnocentric attitude patterns to be politically mobilised above all there. Their points of reference are derived from a long history of political independence, a tradition of Saxony's 'splendour' and (courtly) displays of pomp as well as the "ingenuity" of its engineers. A flourishing strong "homeland solidarity" on this basis produces a particular tendency to be collectively introspective and stubborn. This identity was even successfully preserved under the regime of the German Democratic Republic (GDR), which facilitated the maintenance of a certain inner distance to the socialist rulers for many Saxons. Due to the political self-determination the Saxons achieved in 1989 through their own efforts, this feeling was eventually further strengthened and, in the difficult years of the socio-economic upheaval after 1990, further promoted by (the without exception CDU-led) policy of Saxon assertiveness and the consciously displayed pride about one's own role at the forefront of the economic, social and cultural development in eastern Germany. The obvious willingness to collectively, even publicly, articulate hostile attitudes towards "foreigners" but also the willingness to publicly exhibit one's own feelings of resentment towards a political and media elite perceived to be "foreign", could be interpreted in this context as a statement of a particularly overtly maintained *ethnocentrism*—a kind of "Saxon chauvinism", which is accompanied by the excessive elevation of one's own group and the clear setting of privileges for the indigenous Establishment over newcomers and foreigners. This special Saxon mentality probably

[12] The turnout at the state elections in Saxony in 2014 was just 49.1 per cent; cf. State Statistical Office of the Free State of Saxony (2014). Of the valid second votes 9.7 per cent went to the AfD and 4.9 per cent to the NPD.

strengthened the tendency to express one's anger and indignation, one's distrust felt towards the media and politics, and one's xenophobic prejudices, not only at home or at "the regulars' table", but to also take these feelings to the streets as open criticism and to emphasise such criticism by the symbolic occupation of public space. PEGIDA itself also repeatedly tried to specifically address "Saxon national pride" and to use it for its own purposes. The defiant slogan "Saxony shows how it goes" became a motto for the protests early on. When the worst fears regarding unregulated Muslim immigration then seemingly materialised with the refugee crisis in summer 2015 and the events in Cologne on New Year's Eve 2015/2016, at PEGIDA this was seen as a confirmation and proud reference was made to "Saxon foresight" (Vorländer 2016a, p. 105).

The Saxon state capital Dresden also presents an impressive backdrop for all forms of demonstrations. In the course of the annually ritually remembered historic destruction of the "baroque" city by "Anglo-American bomber formations",[13] on the day of remembrance on 13 February, even before PEGIDA, Dresden had already regularly served as a stage for the parades of a neo-Nazi scene mobilised across Europe. At the same time, over decades the citizens of the town have maintained a narrative, which describes Dresden as a constant victim of circumstances beyond its control. Thus, on the one hand, it was possible to not talk about the city's National Socialist past, and on the other, a nostalgic vision of the restoration of the past beauty of the city could be conceived. With this self-affirming narrative, parts of the Dresden educated middle class knew how to immunise themselves against some of the impositions of the *Socialist Unity Party of Germany* (SED) regime, but at the same time they spun themselves into a cocoon of nostalgic idealisations, which outlasted the GDR period. These formative constellations result in a conservatism, typical for Dresden, which is committed to highlighting and preserving one's own culture, tradition and identity, but which at the same time also produces strong defensive reflexes against the supposed dangers or threats to these "yearnings for an intact world". As such, the current consequences of globalisation, Islamic terrorism and large-scale migratory and refugee movements are interpreted here as scenarios posing an immediate threat—

---

[13] This is according to an inscription dating back to GDR times, which is still today prominently placed at the entrance to the Porcelain Collection in the Zwinger museum complex of the Dresden State Art Collections.

a threat to a situation of normality, stability and security, which had only just been restored after the profound biographical, socio-economic and demographic upheavals of the past decades. In addition, a concrete reason that provides part of the answer as to why PEGIDA could be successfully mobilised specifically in Dresden is that an organisationally compact, well-interconnected, protest initiative was found only there.

6.2   EASTERN GERMAN SENSITIVITIES

Beyond these regional characteristics the new German right-wing populism which openly emerged in the PEGIDA movement also points to existing politico-cultural lines of conflict between eastern and western Germany. The starting points, which were vastly different for historical reasons, but also the continuing inequalities after 1990, have caused a feeling among many in the new federal states that they are economically, socially, but also politico-culturally, disadvantaged in relation to their western German compatriots. While the democratisation in West Germany after 1945 has mainly positive connotations in the collective memory of the western German population because it was connected with an enormous economic boom, this experience, despite initial euphoria in 1990, is lacking to this day in many parts of eastern Germany. Here the introduction of representative democracy did not go hand in hand with an economic boom and the synthesis of the West German mark, freedom and social security which many East Germans had been dreaming of. On the contrary, many eastern German families were affected by unemployment, a loss of social status as well as the feeling of the devaluation of personal achievements in one's life during GDR times (Borstel 2012, p. 258f.). These experiences with "real existing capitalism" were connected directly with the new social and political model and contributed to the fact that although democracy is firmly established as a political idea in the new federal states, in its concrete form it is still experienced by many as "foreign". From an eastern German perspective the feelings of security which have finally been achieved after the lengthy transformation and establishment phase now seem threatened by new changes in these times of the refugee, finance and Euro crises, as well as by externally determined political agendas, which seemingly cannot be influenced.

However, it is not only the long-term effects of the transformation after 1989, but also the specific formative historical influences from before this time that enable PEGIDA to be put into an explanatory context. One must conclude here that in parts of eastern German society there is a far greater tolerance towards everyday expressions of xenophobic and nationalistic attitudes, than in the western German population. To explain such specific features the different historical influences in East and West Germany can be cited and one can refer to the specific peculiarities of the history of the GDR. This includes, for example, an intentionally patriotic education, an East German nationalism promoted by the SED regime, which understood the GDR to be a "socialist nation" that should also distinguish itself from its socialist brothers—while in West Germany the zeitgeist from the 1970s onwards orientated itself more towards visions of a post-national future and seemed to declare the German identity obsolete in view of the processes of European unification and global fraternisation. Added to this was the ambivalent handling of new right-wing extremist phenomena like skinhead groups in the GDR and a policy which strived for the separation of foreigners, such as international guests and "guest workers" that the GDR leadership tried to isolate from the population as much as possible seeing in them a potential threat to its own citizens' ideological reliability (cf. Poutrus et al. 2000). All these elements are likely to have contributed to the fact that, even today, positions which range from nationalistic to xenophobic are considerably more prevalent in eastern Germany.[14]

Furthermore, the hostility towards the elite which is typical of supporters of right-wing populist movements, and which was expressed in a particularly aggressive manner at the PEGIDA demonstrations with disparaging slogans like "lying press", "journalist rabble" or "traitors of the people", could in part be explained by existing lines of conflict between eastern and western Germans or were at least heavily dominated by them. Among the PEGIDA demonstrators it could be established that specifically the hostile feelings of resentment towards the elite, that were in part loudly articulated, often had a clear target: they were directed, not least, against the representatives of those politico-cultural attitudes, whose typically West German origin was clearly named, who were still

[14] Shaped by similar historical experiences—like the recent recovery of political self-determination, the continuing long-term effects of the socio-economic transformation or the lack of experience with (Muslim) immigration—comparable attitude patterns of ethnocentrism seem to be politically effective in many of the formerly socialistically governed countries of central and eastern Europe, for example in Poland, the Czech Republic, Hungary or the Baltic states. This can be seen not least in light of eastern and western European countries' completely different positions on refugee policy.

perceived as "foreign" by parts of the eastern German population, and whose claims to discursive hegemony were seen as political and moral paternalism and an attempt to establish language taboos and new censorship of free speech. For a description of the socio-cultural context of the feelings of alienation expressed by PEGIDA participants it is therefore not unimportant that in eastern Germany, and specifically in Saxony, the political, media and cultural elite after 1990, and still today, consists to a significant extent of former West Germans who had moved there. This applies—as confirmed by recent studies—not only to the senior management level of important companies, but also to numerous key positions in the authorities and ministries and through to chief editors of the print media.[15] In this way, after 1990 an impression became entrenched in the population, namely, that the institutions adopted from the old *Bundesländer* were not one's "own", the rules of the democratic process were not "self-created" ones. Instead they were essentially defined by people who exemplified typical West German socialisation, attitudes and behaviour. Geiges et al. (2015, p. 187f.) even speak here of "import elites from the West" who came from the privileged and secure life contexts of western society's educated middle class, and who after 1989—"not seldom with a domineering and arrogant presence"—had only rarely developed a sense of the enormous social, economic and biographical adjustments that the eastern German population had gone through. In the face of new demographic migratory movements their laboriously gained satiety and routines in turn seemed for many to once again be in danger. The attempt at a political expression of these perceptions, however, only led to being denigrated by the same elites as people "who know nothing about democracy, openness to the world, cosmopolitan tolerance, and the joy of global-cultural integration".[16]

---

[15] Cf. Bluhm and Jacobs (2016).

[16] Similarly, Patzelt and Klose (11.05.2015) also use the politico-cultural experiences of humiliation and deprivation after 1989 in their explanation of PEGIDA. They claim that the peaceful revolution after 1989 led to a massive "reorganisation of power structures in the whole society" of eastern Germany, which from the point of view of many eastern Germans "was connected with clear losses". Because of a sweeping change in the elite as well as "the massive difficulty fitting East German biographies into West German probation and promotion schemata", ultimately a whole generation of eastern Germans was "over a long period of time excluded from prominent economic, societal and political power"—which could for instance explain why in the case of PEGIDA, despite relative material wealth, an outright "dismissal of the political system" was repeatedly registered.

These differences in opinions and attitudes point to further *social psychological structures of prejudice*, which even today still shape the coexistence of eastern and western Germans in parts of the new *Bundesländer* and which define the perception they have of each other. On the one hand, the western Germans' feeling of not being able to be fully accepted in an environment that operates with subtle forms of exclusion of "unestablished non-locals"—on the other hand, seen from the eastern German side, the perception of an air of superiority and latent arrogance of the "Wessis" (slang for West Germans), combined with the implicit and unquestioned assumption of a new unified German identity which is purely built on memory spaces *(lieux de mémoire)*, views of history, standards of evaluation and rules of discourse of West German origin.[17] Along the lines of these prejudice patterns, specifically in Dresden, one has for years been able to observe a constantly recurring situation where political issues become politico-ideologically charged, escalate to a division of the citizens, and then become entrenched milieu structures (Vorländer 2016c).[18] With regard to the PEGIDA demonstrations, these front lines were further consolidated. On the side of the PEGIDA supporters, mainly older, employed, politically more right-leaning eastern Germans, who were pointing out the privileges of the "native population" and who were stubbornly prepared to react negatively towards any form of supposed moral paternalism that, according to their view, evoked old memories of their former lives in the GDR. On the other side, the counter-demonstrators were typically younger people, mostly rooted in an academic environment, who tended politically to be left-leaning, a significant share of whom were recruited from those who had moved to the region (mostly from western Germany).[19] Conversations with

[17] Against the backdrop of these east–west sensitivities many episodes of the Dresden "PEGIDA winter" 2014/2015 can be explained—for example the outrage with which parts of the Dresden population reacted to the invitation made by the organiser of the "Dresden—place to be" concert on 26.01.2015, which was directed against PEGIDA. The doctor Gerhard Ehninger, originally from Baden-Württemberg, had declared to PEGIDA sympathisers that everyone was welcome "who was open and would let themselves be taught" (Bonß 17.01.2015).

[18] Cf. the similar formation of opposing camps, the charged atmosphere related to political identity, and heated discussion about urban planning issues like the Waldschlösschen Bridge (opened 2013) or the development of the Dresden Neumarkt around the Frauenkirche.

[19] Cf. Vorländer, Herold and Schäller (2016, p. 133); Geiges et al. (2015, p. 71ff.) Empirical findings about the NoPegida demonstrators can be found in Geiges et al. (2015, p. 71ff.).

members of the editorial staff of regional media in and around Dresden indicate that this division between predominantly eastern German PEGIDA sympathisers and their opponents, who were often socialised in West Germany or unified Germany, was also reproduced within the editorial staff of regional daily newspapers. While native local news editors often harboured sympathy for the Dresden demonstrators, the leading positions like heads of department, cross-regional editors and chief editors were mainly occupied by western Germans and they were strongly critical of PEGIDA.

The role of such east–west fault lines reveals itself not only in the differing success of PEGIDA in the two parts of the country, but also in the evaluation of the protests. In a survey by the opinion research institute Infratest Dimap in autumn 2016, about a third of the western Germans stated that the events of the past two years had harmed Dresden's reputation, whereas the view among eastern Germans was precisely the opposite. Here more than 30 per cent were even of the opinion that Dresden had improved its image during the PEGIDA protests (Fig. 6.3).[20]

By adopting positions which were tailored to the eastern German point of view, the PEGIDA organisers initially attempted to specifically address these feelings of being dictated to. This was also reflected in PEGIDA's position papers of PEGIDA. There a perspective (reinforced with strong feelings of resentment) on the issues of the immigration, asylum and integration policies was expressed, which, in that form, would probably only have resonated so widely in eastern Germany. In addition, there were demands for a halt to the "warmongering against Russia" as well as an end to the "obsessive politically correct gender-neutralisation of our language"— demands that were connected with typically eastern German socialisation patterns. The criticism expressed by the PEGIDA movement was however

---

[20] Due to historical reasons pronounced sympathies for Russia (as well as Russian language skills) are still widespread among the eastern German population. The criticism of so-called "gender mainstreaming" in turn points to a view of emancipation that is shaped in no small part by experience of the GDR as well—a view, which is mainly orientated towards the picture of working mothers (with all-day childcare available even for young children who needed a crèche), and has little to do with the conviction (shaped primarily by the experiences of the western German emancipation movement since the 1960s), that equality of the sexes must manifest itself in a changed way of using and writing the language. Cf. PEGIDA's *19 points* as well as the *Dresden theses*. For an account of the PEGIDA participants' perceptions of "speaking bans" cf. Vorländer, Herold and Schäller (2015, p. 68). Source: Infratest Dimap (2016a), survey period: 04–05.10.2016.

How has the reputation of Dresden changed during the PEGIDA protests?
Figures in percent

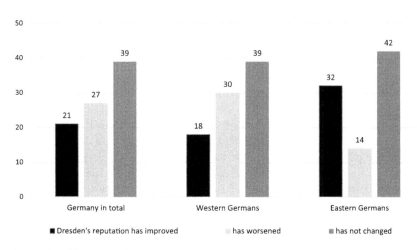

Fig. 6.3 Change in the reputation of Dresden due to PEGIDA

also directed at those eastern German politicians, who—in their evaluation of political disputes, but also in their evaluation of PEGIDA itself—had proven to be as "adapted" as their western German colleagues. A vague hope, connected in particular with Angela Merkel, Joachim Gauck, Stanislaw Tillich and others, was that through their political action they would more strongly assert a specifically eastern German perspective, however that may look.[21] Not least on the basis of these patterns of expectation and disappointment it has become clear that parts of the eastern German population still do not feel emotionally at home in the political system of the *Basic Law*. However, paradoxically, as a kind of "cunning of reason", in this respect PEGIDA specifically could have contributed to its adoption, because the people who came to PEGIDA have by now, as an indignant protesting collective, had their voices heard and received attention and recognition.

---

[21] At the demonstrations at the beginning of 2015, a sign repeatedly appeared which read: "Oh Angela, no Ossi [slang for East German] has disappointed us as much as you—actually yes: Joachim" (12.01.2015). Around the turn of the year both the German Chancellor Angela Merkel and the then Federal President Joachim Gauck had strongly criticised the organisers and participants of PEGIDA.

6.3   THE CRISIS OF REPRESENTATIVE DEMOCRACY

Beyond these regional or country-specific attempts to find an explanation, the empirical findings from the surveys of PEGIDA participants also reflect the facets of a discourse which describes the strengthening of right-wing populist movements above all as a symbol of an ongoing crisis in the system of representative democracy.[22] In view of the integration into increasingly complex federal, supranational and international governance structures the system of representative consensus-building and decision-making has by now become so complex, time-consuming and non-transparent that politics today can barely satisfy the democratic principles of a clear attribution of responsibilities. Consequently, from the point of view of the citizens, the political processes are barely transparent, political decisions seem as though they were agreed on in back rooms and the interests of "the men and women on the street" are hardly represented any more. Furthermore, the public arena of political opinion-forming and decision-making processes has transformed so much that—to meet the needs of a new form of "media democracy"—now the complexity of politics is undermined by a "dramaturgy of the visual". What cannot be adequately staged therein remains beyond the horizon of the citizens. In addition to this, there are the new social media, which for their part are bringing about a transformation of the public. The considerably faster mode of communication provided by the internet lowers the access threshold for situation-related political expression. Protest in the form of eruptive surges of political sentiments can be more easily organised. Hermetically sealed networks, so-called echo chambers, establish a specific view, in which rage, anger, aggression, scandal-mongering and also conspiracy theories thrive. Like-minded people communicate only with each other, they are no longer contradicted and this fuels a group polarisation. The communicative power that emerges in social media, however, has no institutionalised interface with the political system of representation, which, for its part, sees itself as being put under considerable time pressure, and obliged to react and make decisions.[23]

---

[22] For the following see Vorländer et al. (2018).
[23] Cf. Vorländer (2011a, p. 475, 2011b, p. 8, 2013, 2016b, p. 13); Dörner (2001); Sunstein (2002).

In addition to this are processes of change that have been observed, which are mainly tied to the political parties themselves and are often termed the "crisis of the people's parties". Instead of representing the interests of their members or voters, all that is said to count for today's "cartel parties" is holding on to power—and in a negative sense: it is not a successful debate about policy making that is the top priority of their actions, instead it is preventing their competitors from coming to power. Instead of political debate and the emphasis on ideologically motivated differences, processes of mutual policy adjustment and convergence can be observed, unanimity and rational problem-solving are invoked and election campaigns are run with the goal of an "asymmetric demobilisation".[24] The effects of this strong programmatic fixation of the major political parties on the "centre" of the political spectrum are likely to have been strengthened during the past decade in Germany, specifically by a certain shift to the left in the discourse of the media, politicians and the elite in comparison with the real distribution of opinions in the population. In particular, on the right of the political spectrum, beyond the Christian Democratic Union (CDU) and the Christian Social Union in Bavaria (CSU), a widespread feeling has taken hold that there is an under-representation of one's own political orientations—a feeling that could easily be picked up by parties like the Alternative for Germany (AfD) or movements like PEGIDA.[25]

The consequence of such developments as a whole can be described as a decoupling of democracy as a representative political decision-making system and democracy as a social way of life. On the part of many citizens there is a growing oppressive feeling of a steadily progressing loss of sovereignty to politics—a feeling of political alienation, one which is reacted to not least with a blanket hostility towards the elite and a new need for national self-assertion. Fitting this pattern, a majority of the PEGIDA demonstrators—reminiscent of 1989—understood their own protest specifically as a form of democratic self-empowerment of the citizens against the rule of a media-political elite detached from the will of the people. The feeling of "finally being heard" combined here with the claim of a shared political will, as well as the discovery of public visibility as a resource of communicative power. Also, the slogan "Putin, help!" shown again and again in the media, yet unique and always with the same people responsi-

---

[24] Nachtwey (2016, p. 302); Jörke and Selk (2015, p. 488).
[25] For this theory of a "representation gap" see Patzelt and Klose (2016, pp. 42–43).

ble, must be seen in this context. It was not a call for the authority of a strong leader that was behind PEGIDA, but instead the "vulgar" conception of democracy in which politicians are seen as weak, dependent and directly accountable "employees of the will of the people".[26]

The reaction of the much-criticised elites to phenomena like PEGIDA plays into the hands of this development—when, in the face of populist arguments, they refuse to conduct a substantive debate and instead rely on strategies of moralisation, marginalisation and social exclusion. However, anyone who confronts feelings of powerlessness with the accusation that people have simply not recognised the "true complexity" of a political issue, that they are on the "dark side" of society, or that they are arguing "post-factual" would, in doing so, only further fuel the anger of the enraged citizens.[27]

In the meantime, major societal developments have further exacerbated the crisis of the system of representative democracy. They include the processes of globalisation, liberalisation and digitalisation, in particular the opening of borders for goods and migration flows, the digital revolution that occurred with the establishment of the internet, the achievement of a 'real-time level' for information transfer, as well as the development of a new economic culture aligned with the financial markets and their players. The accompanying acceleration of time structures should already prove to be politically problematic. Since a democratic order, under these conditions, with its often time-consuming political opinion-forming, decision-making and adoption processes, can no longer keep up with the constant rapid change of the living environment, the legitimising connection of political decisions and politically-indexed changes to the opinions and needs of citizens seems increasingly difficult to establish. Democracy as a sphere of resonance is in danger of going silent. Consequently, there is an increasing perception that the political institutions and structures of public life do not trace back to an act of collective foundation and consent.

---

[26] This was reinforced by numerous placards at the demonstrations. Cf. for example slogans like "Courage for democracy. Now" (01.12.2014); "Parties good night, citizens to power", "Plebiscites into the Basic Law" (15.12.2014); "All politicians are elected SERVANTS of the people! And not the other way round" (12.01.2015) or "End the dictates of the EU—introduce direct democracy" (12.01.2015). Cf. also statements of PEGIDA supporters like "we citizens [are] the employers and the politicians the employees and if they [the politicians] don't perform well, then they will be fired" (Observation protocol of the 2nd dialogue forum "Together in Saxony" on 10.03.2015).

[27] Cf. Jörke and Selk (2015, pp. 491–495).

Instead, the individual feels like a powerless victim of processes of domination and paternalism controlled by the elite (Rosa 2005, p. 336; 20.04.2015). Soaring numbers of immigrants and asylum seekers act in such a situation as a "catalyst" for the alienation between the political establishment and citizens. The result is said by now to be observable almost everywhere in Europe. It becomes obvious that in part of the population one now finds a striking lack of experience of political self-efficacy—a psychological prerequisite "to engage in an active encounter with something foreign (whether it be a person, an idea, an experience or a practice)". Consequently, the relationship the supporters of PEGIDA and AfD have with the world is seen to be precarious and repulsive: "they feel unheard, unseen, isolated and voiceless in an indifferent or even threatening environment, in which what matters is literally keeping this same world away from them as best they can"—if need be, even with walls, fences and guns (Rosa 2016, p. 291).

6.4   SOCIO-ECONOMIC AND CULTURAL ANXIETIES

Developments in society as a whole, or even global developments, are often also held responsible in socio-economic and socio-cultural terms for phenomena of collective alienation and are seen as underlying causes of right-wing populist forms of politics and protest movements. In 2016, a study by the Bertelsmann-Stiftung determined, through the analysis of secondary data, that concerns about globalisation are particularly strongly pronounced in people who identify with right-wing populist parties.[28] Disproportionately many of these people would, for example, support a withdrawal from the European Union (EU) in a referendum (47 per cent) or at least express their opposition to a deepening of the EU (40 per cent). Only 38 per cent of them are satisfied with the democracy in their country, just 9 per cent trust their politicians. A 57 per cent majority of the people who are afraid of globalisation consider, however, that there are too many foreigners in their country. The proportion of these globalisation sceptics relative to the population as a whole varies greatly however from one country to another. Whereas in Austria and France even a majority of

---

[28] According to the data 78 per cent of AfD voters, 76 per cent of FN voters, 69 per cent of FPÖ voters, 66 per cent of Lega-Nord voters, 57 per cent of PVV voters, 58 per cent of PiS voters, 61 per cent of Fidesz voters, 50 per cent of Jobbik voters and 50 per cent of UKIP voters see globalisation as a threat. Cf. de Vries and Hoffmann (2016, p. 20ff).

respondents regard globalisation as a threat (55 or 54 per cent respectively), in Italy, Spain and Great Britain the percentage share is relatively small (39 per cent, 39 per cent and 36 per cent respectively). With 40, 45 and 47 per cent respectively, the Netherlands, Germany and Hungary are in midfield (de Vries and Hoffmann 2016, p. 3f.).

The right-wing populist protest events held by PEGIDA and the xenophobic feelings of resentment and feelings of political alienation that were openly displayed there were also often interpreted as the response of an unsettled middle class to diffuse concerns about globalisation, modernisation and loss of social status. The approaches available here are in particular based on criticism of society and capitalism. Accordingly, right-wing populism is understood to be the consequence of a socio-economic dynamic which, in recent decades, has intensified in a very particular way. The markets have gained primacy over politics, thereby becoming a "social and political supervisory body", which no longer tolerates contradictions to its economically liberal world view. Thus, the "invisible hand" for many now takes the form of a "fist". Capitalism has become authoritarian and has led to a "denormativisation" and social conflicts "running wild". In this manner a "market-conforming extremism" is said to have arisen, which, in connection with "norms of entrepreneurial self-optimisation" unleashes a collective fear of social descent and thereby promotes the treatment of others as inferior. On the part of the individual, this capitalist world view, with its rules tied to economic rationality and effectivity which directly affect the individual, has taken the place of parental upbringing using corporal punishment. The "rule of market logic" is said to have initiated an authoritarian dynamic in which submission is demanded, thereby creating aggression, which is eventually released in the form of feelings of resentment towards minorities. This is noticeable above all in the eastern European states, because the social pressure for change that the people there have been put under since 1990 is particularly extreme. Against this backdrop the PEGIDA demonstrators have also been interpreted as an expression of a new "authoritarian syndrome of the middle class" (Decker et al. 2015, p. 29ff.; Nachtwey 2015, p. 86ff., 2016, p. 306ff.).

If the most recent successes of right-wing populism are associated in this manner with a spread of expectations of economic rationality and efficiency, then they also seem to seamlessly fit into the predictions from the debate about the phenomenon of a so-called *post-democracy*. According to Colin Crouch, this term describes a deteriorated form of democracy which is currently an imminent threat. In a post-democracy, democratic processes and institutions are hollow and have degenerated to the point of being forms of superficial staging. The true power is instead in the hands of economic concerns and lobby groups, which act behind citizens' backs. Post-democracies are democratic orders in which "boredom, frustration and disillusion have settled in after a democratic moment; when powerful minority interests have become far more active than the mass of ordinary people in making the political system work for them; where political elites have learned to manage and manipulate popular demands; where people have to be persuaded to vote by top-down publicity campaigns" (Crouch 2004, p. 19f.). The preferred form of government in this "post-democratic era" is often referred to as market-compliant democracy. In it the hollowed and eroded institutional order of the old representative system has merged with the primacy of market-conforming coordination mechanisms in society as a whole, to become a political form, which *inter alia* is prone to the permanent claim that there is no alternative to specific political decisions. The consequence is that although democratic norms are emphasised and in public discourse always demanded, ultimately all actors evade these norms and the political system more resembles a "simulation" (Blühdorn 2013). Not only economic and political-administrative elites, but also social actors and citizens, are no longer prepared to bear the costs of a (constant) political commitment and instead leave themselves in the hands of the efficiency logic of the market and consumption. Against this backdrop right-wing populist positions are interpreted as desperate reactions of the citizens, as resentment-laden rebellion against this market-compliant democracy. Phenomena like PEGIDA are referred to as "post-democratic social movements" (Nachtwey 2015, p. 87ff.).

Other approaches have suggested that cultural anxieties are the main reasons for the latest protests and upheavals. The theory that the successes of right-wing populist movements can mainly be explained socio-economically has been called into question, especially by several empirical studies. In Germany, for instance, the number of people who for economic reasons had a generally more pessimistic view of the future has dropped considerably in the past decade. Consequently, according to Lengfeld and Ordemann (2016, p. 21) it is very "unlikely that it was a fear of losing social status of all things, which brought PEGIDA and AfD considerable success". Thus, the theory of the "fear of losing social status among the middle class, which was popular in recent years", should consequently be revised. Furthermore, in the comparative study by Lengfeld

(2017), among the group of people who are considered to be the typical losers of the processes of globalisation and modernisation a significantly higher level of intent to vote for the right-wing populist AfD could not be identified. The theory that right-wing populist movements, parties or election campaigns are mainly supported by the typical losers of modernisation, the underprivileged and low-income earners, is therefore to be rejected.[29]

In the case of PEGIDA, the assumption that right-wing populist protest movements like PEGIDA can above all be traced back to socioeconomic explanatory factors, is also opposed by the finding that here it was less the socially disadvantaged but rather parts of a financially average to well-off middle class who were expressing their indignation about mainstream politics (cf. Sect. 4.1 in Chap. 4 above). Although socioeconomic fears about the future and losing status were also identified here, with a focus, for instance, on job security, pensions or savings, these fears were however barely named as motivations for protesting. Instead, respondents tended to make a positive assessment of their current and individual living conditions in their own family and in their spatial and social surroundings. Both in the evaluation of their own economic situation as well as with regard to the opinion that they receive "their fair share compared to others in Germany", there was hardly any difference between PEGIDA supporters and the general population. Even in response to the question of whether they were satisfied with themselves and their own living conditions, about 70 per cent expressed their satisfaction, which also almost exactly matched the figure for the general population (Reuband 2016, p. 172).[30] Fears that in the future one could lose a social status currently assessed as positive were not linked to the presumed socio-economic consequences of mass immigration. Instead, this immigration was responsible for growing concerns about German culture and identity: As the country supposedly became more and more infiltrated by Muslims, its own traditions were thought to be doomed to fade, its everyday life would suffer from a growing number of terrorist attacks and its liberal way of life would rapidly be corrupted. In interviews and surveys what arose most of all was vague fears of cultural expropriation, in which both the figure of the left-

---

[29] In the case of the election of Donald Trump as President of the United States on 08.11.2016 an analysis of the exit polls was already able to dismiss similar assumptions. Cf. http://edition.cnn.com/election/results/exit-polls (Accessed 05.07.2017).

[30] This seems to also apply to AfD sympathisers; for this cf. Bergmann et al. (2016).

wing liberal guardians of virtue and the North African or Muslim asylum seekers were perceived as a source of irritation, a threat to one's lifestyle. The public perception of western European (but also western German) cities operated as a cautionary example of the disintegration of social structures, an erosion of state order and a tolerance of parallel societies, the spread of which into one's own living environment accordingly needed to be prevented.[31] From the point of view of the PEGIDA supporters, in particular due to the mass immigration of Muslims and Africans, a central promise of affluent western societies, the hope for an equally good or even better life for oneself and one's own children and grandchildren, was at risk of being called into question. There were, however, equally clear contrasts between the evaluation of current and future threat scenarios, as is also symptomatic for the population as a whole. Whereas, for example, talk was of a general increase in crime (mainly by refugees and migrants), the immediate area was mostly (still) considered safe. Whereas, in view of the rising number of asylum seekers, Germany was seen as being overwhelmed by foreigners to a "dangerous degree", one's own concrete living conditions were considerably less often seen to be threatened by this development.[32]

REFERENCES

Bartsch, Michael. 29.02.2016. Sächsische Verhältnisse. Erklärungsversuche für ein Bundesland, in dem der rechte Mob immer wieder Schlagzeilen macht. *Das Parlament*: 3.

Bergmann, Knut, Matthias Diermeier, and Judith Niehues. 2016. Die AfD—eine Partei der Besserverdienenden? *IW-Kurzberichte*: 19. Accessed 3 July 2017. https://www.iwkoeln.de/_storage/asset/280649/storage/master/file/9381123/download/IW-Kurzbericht_2016-19-AfD.pdf

Best, Heinrich, Steffen Niehoff, Axel Salheiser, and Lars Vogel. 2016. *Gemischte Gefühle: Thüringen nach der "Flüchtlingskrise". Ergebnisse des Thüringen-Monitors 2016*. Thüringer Staatskanzlei. Accessed 3 July 2017. http://www.thueringen.de/mam/th1/tsk/thuringen-monitor_2016_mit_anhang.pdf

Blühdorn, Ingolfur. 2013. *Simulative Demokratie: neue Politik nach der postdemokratischen Wende*. Berlin: Suhrkamp.

[31] Cf. Vorländer, Herold and Schäller (2015, pp. 62, 69) as well as the findings from the focus group discussions in Geiges et al. (2015, p. 89ff.).

[32] State Chancellery Saxony (2016, pp. 37f., 81f., 83f., 91f.).

Bluhm, Michael, and Olaf Jacobs. 2016. *Wer beherrscht den Osten? Ostdeutsche Eliten ein Vierteljahrhundert nach der deutschen Wiedervereinigung.* Universität Leipzig. Accessed 3 July 2017. http://www.mdr.de/heute-im-osten/wer-beherrscht-den-osten-studie-100-downloadFile.pdf

Bonß, Annechristin. 17.01.2015. 4000 Dresdner sollen zu Konzert für Weltoffenheit kommen. *Sächsische Zeitung.* 15.

Borstel, Dierk. 2012. Rechtsextremismus und Demokratieentwicklung in Ostdeutschland. Eine Zwischenbilanz nach zehn Jahren. In *Deutsche Zustände. Folge 10*, ed. Wilhelm Heitmeyer, 246–260. Frankfurt a.M.: Suhrkamp.

Cramer, Katherine. 2016. *The Politics of Resentment: Rural Consciousness in Wisconsin and the Rise of Scott Walker.* Chicago: University Press of Chicago.

Crouch, Colin. 2004. *Post-Democracy.* Cambridge: Polity.

de Vries, Catherine, and Isabell Hoffmann. 2016. *Globalisierungsangst oder Wertekonflikt? Wer in Europa populistische Parteien wählt und warum.* Bertelsmann Stiftung. Accessed 3 July 2017. https://www.bertelsmann-stiftung.de/fileadmin/files/user_upload/EZ_eupinions_Fear_Studie_2016_DT.pdf

Decker, Oliver, Johannes Kiess, and Elmar Brähler. 2015. *Rechtsextremismus der Mitte. Eine sozialpsychologische Gegenwartsdiagnose.* Gießen: Psychosozial-Verlag.

Decker, Oliver, Johannes Kiess, Eva Eggers, and Elmar Brähler. 2016. Die 'Mitte'-Studie 2016: Methode, Ergebnisse und Langzeitverlauf. In *Die Enthemmte Mitte. Autoritäre und rechtsextreme Einstellung in Deutschland*, ed. Oliver Decker, Johannes Kiess, and Elmar Brähler, 23–66. Gießen: Psychosozial-Verlag.

Dörner, Andreas. 2001. *Politainment. Politik in der medialen Erlebnisgesellschaft.* Frankfurt a.M.: Suhrkamp.

Eddy, Melissa. 25.01.2015. German Quandary of How to Deal With Anti-Immigration Movement. *The New York Times Online.* Accessed 3 July 2017. http://www.nytimes.com/2015/01/26/world/german-quandaryof-how-to-deal-with-anti-immigration-movement.html

Federal Ministry of the Interior. 2016. *Verfassungsschutzbericht 2015.* Bundesministerium des Inneren. Accessed 3 July 2017. https://www.bmi.bund.de/SharedDocs/Downloads/DE/Broschueren/Multimedia/vsb-2015.pdf?__blob=publicationFile

Gathmann, Florian. 14.10.2016. Failed Freistaat. *Spiegel Online.* Accessed 3 July 2017. http://www.spiegel.de/politik/deutschland/jaber-al-bakr-suizid-in-sachsen-failed-freistaat-kommentar-a-1116399.html

Gathmann, Florian, and Oliver Trenkamp. 03.11.2015. Goebbels-Vergleich bei Pegida-Demo: SPD-Generalsekretärin nennt Bachmann "wahnsinnigen Faschisten". *Spiegel Online.* Accessed 3 July 2017. http://www.spiegel.de/politik/deutschland/pegida-yasmin-fahimi-nennt-lutz-bachmann-wahnsinnigen-faschisten-a-1060780.html

Geiges, Lars, Stine Marg, and Franz Walter. 2015. *PEGIDA. Die schmutzige Seite der Zivilgesellschaft?* Bielefeld: Transcript.

Infratest Dimap. 2016a. *Dresden trotz leichter Ansehensverluste weiterhin beliebtes Reiseziel.* Infratest Dimap. Accessed 3 July 2017. http://www.infratest-dimap. de/umfragen-analysen/bundesweit/umfragen/aktuell/dresden-trotz-leichter-ansehensverluste-weiterhin-beliebtes-reiseziel/

———. 2016b. *Sachsen Monitor 2016. Ergebnisbericht.* Infratest Dimap. Accessed 3 July 2017. https://www.staatsregierung.sachsen.de/download/staatsregierung/Ergebnisbericht_Sachsen-Monitor_2016.pdf

Jörke, Dirk, and Veith Selk. 2015. Der hilflose Antipopulismus. *Leviathan* 43 (4): 484–500.

Kern, Holger L., and Jens Hainmüller. 2009. Opium for the Masses: How Foreign Media Can Stabilize Authoritarian Regimes. *Political Analysis* 17 (4): 377–399.

Lengfeld, Holger. 2017. Die "Alternative für Deutschland": eine Partei für Modernisierungsverlierer? *Kölner Zeitschrift für Soziologie und Sozialpsychologie* 69: 209–232.

Lengfeld, Holger, and Jessica Ordemann. 2016. *Die Angst der Mittelschicht vor dem sozialen Abstieg revisited. Eine Längsschnittanalyse 1984–2014.* The German Socio-Economic Panel-Study. Accessed 3 July 2017. https://www.diw.de/documents/publikationen/73/diw_01.c.541642.de/diw_sp0862.pdf

Lühmann, Michael, Danny Michelsen, and Marika Przybilla-Voß. 2017. *Ursachen und Hintergründe für Rechtsextremismus, Fremdenfeindlichkeit und fremdenfeindlich motivierte Übergriffe in Ostdeutschland sowie die Ballung in einzelnen ostdeutschen Regionen.* Institut für Demokratieforschung Göttingen. Accessed 3 July 2017. http://www.demokratie-goettingen.de/content/uploads/2017/05/Studie-Rechtsextremismus-und-Fremdenfeindlichkeit-in-Ostdeutschland-Abschlussbericht.pdf

Nachtwey, Oliver. 2015. Rechte Wutbürger. Pegida oder das autoritäre Syndrom. *Blätter für deutsche und internationale Politik* 3: 81–89.

———. 2016. PEGIDA, politische Gelegenheitsstrukturen und der neue Autoritarismus. In *PEGIDA—Rechtspopulismus zwischen Fremdenangst und "Wende"-Enttäuschung?* ed. Karl-Siegbert Rehberg, Franziska Kunz, and Tino Schlinzig, 299–312. Bielefeld: Transcript.

Packer, George. 2013. *The Unwinding: An Inner History of the New America.* New York: Farrar, Straus and Giroux.

Patzelt, Werner. J., and Joachim Klose. 11.05.2015. Die Ursachen des Pegida-Phänomens. *Frankfurter Allgemeine Zeitung:* 13.

Patzelt, Werner J., and Joachim Klose. 2016. *PEGIDA. Warnsignale aus Dresden.* Dresden: Thelem.

Pleul, Clemens, and Stefan Scharf. 2016. Pegidas Entwicklung auf der Straße und im Netz. In *PEGIDA: Warnsignale aus Dresden*, ed. Werner J. Patzelt and Joachim Klose, 295–368. Dresden: Thelem.

Poutrus, Patrice G., Jan C. Behrends, and Dennis Kuck. 2000. Historische Ursachen der Fremdenfeindlichkeit in den neuen Bundesländern. *Aus Politik und Zeitgeschichte* 39: 15–21.

Quent, Matthias. 2016. Rechte Gewalt in Sachsen: Lokale Unterschiede. In *Extremismus in Sachsen*, ed. Gert Pickel and Oliver Decker, 74–85. Leipzig: Edition Leipzig.

Reuband, Karl-Heinz. 2015. Wer demonstriert in Dresden für Pegida? Ergebnisse empirischer Studien, methodische Grundlagen und offene Fragen. *Mitteilungen des Instituts für Deutsches und Internationales Parteienrecht und Parteienforschung* 21: 133–143.

Reuband, Karl-Heinz. 2016. Außenseiter oder Repräsentaten der Mehrheit? Selbst- und Fremdwahrnehmungen der Teilnahmer von PEGIDA-Kundgebungen. In *PEGIDA—Rechtspopulismus zwischen Fremdenangst und "Wende"-Enttäuschung?* ed. Karl-Siegbert Rehberg, Franziska Kunz, and Tino Schlinzig, 165–187. Bielefeld: Transcript.

———. 2017. Pegida, Sachsen und die Fremdenfeindlichkeit. Warum es komplexerer und regionalspezifischer Analysen bedarf. *Forschungsjournal Soziale Bewegungen* 30: 101–106.

Rosa, Hartmut. 2005. *Beschleunigung. Die Veränderung der Zeitstrukturen in der Moderne*. Frankfurt a.M.: Suhrkamp.

———. 20.04.2015. Fremd im eigenen Land? *Frankfurter Allgemeine Zeitung*: 6.

———. 2016. Der Versuch einer sklerotischen Gesellschaft, sich die Welt vom Leibe zu halten—und ein Vorschlag zum Neuanfang. In *PEGIDA—Rechtspopulismus zwischen Fremdenangst und "Wende"-Enttäuschung?* ed. Karl-Siegbert Rehberg, Franziska Kunz, and Tino Schlinzig, 289–296. Bielefeld: Transcript.

Schütz, Dieter. 18.09.2000. Interview mit Kurt Biedenkopf: "Staat kann Zivilcourage der Bürger nicht ersetzen". *Sächsische Zeitung*: 6.

State Chancellery of Saxony. 2016. *Auswertungstabellen Sachsen Monitor 2016*. Sächsische Staatskanzlei. Accessed 3 July 2017. https://www.staatsregierung. sachsen.de/download/staatsregierung/Tabellen_SN-Monitor_2016_Final. pdf

State Statistical Office of the Free State of Saxony. 2014. *Landtagswahl 2014. Endgültiges Landesergebnis*. Statistisches Landesamt Sachsen. Accessed 3 July 2017. https://www.statistik.sachsen.de/wpr_alt/pkg_s10_erg_lw.prc_erg_lw?p_bz_ bzid=LW14&p_ebene=SN&p_ort=14

Sunstein, Cass. 2002. The Law of Group Polarization. *The Journal of Political Philosophy* 10 (2): 175–195.

Vorländer, Hans. 2011a. Der Wutbürger—Repräsentative Demokratie und kollektive Emotionen. In *Ideenpolitik: geschichtliche Konstellationen und gegenwärtige Konflikte*, ed. Harald Bluhm, Karsten Fischer, and Marcus Llanque, 467–478. Berlin: Akademie Verlag.

———. 2011b. Spiel ohne Bürger. *Frankfurter Allgemeine Zeitung*: 8, July 12.

———. 2013. Kritik, Krise, Szenarien. Zur Lage der Demokratie. *Zeitschrift für Politikwissenschaft* 2: 267–277.

———. 2016a. PEGIDA—Provinzposse oder Vorbote eines neudeutschen Rechtspopulismus? In *PEGIDA—Rechtspopulismus zwischen Fremdenangst und "Wende"-Enttäuschung?* ed. Karl-Siegbert Rehberg, Franziska Kunz, and Tino Schlinzig, 99–111. Bielefeld: Transcript.

———. 2016b. Wenn das Volk gegen die Demokratie aufsteht: Die Bruchstelle der repräsentativen Demokratie und die populistische Herausforderung. In *Vielfalt statt Abgrenzung. Wohin steuert Deutschland in der Auseinandersetzung um Einwanderung und Flüchtlinge?* ed. Bertelsmann Stiftung, 61–76. Gütersloh: Verlag Bertelsmann Stiftung.

———. 2016c. Zerrissene Stadt. Kulturkampf in Dresden. *Aus Politik und Zeitgeschichte* 66 (5–7): 22–28.

Vorländer, Hans, Maik Herold, and Steven Schäller. 2015. *Wer geht zu PEGIDA und warum? Eine empirische Untersuchung unter PEGIDA-Demonstranten in Dresden*. Dresden: ZVD.

———. 2016. *PEGIDA. Entwicklung, Zusammensetzung und Deutung einer Empörungsbewegung*. Wiesbaden: Springer VS.

———. 2018. Entfremdung, Empörung, Ethnozentrismus. Was PEGIDA über den sich formierenden Rechtspopulismus verrät. In *Das Volk gegen die (liberale) Demokratie. Die Krise der Repräsentation und neue populistische Herausforderungen*. Leviathan Sonderband 18, ed. Dirk Jörke and Oliver Nachtwey, accepted. Baden-Baden: Nomos.

Yendell, Alexander. 2016. Islamfeindlichkeit und negative Haltungen gegenüber Muslimen, dort wo kaum Muslime leben—einige Fakten und Erklärungsversuche. In *Extremismus in Sachsen. Eine kritische Bestandsaufnahme*, ed. Gert Pickel and Oliver Decker, 119–129. Leipzig: Edition Leipzig.

Yendell, Alexander, Oliver Decker, and Elmar Brähler. 2016. Wer unterstützt Pegida und was erklärt die Zustimmung zu den Zielen der Bewegung? In *Die enthemmte Mitte. Autoritäre und rechtsextreme Einstellungen in Deutschland*, ed. Oliver Decker, Johannes Kiess, and Elmar Brähler, 137–152. Gießen: Psychosozial-Verlag.

Zick, Andreas, Daniela Krause, Wilhelm Berghan, and Beate Küpper. 2016. Gruppenbezogene Menschenfeindlichkeit in Deutschland 2002–2016. In *Gespaltene Mitte, Feindselige Zustände. Rechtsextreme Einstellungen in Deutschland 2016*, ed. Andreas Zick, Beate Küpper, and Daniela Krause, 33–81. Bonn: Dietz Verlag.

CHAPTER 7

PEGIDA as Part of Right-Wing Populism in Germany and Europe

What is PEGIDA, why has the movement attracted so much attention, and why was PEGIDA so successful in Dresden in particular? Many observers from the media and academia have attempted to explain the phenomenon in recent years and at the same time expressed their political concern that PEGIDA was a quintessentially right-wing extremist movement, which made use of xenophobic, chauvinistic and racist feelings of resentment, strengthening and instrumentalising them. The organisers and participants of the protests did little in order to allay these fears. Yet the majority of the explanations for why PEGIDA was formed remained unsatisfactory and inadequate because they simply took the outward appearance—the crowds marching in the dark and chanting militant slogans at rallies—to be the core of the movement and blocked out both the varied motivations of the participants and the complex mix of their protest.

PEGIDA was not a uniform movement when it began, either in terms of organisation and personnel, or in terms of its motivation and its programme. The local or regional offshoots of PEGIDA differed in terms of the make-up of the protest groups, but above all also with regard to their success on the streets. The link between the organisations was based on partly diffuse and critical, at times aggressively expressed, feelings of resentment towards Muslims, asylum seekers and refugees, but above all

© The Author(s) 2018   195
H. Vorländer et al., *PEGIDA and New Right-Wing Populism in Germany*, New Perspectives in German Political Studies,
https://doi.org/10.1007/978-3-319-67495-7_7

towards the political and media elite of the Federal Republic. The movement had its beginnings in Dresden. The initial backbone of the movement was a circle of friends and acquaintances, the mobilisation took place through Facebook and the strong response by the media then generated an amplifying effect. Public criticism, media attention and a "now more than ever" reaction from the demonstrators helped the protest movement grow to as many as 25,000 participants at its peak. The original grounds for the emergence of the PEGIDA protests in autumn 2014 had been provided by religiously motivated acts of violence committed by the Islamic State (IS) and local plans for the housing of asylum seekers and refugees. With these sensitive issues there was a current focal point around which various motivations for anger and indignation could accumulate and be mobilised. Firstly, it was possible to connect with widespread structures of nationalistic and xenophobic resentment which are identifiable throughout Germany. Secondly, this emotionally charged catalyst released what was evidently a long pent-up rage about the political and media elite and caused it to collectively and publicly erupt as a generalised blanket indignation. These powerful emotions seemed to have less of a socio-economic justification, along the lines of a fear of economic disadvantage and a loss of social status, instead they were to be understood above all as diffuse fears of cultural expropriation, of a loss of traditions and regional or national identity due to Islam, a religion which was actually little known in terms of day-to-day experiences. Criticism of Islam and Islamophobia thus served as the "spark" for PEGIDA, which caused outrage about a poorly communicated and administered asylum policy and direct concern about one's personal surroundings to shift into something fundamental, and thereby opened floodgates through which all kinds of disappointments and frustrations could be publicly presented in the form of abuse of "policies", "politicians" or "the media".

At the time of its early peak, around the turn of 2014/2015, PEGIDA in Dresden was, contrary to initial speculation, for the most part not a movement of right-wing extremists, Islamophobes and xenophobes. Approximately a third of the participants at the rallies and on the "evening strolls" indicated diffuse xenophobic motivations and attitudes. The majority fundamentally criticised policies, the media and the concrete functioning of practised democracy in Germany. PEGIDA recruited participants from the middle class of Dresden and Saxony, and from the fragile segments of their societies. Something that stood out in the socio-demographic make-up was the comparatively high proportion of self-employed people and salaried employees, the high participation rate of academics and—with regard to the income structure in Saxony—an average income situation. At the same time, the organisers' biographical backgrounds pointed in many cases to an unstable, precarious working life in various fields within the service sector and small business.[1]

After internal disputes about the political profile and the subsequent split of the organisational team, in spring 2015 it initially seemed as if PEGIDA was on its last legs. By the end of July 2015 hardly more than two to three thousand people could be mobilised each week. The exception to this was the appearance of Geert Wilders with an audience of about 10,000. The refugee crisis of late summer 2015 and the decision made by Angela Merkel to admit hundreds of thousands of migrants then breathed new life into PEGIDA. The movement now presented itself as a clearly anti-asylum and anti-immigration movement and attempted to thereby establish itself as the political platform of an extra-parliamentary protest against the refugee policy of the Federal Government. It took on a clearly Islamophobic profile and intensified political provocation through rhetoric which became increasingly radical. The organisers attempted in this way—with little success—in terms of their programme and organisation to connect with international right-wing and right-wing populist networks. The electoral successes of the right-wing populist Alternative for Germany (AfD)—reorganised in the meanwhile as the "PEGIDA party"—have, since 2016, seen PEGIDA then successively disappear from the spotlight of public attention. Attempts to attract attention again with abusive campaigns, as on the Day of German Unity in October 2016, were in the end unable to change this. The right-wing populist protest in Germany had found its parliamentary representation through the AfD. Border controls in the Balkans and an agreement with Turkey had seen the refugee numbers decline sharply again. Not even terrorist attacks like that in Berlin during the Christmas period 2016 led to a revival of PEGIDA. The issue of the display of anger and indignation on Germany's streets thereby appeared to have resolved itself for the time being. What remained was a protest ritual every Monday with between one and two thousand participants.

As a phenomenon PEGIDA either did not fit or fitted only with reservations into the usual scheme of analysis provided by the hitherto established protest and social movement research in Germany, which

[1] Cf. Vorländer, Herold, Schäller (2016, pp. 10ff., 57ff.).

had primarily devoted itself to the classic "good" protest movements, which occasionally make use of forms of civil disobedience. Terms like "grass-roots movement", "social movement" or even "new social movement" were accordingly ruled out for PEGIDA because they were too clearly predefined and were used above all to describe theme-based protest projects wishing to be seen as "progressive", "enlightening" and "emancipatory", with focal areas such as peace, equality, saving the environment, or criticism of capitalism.[2] The type of protest organised by civil society, which appeared on the streets and squares of German cities for the first time through PEGIDA, then, against this background, inevitably had to be seen as "the ugly face of civil society"[3]—especially because this tied in with the justified criticism of publicly articulated forms of intolerance, national patriotism and "group-focused enmity". However, to take this "dark side" of the demonstrations in winter 2014/2015 to be the whole, could not do justice to the complex appearance or the mix of factors which enabled a small group of friends on Facebook to develop into a mass movement within just a few weeks. The high emotionality, the confrontational air, the mode of putting one's indignation on display, and the successful attempt to generate communicative power on prominent squares and streets, had made PEGIDA into a new style of protest movement, a right-wing populist movement of indignation. Such forms of publicly expressed outrage had originally emerged as a protest critical of globalisation, such as in the case of Occupy Wall Street or Indignados, held in order to confront the domination of globally active financial actors. This kind of protest had previously exclusively been classed as belonging more to the left-wing political camp, both according to self-attribution and the ascription made by others.[4]

PEGIDA certainly employed similar mechanisms and symbolic forms in order to generate public attention as a movement. Social media played a decisive role both in the emergence and during the peak, namely as a virtual space for communication and organisation. But it was not until

---

[2] For an investigation of these kinds of protest movements cf. Rucht (2011).

[3] This is the title of the book by Geiges et al. (2015).

[4] The current state of research and literature on social and protest movements as well as movements of indignation has been covered by Kneuer and Richter (2015). Cf. on this topic also Castells (2015), who understands these movements to be a phenomenon of a "networked society". For the classification of PEGIDA as a movement of outrage and indignation cf. Vorländer et al. (2016, p. 137ff., 2018).

the moment that PEGIDA entered real space, to publicly and effectively occupy prominent streets and squares, that it became a movement. And because it did so, it was able to attract a wide range of participants. The performative act and constitution of PEGIDA as a mass movement went hand in hand. The public event every Monday, structured with a rally and "evening stroll", established a ritual which through its regular repetition gave the participants the feeling of belonging to a community of like-minded people. It was through the public staging that they were able to overcome their own feelings of powerlessness and to achieve communicative power. Yet PEGIDA was not about a protest tied to a concrete *issue*, not about clear proposed solutions for concrete political problems; instead it was about the display of collective anger and outrage. Against this background, the findings of a diffuse fear of Islam can be merged with a mixture of national and regional patriotic and xenophobic orientations, which were identified among many demonstrators, as well as dissatisfaction with the concrete state of representative democracy, which has turned aggressive. PEGIDA is then to be understood first as a successful *populist* attempt to mobilise from existing *ethnocentric* attitude patterns, not directed at specific political concerns, but instead as a public expression of general dissatisfaction—a *movement of indignation*.

PEGIDA can be understood to be a *populist revolt* (Hicks 1931). A decisive role was played, above all, by the feeling of being excluded and left behind. This is likely to be similar for the emergence of all populisms—even though the specific, also underlying causes, are to be determined differently in each case, whether it be economic inequality, social exclusion or cultural expropriation. In the case of PEGIDA, economic and social reasons cannot be readily identified as the deciding causes for the emergence of the movement, whereas the perception that there is a gaping unbridgeable distance between politics and media, on the one hand, and the people on the other, seemed to be a widespread motivation. This was joined by the feeling that policy makers had lost control over developments perceived as threats—above all immigration, Islam, changes in the geopolitical situation, but also the economic and social change brought about by globalisation—and that the media falsely portrayed and classified these processes.

In eastern Germany these perceptions were strengthened by the after-effects of the transformation, which in the past decades had already once lastingly changed political, economic and social living conditions. There, in the course of the Peaceful Revolution of 1989, some, in part, strongly simplified notions of democratic decision-making processes were formed, but to some extent there were also entirely justified expectations of the new free and democratic system, which, against the backdrop of experiences of social and economic deprivation, have by now produced equally strong patterns of political disappointment. In addition, the various motivations of PEGIDA supporters were also an expression of unresolved socio-economic transformation experiences in the time after 1989/1990 in eastern Germany, where the changes had taken place rapidly as if in a time-lapse recording. Experiences of social and economic deprivation, the perception of a "structural disadvantage" compared to western Germans as well as the feeling of one's own life achievements being held in low regard—all these things are also likely, in an underlying structure, to have contributed to the strong response to PEGIDA's calls to protest. Added to this were the consequences of an incomplete and also partly unachievable adoption process of a unified political culture, which—from the point of view of many PEGIDA demonstrators—was still defined by typically western German memorial sites, horizons of experience and interpretation paradigms and so, in the media-political discourse of the Berlin Republic, only scant attention was paid to one's own, possibly differing, assessments. The resulting collective feelings of alienation, in particular the loss of the sovereignty of interpretation over one's own life, were experienced as a cultural-communicative expropriation by an elite of politicians and opinion leaders and caused the resentment-laden hostility towards the elite which PEGIDA expressed in an aggressive form. The perception of a cultural lifestyle seemingly threatened from the inside and the outside, the feeling of political powerlessness, as well as the aggression stemming from dissatisfaction with the concrete media-political state of practised democracy can be understood to be a common denominator with contemporary populisms in Europe and North America.

PEGIDA has hardly achieved anything, yet it has changed a lot. The movement was neither able to transform into a political party nor did it manage to establish itself internationally as a partner in the phalanx of right-wing populist groups. It lacked the necessary organisational ability and skill among its personnel. The movement was too heterogeneous, the group backing it was too divided. It was thus not surprising that PEGIDA never managed to develop a relatively coherent programme. Apart from the protest, first against the Establishment, then against the refugee and migration policy, there was little that united the movement; but paradoxically that was, at the same time, also the prerequisite for its success on the streets.

PEGIDA was a melting pot for feelings of resentment, attitudes and trends which needed a signal in order to be mobilised. Its founder Lutz Bachmann and his team were the political entrepreneurs who were able to bring the dissatisfied, the xenophobes, the critics of Islam, and those opposed to refugees (and to some extent also right-wing extremists) out onto the streets—and at the same time they were able to arouse sympathy for their protest in the German population and to attract attention in the national and international media. PEGIDA became the voice of a muffled and diffuse protest. The signal event of the refugee crisis in autumn 2015 reinforced the movement in a two-fold sense: by supposedly giving legitimacy to the protest, which had already commenced a year before, and as a "second wind" for a movement which had already begun to falter.

PEGIDA took up something which was already present but not visible and then joined everything together. People with right-wing populist, xenophobic and Islamophobic attitudes, critics of democracy and right-wing extremists could get behind the movement, but also sceptics and those dissatisfied with their situation found a platform in PEGIDA which allowed them to finally unleash their criticism of "the" policies and "the" media, which had previously been suppressed or held back. The organisers and speakers provided the catchwords, symbols and rituals, as well as a framework and formed a movement out of what had previously only been a mass of people who felt unheard and unrepresented. At the same time, PEGIDA also provided semantic hinges to bring together the anti-Establishment mood, the loathing of the opinion diktat of the press, the perception of being overwhelmed by Islamic influence and the assumption of a conspiracy of the European Union (EU), in an expression of resistance and defence of the cultural identity of one's home, region and nation. That made PEGIDA an *identity populist movement*, allowing it to emanate beyond Dresden and find—partly tacit, partly open—support even in the centre of German society.

PEGIDA made feelings of resentment socially acceptable and as a "regulars' table" of the streets made a decisive contribution to a coarsening of the discourse and to a disinhibition of the protest culture. The lines between rhetorical radicalisation and violent assaults became brittle. PEGIDA demonstrations indirectly led to a sudden increase in violent attacks on accommodation for asylum seekers, especially in Saxony. Additionally, on social networks, there was an alarming "normalisation" of aggressive abuse of the elite and uninhibited xenophobic statements, of hate speech.

PEGIDA was able to combine and express the protest of a dissatisfied, mistrustful and latently xenophobic population, which had neither a location nor representation in Germany. This applied in particular during the refugee crisis, when there were grave concerns that Germany could lose state control of the migration flows, and all the established parties supported the asylum policy of the Federal Chancellor, but did not express these fears. The Patriotic Europeans against the Islamisation of the Occident were able to make the crisis of confidence visible on the street; the Alternative for Germany filled the void in parliament. In this respect PEGIDA also gave the AfD a boost.

Thus the new German alliance of street and parliament, of movement and party is taking on the function that has been performed for a long time in other European countries by right-wing populist, extreme right-wing and national-conservative movements, parties and governments. In the rejection of uncontrolled immigration, mistrust of "the" religion of Islam, dissatisfaction with the "established" elite in politics and media, criticism of liberal and representative democracy and the fear of heteronomy and foreign control by the EU, a common European right-wing populism has emerged, one which is seeking to radically change societies in Europe through the reactivation and redefinition of central linguistic themes, through cultural and national identity, patriotic and ethnic nationalism, the restoration of sovereign statehood and the establishment of direct, plebiscitary democracy. Whether PEGIDA marked the beginning of the long-term establishment of right-wing populist positions and parties in the democratic system of the Federal Republic of Germany remains to be seen.

References

Castells, Manuel. 2015. *Networks of Outrage and Hope: Social Movements in the Internet Age*. New York: John Wiley & Sons.

Geiges, Lars, Stine Marg, and Franz Walter. 2015. *PEGIDA. Die schmutzige Seite der Zivilgesellschaft?* Bielefeld: Transcript.

Hicks, John D. 1931. *The Populist Revolt: A History of the Farmers' Alliance and the People's Party*. Minneapolis: The University of Minnesota Press.

Kneuer, Marianne, and Saskia Richter. 2015. *Soziale Medien in Protestbewegungen. Neue Wege für Diskurs, Organisation und Empörung?* Frankfurt a.M.: Campus.
Rucht, Dieter. 2011. Zum Stand der Forschung zu sozialen Bewegungen. *Forschungsjournal Soziale Bewegungen* 24: 21–47.
Vorländer, Hans, Maik Herold, and Steven Schäller. 2016. *PEGIDA. Entwicklung, Zusammensetzung und Deutung einer Empörungsbewegung.* Wiesbaden: Springer VS.
———. 2018. Entfremdung, Empörung, Ethnozentrismus. Was PEGIDA über den sich formierenden Rechtspopulismus verrät. In *Das Volk gegen die (liberale) Demokratie. Die Krise der Repräsentation und neue populistische Herausforderungen*, Leviathan Sonderband 18, ed. Dirk Jörke and Oliver Nachtwey, accepted. Baden-Baden: Nomos.

INDEX[1]

---

[1]Note: Page numbers followed by 'n' refers to notes.

© The Author(s) 2018
H. Vorländer et al., *PEGIDA and New Right-Wing Populism in Germany*, New Perspectives in German Political Studies, https://doi.org/10.1007/978-3-319-67495-7

Printed by Printforce, the Netherlands